Westminster Pelican Commentaries
Edited by D. E. Nineham

Paul's First Letter to Corinth

Westminster Pelican Commentaries

Paul's First Letter to Corinth

JOHN RUEF

The Westminster Press

PHILADELPHIA

© John Ruef 1971, 1977

First published in 1971 by Penguin Books Ltd.

First published in 1977 in SCM Pelican Commentaries series
by SCM Press Ltd.

Published by The Westminster Press ®
Philadelphia, Pennsylvania

PRINTED IN THE UNITED STATES OF AMERICA

Library of Congress Cataloging in Publication Data

Ruef, John Samuel.
    Paul's first letter to Corinth.

    (Westminster Pelican commentaries)
    Includes bibliographical references and index.
    1. Bible. N.T. 1 Corinthians — Commentaries.
I. Bible. N.T. 1 Corinthians. English. Revised
standard. 1977. II. Title. III. Series.
BS2675.3.R8 1977   227′.2′077   77-24086
ISBN 0-664-21348-0
ISBN 0-664-24183-2 pbk.

*This work is dedicated to the memory of one who
was the author's teacher and friend*

THE REVEREND ROYDEN KEITH YERKES

Contents

Editorial Foreword

The general aim and scope of the Pelican Commentaries on the later books of the New Testament will be similar to those of the Pelican Gospel Commentaries. Each volume will contain an introduction designed to provide non-specialist readers with sufficient background information to enable them to understand the situation to which the author was addressing himself and the way his original readers are likely to have understood what he wrote. The more detailed information necessary for the understanding of individual passages will be provided in the body of the commentary.

As in the case of the Gospel Commentaries, the basic endeavour will be to elucidate the religious meaning of the text, but it is hoped at the same time to give the reader a fair indication of current scholarly opinion on the various historical, critical, and linguistic questions raised by each book.

This book was written in the library of the Yale Divinity School. I express my sincere thanks to the staff of the library for their generous help and co-operation. The typing and preliminary editing of the manuscript were done by my wife, whose services are beyond price.

New Haven, Connecticut
Christmastide 1969

Abbreviations

Allo	B. Allo, *Saint Paul, Première Épître aux Corinthiens*, 1956
Barrett	C. K. Barrett, *A Commentary on the First Epistle to the Corinthians*, 1968
BZ	*Biblische Zeitschrift*
CTM	*Concordia Theological Monthly*
Edwards	T. C. Edwards, *A Commentary on the First Epistle to the Corinthians*, 4th ed. 1903
ET	*Expository Times*
E.T.	English translation
Ev Theo	*Evangelische Theologie*
Godet	F. Godet, *Commentary on St Paul's First Epistle to the Corinthians* (E.T. by A. Cusin), 1886
Goudge	H. Goudge, *The First Epistle to the Corinthians*, 1903
Héring	J. Héring, *The First Epistle of St Paul to the Corinthians* (E.T. by A. W. Heathcote and P. J. Allcock), 1962
HTR	*Harvard Theological Review*
Hurd	J. Hurd, *The Origin of I Corinthians*, 1965
Int	*Interpretation*
J.B.	Jerusalem Bible
JBL	*Journal of Biblical Literature*
JBR	*Journal of Bible and Religion*
JTS	*Journal of Theological Studies*
Ker u Dog	*Kerygma und Dogma*
Lietzmann	H. Lietzmann, *An die Korinther I, II* (Handbuch zum Neuen Testament), ed. W. G. Kümmel, 4th ed. 1949
LXX	Septuagint – the Greek version of the Old Testament
Moffatt	J. Moffatt, *The First Epistle of Paul to the Corinthians* (The Moffatt New Testament Commentary), 1938
N.E.B.	New English Bible
NKZ	*Neue Kirchliche Zeitschrift*
Nov Test	*Novum Testamentum*
NTS	*New Testament Studies*

par(r).	parallel(s), i.e. synoptic parallel
Rhpr	*Revue d'histoire et philosophie religieuse*
R.-P.	A. Robbinson and A. Plummer, *A Critical and Exegetical Commentary on the First Epistle of St Paul to the Corinthians* (International Critical Commentary), 1914
R.S.V.	Revised Standard Version
S.-B.	H. L. Strack and P. Billerbeck, *Kommentar zum Neuen Testament aus Talmud und Midrasch*, 1922–8
Schlatter	A. Schlatter, *Paulus der Bote Jesu*, 1962
SJT	*Scottish Journal of Theology*
s.v.	See under word in the dictionary to which reference is made
ThLZ	*Theologische Literaturzeitung*
ThWbNT	*Theologisches Wörterbuch zum Neuen Testament*
TZ	*Theologische Zeitschrift*
Weiss	J. Weiss, 'Der erste Korintherbrief', *Kritisch-exegetischer Kommentar über das Neue Testament*, ed. Meyer, 1910
Wendland	H. D. Wendland, *Die Briefe an die Korinther* (Das Neue Testament Deutsch), 1946
ZNW	*Zeitschrift für die neutestamentliche Wissenschaft*

Comparison: cp. is used where the contrast serves to bring out the point of an argument; cf. is used in cases where there is confirmation by similarity or identity.

Introduction

Many people associate the modern, critical study of the Bible with the translations into the vernacular in the time of the sixteenth-century Reformers. Actually, the type of critical study of the scriptures which we take for granted today did not begin until the end of the eighteenth century. Translation into the vernacular, important as that is, constitutes only one form of interpretation of the text and one step in the entire critical enterprise. We welcome the newer translations into English, such as the Revised Standard Version (R.S.V.), which serves as the basis for this series of commentaries, as well as the New English Bible (N.E.B.) and, most recently, the Jerusalem Bible (J.B.). But, important as these translations are, we must remember that behind each one is much critical study, as well as the point of view of those who did the studying. The study and translation of the Bible, therefore, are a continuous process, as each age attempts to understand anew the meaning of the scriptures.

Once the critical study of the Bible had begun, and men were willing to treat the Bible, for purposes of scientific examination, as they would any other book, a number of problems began to emerge. First and foremost, there was the problem of the identity of Jesus. In many places in the Gospels he appears as a human, a Jew, a teacher of religion who wandered through Palestine gathering a small band of followers. There are other passages, however, where Jesus is just as clearly depicted as a wonder-worker, or even a divine person. The solution of the nineteenth-century scholars[1] who were at all critical was simple: Jesus was a man, a teacher. He said things which the officials of his own day did not like and was put out of the way as a trouble-maker. The idea that he was a wonder-worker or divine came later, after his followers had had certain visionary experiences which convinced them that somehow God had brought Jesus back to life. The process of criticism then consisted in stripping away the

1. Cf. P. Feine, J. Behm, G. Kümmel, *Introduction to the New Testament* (E.T. by A. J. Mattill, Jr), 1966, 26–30.

later superstitious accretions and uncovering the real human being, Jesus.

Secondly, there was the problem of the early church. While some scholars were trying to uncover the historical Jesus underneath the accretions of later superstition, others were occupied with the problem of how an organization such as the church, represented by the writing of the early Greek Fathers, could have arisen from the group of men whom Jesus had gathered to himself in his lifetime. These men had been Jews, and uneducated ones at that. Their leader had been an itinerant Jewish teacher who had been executed for his unorthodox opinions and practices. How did the Catholic Church emerge from this group? The scholars' answer was that the basically Jewish teaching of Jesus, preserved by his original Jewish followers, was taken over by gentiles and reinterpreted in a radical way. One of the principal agents in this radical reinterpretation of Christianity in gentile terms was Paul the Apostle. According to this theory, which dominated most of the nineteenth century and a good part of the twentieth, because Paul had been raised, not in Palestine, but in the 'Dispersion' (Judaism outside Palestine), he had been taught a more liberal kind of Judaism than that in which the first followers of Jesus had been raised and had also come into contact with many more influences of the Hellenistic world than they had. As a result of this, according to the theory, he was the ideal person to reformulate a basically Jewish message into one which would attract gentile adherents.

So, for instance, according to these critics, Paul reformulated the Gospel of Jesus the Messiah (Christ, literally, 'the anointed one') into the religion of Jesus the Lord (the god venerated in a particular cult).[2] He made the simple cleansing and initiatory rite of Baptism into a mystical ceremony of dying and rising with the cult-god, Jesus.[3] He took the tradition of Jesus's last meal with his disciples and transformed it into a cult ceremony in which the participants ate Jesus's

---

2. Cf. 1 Cor. 12[3]; Rom. 10[91]; Phil. 2[11]. 'Lord' (Greek, *kyrios*) in gentile religious parlance referred to the god venerated in a particular cult. It is also the word used in the Septuagint (the Greek translation of the Hebrew scriptures) for the word *YHWH* (the proper name of God) and the word *'ADON*, 'Lord'. Cf. G. Kittel, *Theological Dictionary of the New Testament*, III, 1048ff.

3. Cf. Rom. 6[3-5]; cp. Col. 2[12].

body and drank his blood.[4] Finally, and most significantly, Paul stated that, for the gentiles, the Jewish scriptures and traditions were no longer legally binding.[5]

Now, according to the dominant theory of the nineteenth century,[6] this last development in Paul's thinking was disastrous for the relations of this new gentile wing of the church with the more conservative group in Palestine. The Jewish Christians, who took James the brother of Jesus as their leader, set about to oppose this Hellenizing of the Christian message. There ensued a struggle between these two factions. The Catholic Church which resulted from the struggle of these two opposing points of view represents a synthesis of both of them. Much of Paul's gentile-oriented reformulation was maintained, but his ideas about the non-binding character of the law were left behind, and Christianity proceeded to formulate its own system of law.

This theory of the development of the early church has persisted well into the twentieth century because it does provide a very convenient explanation for many of the problems which we find in the Pauline epistles. It does so, furthermore, in a way which takes into account the constant pattern of persecution of Paul by those who are thought to be Jews or Jewish Christians in the Book of Acts. This theory, however, depends upon two basic premises, both of which have more recently been called into question: (1) that there was a basic antagonism between the churches founded by Paul and the church in Jerusalem under James the brother of Jesus; (2) that the Judaism out of which Christianity emerged was homogeneous and did not admit of deviation from norms which can be identified in the Jewish traditions which have come down to us in the rabbinic traditions.

The first premise must be called into question. In the first place, Paul himself seems to be unaware of any basic antagonism between himself and the church in Jerusalem. He seems, in fact, to feel that they share the highest degree of unity and fellowship.[7] Furthermore,

---

4. Cf. 1 Cor. 10$^{16-17}$; 10$^{23-5}$ 5. Cf. Rom. 8$^{1-4}$; Gal. 2^{16}.
6. Cf. Feine, Behm, Kümmel, op. cit. (n. 1), 27, and for a thorough critique of Baur's point of view, J. Munck, *Paul and the Salvation of Mankind* (E.T. by F. Clarke), 1959, 69–86.
7. Cf. Gal. 2^9.

as some recent studies have shown,[8] there is a serious problem in accepting the Book of Acts as a reliable historical account of the first days of the Christian church. This book, probably written by the author of the Lucan Gospel, has a strong tendency to make the record exonerate the Romans and condemn the Jews for the troubles which plagued the early church.[9]

The second premise has been placed in real doubt by the discovery of the so-called Dead Sea Scrolls. These documents probably constitute the remains of a library collected by a sect of semi-monastics, Jews who lived in isolation from the rest of Judaism on the northwestern shore of the Dead Sea, not far from Jericho. These writings reflect a Judaism in which there was considerable variety of expression and which was anything but monolithic. The discovery emphasizes what we should already have expected from the New Testament evidence which tells us of the Pharisees, the Sadducees, the Zealots, and the Herodians. It was not just the simple tension between Palestinian, Jewish-Christians and non-Palestinian, gentile-Christians which complicated the picture of the early church and produced tensions within it. The problem is far more complex than such a simple solution would indicate.

In our own century, there are those who would seek a simple solution to this problem of the history of the early church in the religious phenomenon known as Gnosticism.[10] At one time we knew about this mainly from the writings of three early Christian theologians, Irenaeus, Hippolytus, and Epiphanius. From their point of view as defenders of orthodoxy, Gnosticism represented a perversion of the true faith, i.e. Gnostics were considered by these writers to be Christian heretics. However, since 1947 and the discovery of a large cache of Gnostic writings in Egypt,[11] the main outlines of this way

8. H. Conzelmann, *The Theology of St Luke* (E.T. by G. Buswell), 1960; H. Flender, *St Luke: Theologian of Redemptive History* (E.T. by R. and I. Fuller), 1967.

9. Cf. B. S. Easton, 'The Purpose of Acts', *Early Christianity*, ed. F. C. Grant, 1955, 33–115.

10. W. Lütgert, *Freitheitspredigt und Schwärmgeister in Korinth*, 1908; W. Schmitals, *Die Gnosis in Korinth*, 1956; U. Wilckens, *Weisheit und Torheit: Eine exegetischreligionsgeschichtliche Untersuchung zu I Kor. 1 und 2*, 1959.

11. The so-called Coptic Gnostic Library was discovered in a district of Egypt known as the Fayyum near the town of Nag Hammadi and the ancient

of thinking have become clearer. However, their relation to Christianity seems to be much more complex than scholars would have thought, had they only known the writings of the Greek Fathers mentioned above.

The outlines of Gnostic thought are somewhat as follows, stated in the most general terms. Man was in essence a divine being. He existed before Creation. Creation was not the work of the supreme Deity who has no relation to the material world as we know it. Creation was a trick perpetrated by a demi-God. Through a ruse, the divine Man was ensnared by the material Creation and became scattered as little sparks of the Divine throughout Creation.

It was important for a man to have this knowledge, for this was the means of his salvation. Since this saving knowledge stood at the centre of their belief, these people were referred to as 'the ones who have knowledge' (Greek, *gnostikoi*). At his death, man in his divine essence can, because he 'knows', circumvent those demi-gods responsible for the created order and ascend to the purely divine realm where he really belongs.

In the Christian version of Gnosticism, this knowledge is brought to man by the redeemer, Jesus, who descends from heaven, takes human form, transmits the saving knowledge to man, and then, leaving his human form to its ignominious fate, ascends, as all good Gnostics do, to the realm of pure divinity. There are other versions of Gnosticism which are not Christian. These give evidence that Gnosticism may be pre-Christian in origin. The origin of Gnosticism is one of the most debated questions today in the scholarly study of religion, and the view one takes of the origin of Gnosticism plays no small part in the treatment one makes of certain problems basic to the New Testament, particularly in the area of Pauline studies.

If one thinks that Gnosticism is a perversion of Christianity which gradually developed in the form in which we meet it in the second century,[12] this drastically affects the picture which one has of the

---

site of Chenoboskion. Cf. W. C. Van Unnik, *Newly Discovered Gnostic Writings* (E.T. by N. V. Keulen), 1960, 7–271; J. M. Robinson, 'The Coptic Gnostic Library Today', *NTS* 14 (1968), 356–401.

12. This is the position of Irenaeus, Hippolytus, and Epiphanius, which persisted to the early part of this century.

early church. On the other hand, if one holds that Gnosticism is a development within Judaism which finds its way into Christianity[13] this results in quite another picture. If one asserts, as Bultmann does,[14] that Christianity actually 'borrowed' the myth of the descending and ascending redeemer from Gnosticism, it does presuppose that Gnosticism was already a well-developed kind of thought by the time Christianity came on the scene.[15] This is the question which is being hotly debated today.

It is contended, for instance, that this notion of a developed Gnosticism at the time of the primitive Christian church is simply not supported by the evidence, and that, far from providing a simple solution to the New Testament problems, it points to a greater complexity:[16] that is, just as in the case of Judaism and the Dead Sea Scrolls, the discoveries concerning Gnosticism point to a far greater complexity within the early church than we had supposed. There were probably many currents of thought within the early church. Each person or group would attempt to understand the Christian Gospel in terms of his or their own frame of reference and background. Out of this situation eventually developed a norm of faith. Once this norm had been accepted, later writers tended to see it as having existed from the beginning.

The age in which Christianity arose was one of much mutual borrowing, on the part of various religions, which we call 'syncretism'. There are elements in early Christian as well as in pre-Christian Judaism which resemble elements in later Gnosticism. Some of these elements are found in 1 Corinthians. They could represent a developed non-Christian Gnosticism which had been taken over by Christianity. Or they could represent an early form of Gnosticism which would show up later as the more developed heresies of the second century. Current study on the problem points to a third and perhaps more tenable notion: these are some indications of the *milieu*

13. R. M. Grant, *Gnosticism and Early Christianity*, 1959.

14. *Theology of the New Testament*, 1951–5, Vol. I, 172ff.

15. J. M. Robinson, 'Basic Shifts in German Theology', *Interpretation*, 16 (1962), 79ff.; H. Conzelmann, 'Current Problems in Pauline Research', *Interpretation*, 22 (1968), 171–86.

16. R. McL. Wilson, *The Gnostic Problem, A Study of the Relations between Hellenistic Judaism and the Gnostic Heresy*, 1958, 64–85.

in which catholic Christianity, normative Judaism and Gnosticism were all nourished at this time.[17]

The complex situation of the early church will not yield to simplistic solutions. The situation of the world and the church within which Paul preached and in which he wrote his epistles was one in which, from a religious point of view, there was a great deal of activity and interaction. The situation of the early church was one in which there were any number of attempts to understand and interpret the new faith. Paul's was one of these, and he had both his adherents and his opponents.[18] Of those who were his adherents, there were those who pressed some of his positions beyond their logical extreme,[19] while others objected to this interpretation of Paul's teaching and asked him to clarify for them just what he meant.[20]

Two areas of Paul's thought seem to have been particularly open to misinterpretation by the Christians in Corinth: (1) the resurrection, and (2) the possession of the Spirit. For this reason, it will be well in this introductory section to make some general observations about both these subjects.

THE VIEW OF THE RESURRECTION WHICH UNDERLIES PAUL'S THOUGHT

Faith in Jesus's resurrection was basic to Paul's understanding of the Christian faith. Paul's preaching of the resurrection, however, was not interpreted by everyone in Corinth in the same way. This is difficult for us to comprehend, because our understanding of the resurrection of Jesus has been informed primarily from a reading of the Gospels of Matthew, Luke, and John, all of which picture a risen Lord Jesus who appeared to men and lived with them in a recognizable human form in the period after the crucifixion.[21] That is, we think of Jesus as coming out of the tomb and returning in some fashion to life.

Now this idea of resurrection as returning to life from the dead was a belief of the Pharisees of this period. This is what would happen to

17. H. Koester, 'Gnomai Diaphorai: The Origin and Nature of Diversification in the History of Early Christianity', *HTR*, 58 (1965), 279–318.
18. Cf. 1 Cor. 1[12ff.]   19. Cf. ibid., 6[12], 10[23].
20. Cf. ibid., 12[23ff.].   21. Matt. 28[1-20]; Luke 24[1-53]; John 20[1]-21[25].

those who were to have a portion in the world which was to come after the end of this world. We know that this faith in the resurrection was not shared by the Sadducees (Mark 12[18-27] parr.). We also know that there was at least one other way to express the idea that God had placed his sign of approval upon a particularly worthy individual – God would exalt him to heaven (Moses, Elijah, and Enoch are all thought in various strands of Jewish tradition to have been exalted to heaven). So that there lay near to hand, in the time of Jesus and Paul, not just the one idea of resurrection, but also the idea of exaltation to explain how it was that Jesus could appear to his followers after the crucifixion.

The idea of resurrection eventually prevailed as the one which expressed the orthodox position of Christianity. However, in the earlier period there is some evidence which would indicate that the idea of exaltation also found acceptance. There is, for instance, the hymn in Phil. 2[5ff]. This passage speaks of Jesus's death on the cross, but there is not the slightest echo of any resurrection such as we find in the narratives which come at the end of Matthew, Luke, and John. According to Phil. 2[5ff], Jesus dies and God exalts him to heaven.[22] Again, in the three accounts of the appearance of Jesus to Paul on the road to Damascus[23] there is no attempt to picture a Jesus in the sort of way described in Matthew, Luke, and John. There is rather only a bright light, a voice, and a description of the time of day and general location of the place. If we compare these accounts with the simple ones given by Paul, we can only conclude that there has been a considerable amount of elaboration within the tradition by the time these accounts find their way into the Books of Acts. Further comparison would also indicate that the elaboration was along the lines of the notion of exaltation such as we have in Phil. 2[5ff] rather than along the lines of the notion of resurrection in the last three Gospels.[24]

22. Cp. Acts 7[55] and 2[33ff], where Jesus is pictured as exalted.

23. Acts 9[1-19], 22[3-21], 26[12-18].

24. Luke is an exception in one sense, because in the third Gospel there is the tradition of the ascension as well as that of the resurrection. Luke was able to bring these two traditions together by making the ascension follow after and terminate the period of Jesus's earthly stay after his resurrection. It should be noted that he was not entirely consistent in the way in which he did this; cp. Luke 24[49-51] with Acts 1[3]. This inconsistency could represent a retention of two

We must also consider the attitude of the fourth Gospel. While it is true that the author of the fourth Gospel has included at the end of his work a cycle of stories which depict appearances of Jesus after the crucifixion, such as we have in Matthew and Luke, it is also true that the attitude of the Evangelist which we find expressed in the body of the Gospel is more like the exaltation notion seen in Phil. 2⁵ᶠᶠ· and elsewhere. In the body of the fourth Gospel there is no mention of Jesus's death on the cross or his resurrection. There are only the somewhat enigmatic references to his 'coming' into the world and his 'going' from the world to the father.

Finally, it is not without significance that Mark's Gospel, the Christian work written next after Paul, does not have now and probably never did have any cycle of resurrection stories such as we have in Matthew, Luke, and John. So then within the Gospel tradition and also in Paul there is evidence of a tradition concerning what happened to Jesus after the crucifixion which expressed itself in terms of exaltation rather than resurrection.

Eventually, as we said above, the idea of resurrection prevailed. Why this was so is a question whose answer may lie in part in the events reflected in the first epistle to the Corinthians.

I hope that I have shown that there were probably two categories which the earliest church could have used to explain how Jesus could have appeared to his disciples after the crucifixion: resurrection, represented primarily in the last three Gospels; exaltation, the evidence for which I have cited above. Whichever category one fastened upon to explain how Jesus could have appeared after his death to those who would then constitute the nucleus of the earliest Christian community, there were serious problems and incongruities.

a. If, on the one hand, one chose to say that Jesus had been raised from the dead, there were at least two problems which the church would immediately have to face. (1) Resurrection from the dead was associated in the Jewish mind with the end of the world and the coming of God in judgement to inaugurate the new world. It was obvious, after the death of Jesus, that this had not happened, (2) the

---

different traditions concerning the length of this period. But this only pushes the connecting of the resurrection and the exaltation or ascension ideas back into the pre-Lucan period.

concept of resurrection was essentially foreign to the gentile mind. It would have to be understood by them in some other way than it was by the Jews.

b. On the other hand, if one chose the idea of exaltation, there were two problems which would be confronted. (1) The traditional Hebraic notion of exaltation was really that of 'translation', i.e. the person exalted did not die, but was 'assumed' into heaven. Jesus really did die, however, according to the tradition. Some effort would have to be made to accommodate this fact. (2) The gentile convert to Christianity would accept the notion of a translation because it would not involve the death of the individual, but rather, in accord with gentile ideas of immortality, the ascent of the soul, apart from the body.

Much of what Paul says about the resurrection and related matters can be understood if one keeps these problems in mind. For instance, the dilemma with which Paul is confronted in Corinth concerning the resurrection is not that these people denied the resurrection of Christ. What they denied was rather the resurrection of the dead.[25] How could they deny the one while affirming the other? The answer lies in realizing that the Corinthians had come to understand what happened to Jesus after the crucifixion as an exaltation or translation rather than as a resurrection in the Jewish sense. When, therefore, they said, 'Christ is risen,' they understood this in the sense of an ascension or an assumption to heaven from where Christ subsequently appeared or was revealed to those who were to be the nucleus of the infant church. It is only thus that the Corinthians could claim that, while Christ is risen, there is no such thing as the resurrection of the dead. The key word of course is 'dead'. In the thought of the gentiles, the dead are beyond recall. In the mind of the Corinthians, resurrection meant that Jesus avoided death. In the thought of Paul, of course, resurrection meant that Jesus overcame death.

Paul must, therefore, emphasize in his discussion of the resurrection in Chapter 15 and elsewhere[26] that Jesus really did die. Because Jesus overcame death, death itself will eventually be completely overcome

25. Cf. 1 Cor. 15[12].
26. Paul cites Christian tradition in 1 Cor. 15[3] which emphasizes the death of Jesus. Cf. also the emphasis upon the death of Jesus in Paul's discussion of the Eucharist (1 Cor. 11[26]) and in his discussion of Baptism (Rom. 6[3, 5]).

for all. But for now, the believer cannot avoid death any more than Jesus could. Once we understand why Paul emphasized the reality of the death of Christ, we can better understand the course of his argument concerning resurrection.

Paul does not argue, as one might expect, from the premise that Jesus did rise from the dead. What he does say is, if you deny the resurrection of the dead, then you can no longer profess that Christ is risen. And furthermore, you cannot claim anything else for your religion either, such as forgiveness of sins.[27] Paul is most explicit in I Thess. 4[13ff.]: sorrow for the dead is not appropriate to Christians since it implies that they have no hope. On the contrary, one cannot profess that Christ died and rose without also the hope that God will take care of those who have died.

Here again we see Paul stressing that the proper Christian profession is not, as the Corinthian Christians would have it, Christ is risen. The proper profession is, Christ died and is risen. But one cannot make this profession without providing the same basis of hope held out for others who have died. The hope is, after all, not a hope simply for individual salvation. This was a common idea among the gentiles, but it was not the way in which the Jews viewed salvation: salvation lay in God's concern for his people. To belong to the people of God was to share in the hope of the people of God. If one were to affirm this hope for oneself as an individual believer, while denying this hope for the members of the community who had died, one would in effect be shattering the unity of the community in this particular respect. And this kind of threat to the unity of the community was something which Paul would not tolerate.

Now we see why Paul had to emphasize the death of Christ. This is the one element with which the human person, as human person, can identify; Jesus died as all men die. He was also raised from the dead. These two elements together constitute the basis of the Christian proclamation, the expression of the Christian hope. Paul must emphasize the death of Christ in order to bring out the fullness of the expression of Christian hope which he inherited from Pharasaic Judaism, the resurrection of the dead.

27. Cf. I Cor. 15[17].

THE GIFT OF THE SPIRIT IN THE THOUGHT OF PAUL

Paul preached to the Corinthians the Gospel of Jesus died and risen. We have seen that there is reason to believe that what Paul meant by resurrection was what we have come to call the Ascension. We may assume then that this may be the way in which the Corinthians understood Paul's preaching. Now the question may be asked, 'What was their reaction to this preaching?' 'They became Christians', would be a simple and correct answer. But precisely what did this mean in mid-first-century Corinth? One thing we know it meant was trouble for Paul.

It could not have been at all obvious to these newly converted Christians what the expectations or implications of their new faith were. It is for this reason that they have many questions to put to Paul. Some they write in a letter[28] and some are put to him orally.[29] But what do we know about these people in Corinth? The most important thing we know is that they were not Jews. The Book of Acts recounts how it was here in Corinth that the Jews for the most part opposed Paul so that he decided to turn to the gentiles.[30] Whether this is the first time he actually turned to the gentiles might be hard to say on the basis of the evidence from Acts,[31] but Paul himself says that he felt a particular calling to preach the Gospel to the gentiles.[32]

There is some evidence in the Book of Acts which may help us to understand how gentiles reacted to the preaching of the Christian Gospel. There are nine accounts in the Book of Acts which describe how individuals or groups were converted to the Christian Gospel and received into the church.[33] Of these accounts, five have to do with the conversion of gentiles.[34] Further, within this latter group, one account in particular – the conversion of Cornelius the centurion – stands out from the rest for several reasons: (1) Peter, at the council of Jerusalem,[35] makes reference to this event in justifying the reception and equal status of gentiles in the Christian community; (2) the

28. Cf. ibid., 7^1. 29. Cf. ibid., 1^{11}. 30. Cf. Acts 18^{5ff}.
31. Cf. above p. 5 and n. 8. 32. Cf. Gal. 2^{7-9}.
33. Acts 2^{38ff}, 8^{26ff}, 9^{3ff}, 10^{44ff}, (11^{15ff}), 16^{14ff}, 16^{25}, 18^8, 19^{1ff}.
34. ibid., 8^{26ff}, 10^{44ff}, 11^{15ff}, 16^{14ff}, 16^{25ff}. 35. ibid., 15^8.

story of Cornelius's conversion is told twice, once in Chapter 10 and again in Chapter 11; (3) of all the accounts in Acts which deal with the reception of new converts into the church, this is the only one in which the Spirit comes upon the individuals in question prior to their Baptism.

The fact that this story is told twice in the Book of Acts and that it is referred to in the account of the Jerusalem Council in Chapter 15 indicates the importance which it had in the tradition. Its importance may have resided in the fact that it preserved some important elements of the way in which gentiles were first admitted into the church. It is in this account that the Holy Spirit is described as coming upon Cornelius and his household while they 'heard the word'. His presence is known by the fact that they spoke in tongues. According to one story then preserved in the Book of Acts, the gentiles were admitted into the church because they spoke in tongues which indicated that they had received the Spirit. The church in Corinth was also very concerned with speaking in tongues. Paul spent a considerable amount of space in his epistle evaluating and admonishing the Corinthians upon this very subject. Why were the Corinthians so concerned about speaking in tongues? Why did they place such a high value upon it? It may have been that, as is described in the case of Cornelius the centurion, this was the way in which they came into the church in the first place.

We assume then that when the Corinthians received the Gospel of Jesus Christ they did so in a manner not unlike what is described in the case of Cornelius in the Book of Acts. By the time of the writing of Acts, however, the real significance of this is lost upon the writer, who knows only that the story has retained an importance in the tradition. As one can see from Acts 2, that author has quite another notion of what is involved in speaking in tongues. He interprets it as a kind of magical linguistic facility whereby men can understand words spoken in a foreign tongue.[36]

However, one can see from what Paul says in 1 Corinthians about speaking in tongues that it was some kind of hyperenthusiastic vocalization which was quite unintelligible except to a chosen few.[37] If we are right in our surmise about the Cornelius story in Acts, namely that it represents one manner in which gentiles were first

36. ibid., 2^{5-11}.   37. 1 Cor. 14^2.

admitted into the church, then one can readily understand the Corinthians' concern for this particular 'gift of the Spirit'.

However, along with this reception of the Spirit, the gentile Christians also believed that they were free.[38] Paul meant by this of course freedom from the Jewish Law and the necessity to establish one's claim to God's favour by works. What the Corinthians understood by this was evidently something quite different. Their slogan came to be 'All things are lawful for me'. Because they have received the Spirit, they can refer to themselves as the 'spiritual ones'.[39] There is some question whether they would even allow this title to be used by anyone who had not had the experience of speaking in tongues.[40] In this freedom, they can worship Jesus, calling him 'Lord', but they can also continue to frequent pagan temples and partake, if not in the worship, at least in the social life which found its centre there.[41] In the market place, they can still buy meat which may have come from a pagan sacrifice.[42] In their worship, they can indulge in eating and drinking which approaches the proportions of an orgy.[43]

As I have attempted to show in the section on the resurrection above, Paul's faith centred in his experience of the risen or exalted Lord Jesus. The faith of the Corinthians seems to have centred in their experience of the Spirit. For this reason they indulged in what seems to have been a highly individualistic kind of piety. Their thought, as we have shown above, had no room for such ideas as the resurrection of the dead. They were far more concerned about their attachment to the person under whose tutelage they had received the Spirit,[44] or their own possession of some kind of esoteric wisdom,[45] than they were in a concern for other, less gifted, individuals within the community.[46]

Paul, therefore, faces a double problem in writing to the Corinthians. He was, on the one hand, the person who founded the church in Corinth.[47] His was the first preaching of the Gospel to which the Corinthians responded. He therefore does not want to discourage in any way their enthusiasm for the faith. On the other hand, the way in which the Corinthians are expressing their faith has some

---

38. ibid., 6[16], 19[23].   39. ibid., 3[1]; cp. 2[13ff], 12[1ff].
40. Cf. below the introduction to Chapters 12–14.   41. I Cor. 8[10].
42. ibid., 10[25].   43. ibid., 11[20ff].   44. ibid., 1[12], 3[4].
45. ibid., 2[6ff].   46. ibid., 2[6ff].   47. ibid., 4[14ff].

most unfortunate elements connected with it, which Paul feels obliged to correct.

Paul the apostle of Jesus Christ who founded the church in Corinth, who had been raised in the town of Tarsus in the province of Cilicia,[48] wrote this letter during his lengthy stay in Ephesus,[49] perhaps in the year A.D. 55.[50] This was evidently not the first time he had written to them,[51] and it was not to be the last.[52]

Some kind of delegation[53] had come to Paul with a letter from the Corinthian church which contained some questions on specific problems which had arisen since his initial visit. Other information had come to Paul, probably by word of mouth, and he uses this opportunity to comment upon these matters as well as those mentioned in the letter from the Corinthians.

There have been any number of attempts to show that the correspondence which we now possess as 1 and 2 Corinthians is actually a compilation of several letters written by Paul at various times to the Corinthians. As far as 1 Corinthians is concerned, we have found none of these theories particularly helpful or convincing.[54]

48. Acts 22³. On a modern-day map, Tarsus would be just north and a little east of Cyprus in the south-eastern corner of Turkey.

49. Acts 19¹ᶠ·, ¹⁰.

50. This dating is made on the basis of the information in Acts 18¹¹ᶠ·. Paul's stay of 18 months in Corinth is at least partially coincident with the proconsulship of Gallio. Gallio's tenure in office can be dated on the basis of an inscription discovered in Delphi at the beginning of this century. Cf. A. Deissmann, *Paul: A Study in Social and Religious History*, 2nd ed. 1927, 261–86.

51. 1 Cor. 5⁹.

52. Cf. 2 Cor.

53. Cf. 1 Cor. 16¹⁵⁻¹⁸.

54. There is a most adequate summary and critique of the various theories of compilation in Feine, Behm, and Kümmel, op. cit. (n. 1).

Commentary

Chapters 1-4

¹Paul, called by the will of God to be an apostle of Christ Jesus, and our brother Sosthenes, ²To the church of God which is at Corinth, to those sanctified in Christ Jesus, called to be saints together with all those who in every place call on the name of our Lord Jesus Christ, both their Lord and ours: ³Grace to you and peace from God our Father and the Lord Jesus Christ.

Paul follows the conventions of letter writing of his own day by beginning with his own name and status and then the title of those addressed. He expands the greeting form in order to make clear the relation which he has to those addressed.

തരു

I

called by the will of God to be an apostle of Christ Jesus: Paul is conscious of his own peculiar call.[55] He was not a follower of Jesus who subsequently received a commission as an apostle. His call to be an *apostle* came simultaneously with the call to faith.[56] This calling as an apostle is distinct from the calling to be a *saint*.[57] It carries with it authority.

apostle: Literally, 'one who is sent'. This may represent the Jewish practice of making a man a *shaliach* or plenipotentiary with full authority to act for the person represented.[58]

brother: This may have been a technical designation for one who was a Christian,[59] though other religious groups used the term.[60]

Sosthenes: Could be the person referred to in Acts 18[17].

---

55. Cf. below on 15[8f.].   56. Cf. Gal. 1[15ff.]; cp. Acts 9[15], 22[15], 26[16ff.].
57. Cf. below on v. 2.   58. Cf. Mishnah, *Berakoth*, 5. 5.
59. Cf. Matt. 23[8].   60. Cf. 2 Macc. 1[1]; Josephus, *Jewish Wars*, ii, 122.

2

Paul designates those addressed with three titles.

the church of God which is at Corinth: The Greek word translated here as church is *ekklēsia*. It is used in the Greek version of the Old Testament (LXX) to refer to the assembly of Israel, that is those called out to worship the God of Israel.[61] As early as Paul, the church felt itself to be the true Israel.

those sanctified in Christ Jesus: Refers to their coming to faith and their subsequent Baptismal initiation into the assembly.[62]

called to be saints: As with Paul, each of them has been called by God. Paul will work out later how one calling is different from another.[63] It is their call and their resultant admission to the community which constitute the basis of their sainthood.

together with all those who ... call on the name of our Lord Jesus Christ: The connection of this clause is not as clear in the Greek as the R.S.V. has made it by the addition of *together*. The Greek text has only *with*. If we are correct in thinking that Paul designates the Christians in Corinth in three different ways,[64] then this clause should properly be understood with all of them: (1) the Corinthian assembly is one with all Christians; (2) they were sanctified as were all Christians; and (3) they were called along with all Christians. There could be a verbal connection in Paul's mind between the word *called* above and (those who) *call* in this clause.

in every place ... both their Lord and ours: A much more complicated question is raised by these words, which I have omitted from consideration in the clause above *with all those*, etc. In order to make a meaningful translation of this difficult passage, the R.S.V. has added several important words not represented in the original text.

together, both, and *Lord:* This translation has also moved the phrase *in every place* from its position in the Greek text (immediately after the word *Christ*) to stand immediately after the word *who* and before *call*. The word *both* is added on the basis of a late manuscript tradition and should be omitted. The word *Lord* is sheer conjecture and depends upon the connection of the phrase *theirs and ours* with the phrase which immediately precedes it in the Greek text, *in every place*. The Greek word

61. Cf. Deut. 18¹⁶, 23¹, etc.   62. Cf. 6¹¹; cp. 2 Thess. 2¹³.
63. Cf. below on Chapter 12.   64. Cf. above on v. 1.

translated here as *place* is *topos*. There is evidence that this word had a broader meaning than the geographical-spatial sense of 'place'. It could also refer to a passage in a book [65] or it could carry the sense of 'opportunity' (for) or 'occasion' (of).[66] The word *topos* can also mean place in the sense of 'status' or 'function'.[67] If *topos* is taken in this sense here, then the word order is maintained and no additional words need be added. The clause can then be rendered: with all those who call on the name of the Lord Jesus Christ, in every status, theirs and ours.[68]

ours: Would refer to Paul's apostle status, *theirs* to whatever status or calling any one had within the community of faith.[69] This is the first statement which emphasizes the unity of the church, a theme which fairly well dominates much of the epistle.[70]

3

Grace . . . peace: This is the standard blessing at the beginning of Paul's epistles, just as in every case a *grace*-blessing is contained in the concluding remarks. It is possible that this formula of blessing was taken over from Jewish usage.[71] It is also possible that Paul 'Christianized' the Greek form of 'greetings', *chairein*, by using the term *charis*, that is 'grace', and then added the standard Jewish form of a greeting-blessing, 'peace', Hebrew *shalom*, Greek *eirēnē*.

the Lord Jesus: Among Greek-speaking Jews, the word *Lord*, Greek *kyrios*, was familiar as a title for God. It would also have been familiar to gentiles as the title given to the deity of a particular cult. It expresses the relation between the believer and the deity in either case.[72]

---

65. Cf. Luke 4[17].
66. Cf. Acts 25[16].
67. Cf. ibid., 1[25]; W. Bauer, *Griechisch-Deutsches Wörterbuch zu den Schriften des Neuen Testaments und der übrigen urchristlichen Literatur*, 5th ed. 1958, *s.v.* 2b.
68. This meaning is disputed by H. Köster in his article 'Topos', *Th Wb NT*, VIII, 205f., 208. It is supported by W. Nauck, 'Probleme des frühchristlichen Amtsverständnisses', *ZNW*, 48 (1957), 213f.; E. Stauffer, 'Jüdisches Erbe im urchristlichen Kirchenrecht', *ThLZ*, 77 (1952), 203; and cf. also G. H. Whitaker, 'Notes and Studies', *JTS*, 22 (1921), 268.
69. Cf. below on Chapter 12.
70. Cf. U. Wickert, 'Einheit und Eintracht der Kirche im Präskript des 1 Cor.', *ZNW*, 50 (1959), 73–82.
71. Cf. 2 Macc. 1[1]; Apocalypse of Baruch 78[2].
72. Cf. below on 12[3].

⁴I give thanks to God always for you because of the grace of God which was given you in Christ Jesus, ⁵that in every way you were enriched in him with all speech and all knowledge – ⁶even as the testimony to Christ was confirmed among you – ⁷so that you are not lacking in any spiritual gift, as you wait for the revealing of our Lord Jesus Christ; ⁸who will sustain you to the end, guiltless in the day of our Lord Jesus Christ. ⁹God is faithful, by whom you were called into the fellowship of his Son, Jesus Christ our Lord.

After establishing the identity of those to whom he addressed his letter, the relation which he had to them, and the relation which they had to the whole church, Paul proceeds with the thanksgiving. This was usual in the Hellenistic world in a formal letter between those who shared the same religious background.[73] It was customary in such a thanksgiving to indicate the subject matter to be touched upon in the letter.[74] There is some reason to believe that Paul's use of the thanksgiving-form may also have been influenced by current Christian liturgical practice.[75] In all his letters Paul follows the same general formula: he (1) gives thanks, (2) always (3) to God (4) on behalf of the Christians to whom he writes (5) because of things God has done for them, which he proceeds to enumerate.

჻

4

because of the Grace of God which was given you in Christ Jesus: Paul here emphasizes the source of the spiritual riches bestowed upon the Corin-

73. Cf. P. Schubert, *Form and Function of the Pauline Thanksgivings*, 1937, 171ff.

74. ibid., 77.

75. Cf. J. M. Robinson, 'The Historicality of Biblical Language', *The Old Testament and Christian Faith*, ed. B. W. Anderson, 1963, 132, 146, 149, no. 29. Also 'Die Hodayot-Formel in Gebet und Hymnus des Frühchristentums', *Apophoreta, Festschrift für Ernst Haenchen*, ed. W. Eltester, 1964, 194–235.

thians. Paul will re-emphasize this point below in 4⁷ff.. He will be mostly concerned in this letter with the individual manifestations of the Spirit's gifts.[76] *In Christ* can refer both to the *locus*, i.e. the church, but also to the ultimate source of these gifts.[77]

5

enriched . . . with all speech and all knowledge: It is clear that Paul approves of the gifts which the Corinthian Church has received. It is also clear that he does not approve of the manner in which they have exercised them. Note below on 4⁸ the ironic use of the word 'rich'. For now, however, by way of establishing *rapport*, Paul speaks positively.

6f

the testimony to Christ: The preaching of the Gospel.

was confirmed: The passive voice is often used as a circumlocution for the divine activity.

. . . even as . . . so that: The relation of these two verses is not obvious. The point is not simply that as a result of the preaching of the Gospel the Corinthians display and/or experience spiritual gifts. If one examines the thanksgivings at the beginning of Paul's epistles, it is clear that these 'even as' clauses[78] play an important role in them.[79] They seem to indicate, not just response to the preaching of the Gospel, but a sense in which the preaching of the Gospel is carried on in turn by those who respond to it faithfully. There is no such thing as a passive reception of the Gospel. One's response in faith involves one in an active witness. It is in this sense that we must understand the clause.

7

you are not lacking in any spiritual gift: It will become clear, however, that the Corinthians do not understand Paul's meaning here. He will have to explain to them at some length what is implied in his notion of the fullness of the Spirit's operation.[80]

as you wait for the revealing of our Lord: This is the proper posture for Christians. They *wait*. They have not yet arrived. There is a time of waiting between one's entrance into *the fellowship* (v. 9) and the final consummation of God's plan for the world – *the revealing of our Lord Jesus Christ* or *the day of our Lord Jesus Christ* (v. 8). The reference here

---

76. E.g. 3¹⁰.   77. Cf. 2 Cor. 1¹⁹f.; cp. Rom. 3²⁴.
78. 2 Cor. 1⁵; 1 Thess. 1⁵; 2 Thess. 1³f.; cp. John 13³⁴, 17².
79. Cf. Schubert, op. cit. (n. 73), 31.   80. Cf. Chapters 12–14.

as elsewhere in Paul's writings[81] is to the end of the world, an idea which the early church inherited from Judaism.[82]

In a preliminary way Paul sets up his basic message to the Corinthians: if your attention is where it belongs, that is upon Jesus Christ, there will be no problem concerning the working of the Spirit.

8

who will sustain you: The Greek word translated here *sustain* is *bebaiōsei*, and it represents the same verb translated above in v. 6 as *confirmed*. The idea of the continuity of the Saviour's action is thus emphasized: he did act and he will continue to do so until the end of the world.

guiltless: The day of the Lord is traditionally in the Jewish thought of the time the day of judgement.[83] In the same way as he continues to work in the life of the Christian,[84] so the Lord Jesus will be the basis of our acquittal in the final judgement. There is a curious paradox here: in vv. 6f. Paul is concerned to indicate that the Corinthians have not yet arrived at the perfect situation associated with God's revelation at the last day. Their proper posture is one of waiting. On the other hand, the believer may have confidence, on the basis of the continuous operation of the Lord through the Spirit,[85] that he will have no accusations made against him in the final judgement.

9

God is faithful: This sentence suggests a certain liturgical form, as do the concluding sentences of other thanksgiving sections in Paul's epistles.[86] God's faithfulness is the ultimate basis for man's faithfulness.

the fellowship of his son . . . : In the term *fellowship*, Greek *koinōnia*, there is involved something of the same paradox which we noted above on v. 8. There is a sense in which by *fellowship* Paul understands that we share in the status of God's son.[87] But this means that we also share in the whole community-process of salvation, that is there are no passive or solitary recipients of salvation.[88]

81. Rom. 8^{18f.}; 2 Cor. 5^{2ff.}; Phil. 3²⁰.
82. Cf. Amos 5¹⁸.   83. Cf. above on v. 7.
84. Cf. above on vv. 6f.
85. Cf. above on *sustain*.
86. Cf. J. T. Sanders, 'The Transition from Opening Epistolary Thanksgiving to Body in the Letters of the Pauline Corpus', *JBL*, 81 (1962), 348–62; J. M. Robinson, op. cit. (n. 75).
87. Cf. Gal. 4³⁷; Rom. 8^{14f.}   88. Cf. Rom. 8^{17ff.}; 2 Cor. 1⁷; 1 Thess. 1^{5ff.}.

In this brief thanksgiving Paul sets out the economy of salvation. It is against this background that he now proceeds immediately to take up the problems of the Corinthian church. Much of what Paul will say in his letter will show how the Corinthians have misunderstood Paul's conception of the saving operation of God through the fellowship of those who believe in Jesus Christ.

$I^{10}-4^{21}$ THE TRUE BASIS FOR CHRISTIAN BELIEF
PAUL'S INTEGRITY AS A CHRISTIAN PREACHER

Paul is concerned about two things in this first section of the body of the epistle:

1. the way in which the Corinthians understand and express their Christian faith;
2. their relation to him as a preacher of the Gospel.

The first concern has two aspects:

a. a tendency to internal stress and difference of opinion about the expression of the faith;

b. an emphasis upon wisdom of which Paul does not approve.

The second concern is the main thrust of this section. Paul must somehow establish his authority over the Corinthians before he can expect to gain a hearing for the admonitions and counsel which he will offer in the rest of the epistle.

I^{10-17} AN APPEAL FOR UNITY

10 *I appeal to you, brethren, by the name of our Lord Jesus Christ, that all of you agree and that there be no dissensions among you, but that you be united in the same mind and the same judgement.* 11*For it has been reported to me by Chloe's people that there is quarrelling among you, my brethren.* 12*What I mean is that each one of you says, 'I belong to Paul,' or 'I belong to Apollos', or 'I belong to Cephas', or 'I belong to Christ'.* 13*Is Christ divided? Was Paul crucified for you? Or were you baptized in the name of*

Paul? 14I am thankful that I baptized none of you except Crispus and Gaius; 15lest any one should say that you were baptized in my name. 16(I did baptize also the household of Stephanas. Beyond that, I do not know whether I baptized anyone else.) 17For Christ did not send me to baptize but to preach the gospel, and not with eloquent wisdom, lest the cross of Christ be emptied of its power.

Paul appeals to the congregation for unity in *mind* and *judgement*, that is in their thought and in the expression of their thought in specific statements. The *quarrelling* was somehow related to an attachment to one of four figures: Apollos, Paul, Cephas, or Christ. The *quarrels* threaten *dissensions* (N.E.B. is better here: 'divisions', literally 'schisms'). Just how deep were these quarrels, and what did they concern? Scholarly opinion seems to be moving away from the position of F. C. Baur, which dominated the nineteenth and the early twentieth centuries. Using the general thesis which we outlined in the Introduction,[89] Baur linked the Cephas party and the Christ party as representing the Jewish wing of the church. The parties adhering to Paul and Apollos represented the gentile wing. There have been many variations on this thesis. They have all had to reckon, however, with two basic criticisms:

1. The *divisions* so called are not what Paul is immediately concerned about. He specifically says: *that ... there be no dissensions* (schism). . . . He does not say: there is dissension. Rather he says that *quarrelling* is *reported.*

2. The problems in Corinth do not seem to have been of Jewish origin, at least not in 1 Corinthians.[90] Paul is faced in 1 Cor. with problems of a specifically gentile character. If anything the problem is the reverse of Baur's formulation: Paul represents the more Jewish orientation rather than that of his gentile opponents in Corinth.

It seems incongruous in Paul's description of the quarrels that he apparently disapproves of people who claim any special attachment to himself or to Christ. Some analysts have attempted to remove the second problem by claiming that the statement *'belong to Christ'* is a

89. See pp. xviiff.

90. Cf. N. Dahl, 'Paul and the Church at Corinth in I Cor. 1¹⁰–4²¹', *Christian History and Interpretation, Studies Presented to John Knox*, ed. Farmer, Moule, and Niebuhr, 1967, 313ff.

copyist's comment which found its way from the margin of a manu-script into the text.[91] Others have made a distinction between the first three watchwords and the fourth, attributing *I belong to Christ* to Paul himself, that is this is his watchword.[92] It is best to take Paul's statement at face value. He disapproves of all four watch-words. One should not even say *I belong to Christ*. When Paul later comes to his own formulation of this, it is significant that he seems to approve of this fourth watchword when he states *you are Christ's*. But he amplifies this immediately by adding *and Christ is God's*. If saying *I belong to Christ* causes quarrelling, or is an expression of quarrelling in the community, then perhaps it is better left unsaid.

ഇരു

11
Chloe's people: Those who were part of the household of Chloe, perhaps domestic slaves.

12
The character of the connection between one who said, *I belong to Apollos,* and Apollos himself is hard to ascertain. Some suggest by analogy to the mystery cults that a special relation existed between the neophyte and the one who baptized him.[93] This would make Paul's group rather small, since he baptized so few. These names are probably only labels by which people in Corinth designated their point of view. We know that Apollos had been in Corinth. Cephas (Peter) probably had not been in Corinth. However, one can certainly see a point of view represented in his name by the author of the Gospel according to Matthew (cf. 16¹³⁻¹⁹).[94] It may be that the main point of all these designations indicates an attempt to declare independence from Paul's point of view.[95] In this case Paul would include his own name in the list as a matter of rhetoric.

13
Is Christ divided?: Can also be taken as a declarative statement, if it refers to what precedes. If it refers to the discussion of Baptism which follows, then it is a rhetorical question. (N.E.B., 'Surely Christ has not

91. Héring, ad loc.   92. Barrett, ad loc.
93. Cf. Héring, ad loc.
94. C. K. Barrett, 'Cephas at Corinth', *Abraham unser Vater Festschrift für Otto Michel*, ed. O. Betz, M. Hengel, P. Schmidt, 1963, 1–12.
95. Cf. Dahl, op. cit. (n. 90).

been divided among you!') What follows is definitely a rhetorical question in two parts: (a) Was Paul crucified for you? (b) Or were you baptized into the name of Paul?

The connection between Baptism and Christ's death is made clear in Rom. 6³⁻¹¹. Paul will not resume his discussion of the cross until v. 17b. He seems to be arguing still for unity. In vv. 10ff. his reference is to mind and judgement. Here in vv. 13ff. it is to Baptism and the cross. Paul argues against the quarrelling and using slogans of a party nature on two grounds: (a) It is Christ who was crucified, not Paul, Apollos or Cephas. (b) It is in Christ's name they are baptized, not Paul's, Apollos's, or Cephas's. There is a kind of diversity within the church which Paul will discuss later, in Chapter 12. There too he will emphasize not simply diversity, but diversity in unity. Cf. also Gal. 3²⁷ᶠ·.

baptized in the name of: In some other religions there is evidence for a kind of mystical parent–relation between the initiator and the initiate, to which the Corinthians might have appealed.[96]

14ff.
Crispus: Cf. Acts 18⁸. *Gaius:* Acts 19²⁹ (at Ephesus).

Paul's negative concern for Baptism can be explained, if there was a preparation of the neophyte by the person who was to baptize him.[97] All this, as I suggest in the Introduction, is subsequent to the preaching of the Gospel, the faithful reception of it and the coming of the Spirit. Paul's mission is prior to Baptism – he plants, he lays the foundation, others built on it.[98]

17
to preach . . . not with eloquent wisdom, lest the cross of Christ be emptied of its power: This is a transitional section. Paul moves here to his first major subject in the section 1¹⁰⁻4²¹: the way in which the Corinthians understand and express their Christian faith.

with eloquent wisdom: The meaning of the Greek phrase *en sophia logou* (literally in wisdom of word) is not clear. Is the emphasis to be placed on the term *wisdom* as a technical term with a special meaning? That is, are we dealing here with some kind of gnosticism or wisdom-mystique?[99] Or is the emphasis to be placed on *word* as expressing the art of word, that is discourse or rhetoric?[100] So, for instance, N.E.B.:

96. Cf. Héring, ad loc.
97. ibid.; cf. Matt. 28²⁰.
98. Cf. below on 3¹⁰.
99. U. Wilckens, op. cit. (n. 10), 11ff.
100. Cf. Barrett, ad loc.

'the language of worldly wisdom'. Frequent reference to *the world* in the following section would seem to bear out the latter emphasis.

On the other hand, other terms such as *spiritual men, men of flesh,* and *unspiritual man* tend to point in the direction of a more technical meaning for wisdom.[101]

This approach Paul contrasts with his own, which emphasizes *the power . . .* (of) *the cross of Christ.* The question is what is the *power of the cross?*

I^18-25   WISDOM AND PREACHING

[18]*For the word of the cross is folly to those who are perishing, but to us who are being saved it is the power of God.* [19]*For it is written,*
'I will destroy the wisdom of the wise, and the cleverness of the clever I will thwart.'
[20]*Where is the wise man? Where is the scribe? Where is the debater of this age? Has not God made foolish the wisdom of the world?* [21]*For since, in the wisdom of God, the world did not know God through wisdom, it pleased God through the folly of what we preach to save those who believe.* [22]*For Jews demand signs and Greeks seek wisdom,* [23]*but we preach Christ crucified, a stumbling-block to Jews and folly to Gentiles,* [24]*but to those who are called, both Jews and Greeks, Christ the power of God and the wisdom of God.* [25]*For the foolishness of God is wiser than men, and the weakness of God is stronger than men.*

In this section Paul seems to deprecate human wisdom, which would contradict what he says in Rom. 1^18-20. There he states that God reveals himself through his Creation. This deprecation of wisdom also seems to contradict what Paul is to say later in 2^6, where he says that *among the mature we do* impart wisdom. It is not *wisdom per se,* however, which Paul deprecates. Paul speaks here of the fact that even with wisdom man did not recognize God. This is also his point in

101. Cf. B. Gärtner, 'The Pauline and Johannine Idea of "To know God" against the Hellenistic Background', *NTS*, 14 (1968), 209–31; K. Niederwimmer, 'Erkennen und Lieben, Gedenken zum Verhältnis von Gnosis und Agape im ersten Korintherbrief', *Ker u Dog*, 11 (1965), 75–102; H. Conzelmann, 'Paulus und die Weisheit', *NTS*, 12 (1966), 231–44.

Rom. 1$^{21ff.}$, where he makes the point that, even though they knew him, men did not honour him as God. Instead they made idols resembling men or animals.

It is in this situation that God makes wisdom foolish by making *foolishness* (the preaching of the cross) into *wisdom* (v. 21). This is the paradoxical character of the divine action which comes through in the teachings of Jesus.[102] Once man has accepted foolishness as wisdom and wisdom as foolishness, he is prepared to be mature and to receive wisdom (2^6).

ﬡﬡ

18

those who are perishing . . . us who are being saved: It is important to note the present tense. There are no guarantees in just 'belonging'. To those who find objectionable the idea that God allows anyone to perish, one can only ask whether this is worse than having one's freedom taken away. The idea of the 'two ways' is deeply rooted in the Hebrew–Jewish mentality.[103]

19f.

Paul quotes from or alludes to Isa. 29^{14}, Psalm 33^{10}, and Isa. 19^{11} in order to substantiate his previous statement about wisdom.

Where . . . where . . . where: Paul may not depend on rhetorical skill, but he is not without it. This is a typical example of a rhetorical device probably borrowed from the 'diatribe'.[104]

Wise man . . . scribe . . . debater of the age: Some see Paul deprecating all of these. Others would say that he means to deprecate only the *debater*, since Apollos is a *wise man* (Acts 18^{24}) and Paul himself qualifies as a *scribe* (Acts 22^3). It is probable that Paul means to deprecate all three. He is satisfied to designate both himself and Apollos as *servants through whom you believed* (1 Cor. 3^5).

21

The recurrence of the term *wisdom* in this verse is confusing. Are there two kinds of wisdom, God's and man's? Or is the emphasis to be

102. Cf. Mark 9^{35}; 10^{31} par.; 10^{44} parr.
103. Deut. 30$^{15ff.}$; cp. 11$^{26-28}$; Sir. 15$^{11ff.}$; Jer. 21^8; Proverbs 8$^{34-6}$; Did. 1^1.
104. R. Bultmann, *Der Stil der Paulinischen Predigt und die kynisch-stoische Diatribe*, 1910.

placed on the prepositions – *in* the wisdom of God, *through* wisdom – so that we are dealing simply with two aspects of wisdom? The term wisdom seems to have no special content in itself in this section. Paul speaks of the *wisdom of God* here in v. 21, and again in v. 24, the content of which is *Christ crucified* (cf. v. 30; 2^6,7^). On the other hand, there is a wisdom through which man does not know God (1^21^; 1^1,4,5^). It is perhaps most reasonable to conclude that *wisdom* is a neutral term for Paul which depends upon the content given to it for its meaning.

in the wisdom of God: Refers therefore to God's plan of salvation, which does not include man's knowledge of him *through wisdom*.

through the folly of what we preach: On the human level of understanding, God's plan of salvation through the crucified Messiah is foolishness compared to what man thinks he knows of God through wisdom. Through faith, however, man knows just the opposite, that is that it is through this folly that man knows God. The R.S.V. translation here is misleading. The Greek text is literally through the folly of 'the preaching' (N.E.B. has 'Gospel'). The Greek word is *kērygma* and refers not only to what is preached but to the act of preaching itself.[105] The activity of the church is as much a part of God's folly ^s the saving act of Christ's death. Paul will make this point rather strongly in vv. 26ff.

24f.
Greeks and Jews are distinguished here because the inability of the Jews to accept a crucified Messiah found substantiation in their scriptures[106] and was therefore a *stumbling-block* rather than just *foolishness*.

Christ the power of God and the wisdom of God: Power as a description of what God does in the world recurs in 2^4,5^. The Gospel is not something purely intellectual, but something which happens, which involves action. If the Gospel is a message, it must be spelled out in the language of deeds as well as words. Our proclamation of the Good News of salvation in Jesus Christ must and will be expressed as much by what we are and do as by what we say. And this is true even when our action is accounted weakness and foolishness by the standards of the world.

105. Cf. H. Schlier, 'Kerygma und Sophia', *EvTheol*, 10 (1950/51), 481–9.
106. Deut. 21^22f.^

²⁶*For consider your call, brethren; not many of you were wise according to worldly standards, not many were powerful, not many were of noble birth;* ²⁷*but God chose what is foolish in the world to shame the wise, God chose what is weak in the world to shame the strong,* ²⁸*God chose what is low and despised in the world, even things that are not, to bring to nothing things that are,* ²⁹*so that no human being might boast in the presence of God.* ³⁰*He is the source of your life in Christ Jesus, whom God made our wisdom, our righteousness and sanctification and redemption;* ³¹*therefore, as it is written, 'Let him who boasts, boast of the Lord.'*

This section is parallel to what follows in 2¹⁻⁵. Both are descriptions of the activity of God in the church: strong in weakness, wise in foolishness. The purpose of this activity of the church is *to shame* mankind, to turn man's boasting into *boasting of the Lord.*[107]

26f.
your call: It is God who calls. The question is, does God's call include our status in life or is it strictly our call to faith in Christ? It is a common idea in some of the later portions of the Old Testament that the poor, the simple, the downtrodden are particularly favoured in God's sight.[108] There seems even to have been a period when the church – at least that part of it known to the author of Luke–Acts – tried a kind of communal ordering of their life together through a sharing of property.[109] Paul seems to be emphasizing here that the prevailing intellectual, economic, and social strata represented in the Corinthian Church are low and that this is part of God's plan. This will only serve to underscore his ironic statements later on about their wealth and power.[110]

107. Barrett, ad loc.
108. Zeph. 3¹²; Psalms 40¹⁷, 69³²ᶠ·, 86¹, 109²²; Isa. 29¹⁹, 61¹.
109. Acts 2⁴⁴ᶠ·, 4³². There is a negative attitude towards the possession of worldly goods which is found in a number of places in the New Testament. It finds its sharpest focus, however, in the Lucan Gospel. Cf. J. Ruef, 'Ananias and Sapphira: A Study of the Community-disciplinary Practices Underlying Acts 5¹⁻¹¹', thesis (unpublished), Harvard, 1960, 84–111.
110. Cf. below on 4⁸.

28

things that are not: Some would interpret this as a judgement by society on things which it treats *as if* they did not exist. Others take the phrase literally to mean non-existent things. In the latter sense Paul could be referring to the 'creation' of the church.

30

your life in Christ Jesus: The Greek here says literally 'you are in Christ Jesus' (so N.E.B.). This refers to the church and one's membership in it. It stands in marked contrast to *things that are not.*

wisdom . . . righteousness . . . sanctification . . . redemption: It is perhaps too much to see here a parallel to the list in vv. 26ff.: *not wise, not powerful, not of noble birth, things that are not.* The contrast, however, is marked. It has been suggested that the last three terms unfold the ideas suggested by the term *power* (v. 24). They all refer to the action of God-in-Christ and therefore God-in-the-church.

31

Paul here alludes to Jer. 9$^{22ff.}$ or I Sam. 2^{10}. This provides scriptural warrant for the low estate of most Christians. It is so the credit will go to God.[III]

2$^{1-5}$ MAN'S WISDOM – GOD'S POWER

^{1}*When I came to you, brethren, I did not come proclaiming to you the testimony of God in lofty words or wisdom.* ^{2}*For I decided to know nothing among you except Jesus Christ and him crucified.* ^{3}*And I was with you in weakness and in much fear and trembling;* ^{4}*and my speech and my message were not in plausible words of wisdom, but in demonstration of the Spirit and power,* ^{5}*that your faith might not rest in the wisdom of men but in the power of God.*

Now Paul comes to his own particular case. He picks up the idea of I^{17}: eloquent wisdom versus the power of the cross of Christ. This time he refers to lofty words and wisdom, which he contrasts with Christ crucified. Some have tried to see reflected here a decision by Paul which he made after his so-called Sermon on the Areopagus in

III. Cf. above on the beginning of section I$^{26-31}$.

Acts 17: discouraged by the philosophical approach he used in Athens, Paul decided to change his tactics when he confronted the gentiles of Corinth.[112] What is more probable is that it was in Corinth that Paul turned to the gentiles and for the first time perhaps faced the problem of presenting Christianity outside the Jewish milieu. Paul's emphasis upon the death of Christ was probably brought about by the nature of the response made by the Corinthians to his preaching of the Gospel.[113]

the testimony: There is some ancient evidence for the reading 'the mystery'. Most commentators take this as an early attempt to harmonize this verse with v. 7 below.

2
to know nothing among you except Jesus Christ and him crucified: As I have suggested above, this turned out to be the emphasis of Paul in his presentation of the Gospel to the Corinthians. The emphasis should therefore be on the phrase *among you.* Paul here is admitting to a certain tactic in his mode of preaching – an emphasis upon the death of Christ.

3
weakness...fear...trembling: Some have interpreted this as a trembling anxiety to perform his duty of preaching the Gospel. It seems simpler to take his statement at face value. His *weakness* is a counterpart to the prevailing lack of distinguished people among the Corinthians. Its purpose is also parallel: so that their '*faith might not rest in the wisdom of men but in the power of God*' (5). The contrast is parallel to the one in 1¹⁷: *not human wisdom, but divine power.*

4
demonstration of the Spirit and power: There was nothing in Paul's mode of life or presentation of the Gospel which would have moved them to faith (v. 3). Therefore their faithful response must be attributed to the divine power. What form did their faithful response take? Paul has mentioned the Spirit as something which demonstrates or is demonstrated. It is the first of thirty-six instances of the use of the word in 1 Corinthians alone.

112. Cf. Barrett, ad loc.
113. Cf. the section on the Spirit in the Introduction.

We have indicated in the Introduction the peculiar meaning and importance which 'spirit' had for the Corinthian Church. Paul makes no very clear distinction between the various uses of the word spirit and the person of Christ.[114] Both can and do refer to the divine presence and power within the community. This would indicate that the *demonstration of Spirit and power* was the faithful response of the Corinthians to Paul's preaching and that it must have taken forms akin to those mentioned in 12[8ff.]: the utterance of wisdom, the utterance of knowledge, faith, etc. None of this, says Paul, has come about through any particular attribute, either of Paul or his hearers – it is God's doing.

2^6-3^4 THE CHRISTIAN MESSAGE IN
              CORINTHIAN TERMINOLOGY

[6]*Yet among the mature we do impart wisdom, although it is not a wisdom of this age or of the rulers of this age, who are doomed to pass away.* [7]*But we impart a secret and hidden wisdom of God, which God decreed before the ages for our glorification.* [8]*None of the rulers of this age understood this; for if they had, they would not have crucified the Lord of glory.* [9]*But, as it is written,*

     'What no eye has seen, nor ear heard,
     nor the heart of man conceived,
     what God has prepared for those who love him',

[10]*God has revealed to us through the Spirit. For the Spirit searches everything, even the depths of God.* [11]*For what person knows a man's thoughts except the spirit of the man which is in him? So also no one comprehends the thoughts of God except the Spirit of God.* [12]*Now we have received not the spirit of the world, but the Spirit which is from God, that we might understand the gifts bestowed on us by God.* [13]*And we impart this in words not taught by human wisdom but taught by the Spirit, interpreting spiritual truths to those who possess the Spirit.*

[14]*The unspiritual man does not receive the gifts of the Spirit of God, for they are folly to him, and he is not able to understand them because they are spiritually discerned.* [15]*The spiritual man judges all things, but is himself to be judged by no one.* [16]*'For who has known the mind of the Lord so as to instruct him?' But we have the mind of Christ.*

114. Cf. I. Hermann, *Kyrios und Pneuma*, 1961, 74ff.

3 ¹*But I, brethren, could not address you as spiritual men, but as men of the flesh, as babes in Christ. ²I fed you with milk, not solid food; for you were not ready for it; and even yet you are not ready, ³for you are still of the flesh. For while there is jealousy and strife among you, are you not of the flesh, and behaving like ordinary men? ⁴For when one says, 'I belong to Paul,' and another, 'I belong to Apollos,' are you not merely men?*

This section is puzzling. It contradicts what Paul has said about wisdom. We have discussed this contradiction in connection with 1²¹ above. Paul also seems to be making distinctions among the Christians themselves: between those who are mature and (by implication) those who are not (v. 6); between those who possess the Spirit and those who are unspiritual (vv. 13f.). The question is immediately raised, is Paul holding something back? Furthermore, are some Christians on a higher or more 'spiritual' plane than others?

The confusing character of this passage may be somewhat more understandable if we assume that Paul is here employing the Corinthians' own terminology.[115] They refer to *mature* men, *spiritual* and *unspiritual* men and a *wisdom* understood only by such. A wisdom reserved for the mature is their idea, not Paul's. So, says Paul, let's use your terminology. Let's talk about a hidden wisdom known only by the *mature*, the *spiritual*. This kind of idea can certainly be substantiated from sacred writings (v. 9), from what we know of the spirit of man and (by inference) the spirit of God (vv. 106f.). *The Spiritual man judges all things but is . . . judged by no one* (v. 15). And then Paul turns the whole train of thought around and says, in effect, who are the spiritual ones among you? Are they the ones who say, I belong to Apollos or I belong to Paul? One cannot call such people '*spiritual*' (not even '*unspiritual*'), certainly not '*mature*'. These people are '*men of flesh*', '*babes in Christ*'.

ର୍ତ୍ତ

6

. . . mature: The Corinthians probably understood this term in the sense which it has in the Hellenistic Gnostic-philosophical writings: those who had received the true knowledge (Greek, *gnōsis*) were the spiritual ones

115. Wilckens, op. cit. (n. 10), 52–96.

and were 'perfect' (Greek, *teleioi*).[116] Paul accepts the term and then contrasts it in 3^1 with *babes* to bring out its other meaning of *mature*.

7f.

wisdom . . . the ages . . . rulers of this age: These are terms known from later literature to be characteristically 'gnostic'. It is in some such sense that the Corinthians probably used them. This would rule out understanding *rulers* solely as temporal rulers, as do some commentators.[117] Here it may be helpful to think of Paul using a term which has one meaning for the Corinthians (heavenly beings) and another meaning for Paul (earthly rulers). This latter sense is evidenced clearly in Rom. 13^{1-7}. The same thing can be said about *this age*.[118]

secret and hidden . . . decreed before the ages: Paul emphasizes the hiddenness of the plan of salvation (wisdom of God) which not even the heavenly beings (earthly rulers) knew, because had they known it they would not have cooperated with God in carrying it out. The emphasis is on the hiddenness of God's plan, not on the unwitting cooperation of the rulers.

Lord of glory:[119] The hiddenness is substantiated as the mode of God's operation by a quotation (as it is written) from some holy book. Most commentators assume that this is taken from the Apocalypse of Elias to which Origen refers in his Commentary on Matthew 29^9.[120]

10–16

Now Paul's attention turns from hiddenness to spirit. Since the wisdom of God is hidden by God, one must receive it from God, and in order to receive it one must have the Spirit, i.e. be spiritual.

10f.

The Spirit is also God's mode of operation.

the spirit of the man: It is probably best to take this as meaning 'mind'.[121] God, however, does not give us his 'mind' but his spirit – we have the *mind of Christ* (v. 16).

116. R. Bultmann, *Theology of the New Testament* (E.T. by K. Grobel), 1951, I, 181. Also Gärtner, op. cit. (n. 101).

117. J. Schniewind, 'Die Archonten dieses Aons', Kor. 2^{6-8}, *Nachgelasene Reden und Aufsätze*, 1952, 104–9.

118. Cf. the general Introduction, pp. xixf.

119. Cf. Enoch (Ethiopic) 22^{14}; $25^{3,7}$; $27^{3,4}$; 63^2; 75^3.

120. Weiss, ad loc. Also Barrett.

121. But see also Isa. 64^4; $65^{16(17)}$.

12

the spirit of the world: Here again one must assume that Paul is using the Corinthians' terminology. *Spirit of the world* would parallel *rulers of this age.* It does not know God's plan of salvation either.

13

we impart this: Paul is describing, not without irony, the discourse of the Corinthian community.

spiritual truths . . . those who possess the Spirit: The Greek, *pneumatikois pneumatika,* has just the slightest touch of the English, 'sweets for the sweet'. The first *pneumatikois* can also mean 'spiritual matters', if it is taken as a neuter. Most commentators prefer to take it as a masculine. The Greek word behind *interpreting* can also mean 'comparing'. The whole phrase could be rendered, 'comparing spiritual things with spiritual'. This would parallel *they are spiritually discerned* at the end of v. 14.[122]

14

unspiritual man: The Greek term is *psychikos* and means literally 'natural'. In more developed gnostic terminology this would refer to the intermediate variety of men – those who could be saved, as distinguished from the 'hylic' or 'earthly', who could not, and the 'pneumatic', who already were.[123] Some such system may have developed out of the kind of thinking in which, as we see it, the Corinthians were engaged. There is little evidence that such a developed system existed at the time 1 Corinthians was written.[124] The point is that they thought of themselves as *spiritual* and Paul is using their terminology.

15

The spiritual man . . . is . . . judged by no one: This is the theological basis for their watchword, *All things are lawful for me* (6^{12}). One did not presume to judge those who had the Spirit since God spoke through them (Mark $3^{28f.}$ parr.; Did. xi. 7). However, there could be the problem of who really had the Spirit and who was just pretending or had an evil spirit (12^{10}; 1 John $4^{1ff.}$; Did. xi 8f.). It will be clear in $3^{1ff.}$ that Paul does not consider the claim of the Corinthians to have the Spirit to be the end of the discussion.

122. The most thorough discussion of the various possibilities is in R.-P., ad loc.
123. R. McL. Wilson, op. cit. (n. 16), 131, 2.
124. C. Colpe, *Die religionsgeschichtliche Schule,* 1961, 64ff. R. McL. Wilson, *Gnosis and the New Testament,* 1968, 1–30.

16

the mind of Christ: The Corinthians claim to know the divine mind because they know the mind of Christ. The thought of the quotation is parallel to that of the quotation in v. 9 above. Again, *mind* (Greek, *nous*) is one of those terms which are important in the scheme of creation and redemption in Gnosticism. In the more developed Gnostic schemes, *mind* is one of the emanations from the one true God prior to the creation by lesser beings of the material world. In at least one scheme he is identified with Christ and is sent by God to redeem man.[125]

Who has known the mind of the Lord: This parting bit of irony, taken from Isa. 40[13] (LXX), expresses one of the wellsprings of all religion: the desire to know ultimate reality – *the mind of the Lord.* The Jew knew that this longing must ever be unfulfilled (Exod. 34[20]; John 1[18]). God must reveal himself. For the Jew this happened in the Law of Moses. To follow the Law was as much as any man could expect to know of God. But the disciples of Jesus claimed that one could only understand the Law through an understanding of Jesus. The form of this understanding is what is at issue here in 1 Corinthians. The Corinthian Christians, probably because they were gentiles, thought that, because they had the mind of Christ, they knew a good deal more about God than, from a Jewish point of view, was possible. This would be the point of Paul's use of this quotation which ends . . . *so as to instruct him? But we have the mind of Christ,* say the Corinthians. In what follows Paul will examine the legitimacy of their claim to have *the mind of Christ.*

3^{1-4}

Here Paul turns the claim of the Corinthian Christians against them. He was not able to teach any more profoundly than he did, because they had not reached the degree of spiritual maturity of the perfect (*teleioi*, 2^6) then, and they have not reached it yet. This is borne out by their quarrelling (vv. 3, 4). They have not reached the stage of 'pneumatics'. They are still ruled by their fleshly nature (vv. 1, 3). They are *babes* rather than *mature* men.

2

milk . . . not solid food: A Jewish simile found in the rabbis and in Philo.[126] This is Paul's way of emphasizing what he means by 'mature' (cf. above on 2^6).

---

125. R. McL. Wilson, op. cit. (n. 16), 123, 4.
126. Cf. R.-P., ad loc. for references. Cp. Heb. 5[12].

4

Paul . . . Apollos:[127] If the Corinthians had reached the state of maturity and spirituality to which they lay claim (2^{6-16}), they would not be involved in this kind of strife.

5What then is Apollos? What is Paul? Servants through whom you believed, as the Lord assigned to each. 6I planted, Apollos watered, but God gave the growth. 7So neither he who plants nor he who waters is anything, but only God who gives the growth. 8He who plants and he who waters are equal, and each shall receive his wages according to his labour. 9For we are fellow workmen for God;

Paul now describes the true relation between himself and Apollos. There was evidently no antagonism between these two (v. 8), though there is reason to believe, from the account of Apollos in Acts 18^{24-8}, that his initial understanding of Christianity would not have been that of the Apostle.

ॐ

5

Servants:[128] Here Paul defines their function as that of eliciting faith, presumably by preaching. There is an economy in all this activity which Paul describes by an agricultural analogy: he is the one who plants, Apollos is the one who waters. It is God, however, who causes growth, and in comparison with him his servants are not anything. This divine division of labour is much more clearly worked out by Paul in his discussion of the church in 12^{4-31}.

6

planted . . . watered: One should not press an analogy too far, but one cannot help asking what the difference was between the activity of Paul and that of Apollos? That their approaches to the faith were not

127. Cf. above on $1^{12\text{ff.}}$.
128. Cp. servants of God, 2 Cor. 6^4; servants of the New Testament, ibid., 3^6; servants of Christ, ibid., 11^{23}.

the same is evidenced not only by Acts 18²⁴⁻⁸,[129] but by the fact that dissension arose between those who claimed allegiance to Paul and those who claimed allegiance to Apollos. According to Acts, Apollos was learned in the scriptures (18²⁴), he taught about Jesus, knew only the baptism of John (v. 25) and spent his time trying to prove to Jews (from the scriptures) that Jesus was the Messiah (v. 28). When Paul returned to Ephesus (19¹) Apollos was in Corinth, having presumably left Ephesus. Paul found there disciples who had not received the Spirit and who knew only the baptism of John (vv. 2, 3). Paul then baptized them in the name of Jesus, laid hands on them, and they received the Spirit, spoke in tongues and prophesied.

I have tried to point out in the Introduction the significance of the Spirit in the Corinthian community.[130] Paul deals mainly with this and related problems in I Corinthians. He does not need to use the Jewish scriptures to prove that Jesus is the Messiah. His knowledge of who Jesus is is unmediated and comes directly from the Lord.[131] We have suggested that the phenomenon of the Spirit among the Corinthians is not unrelated to the manner in which Paul received his revelation of Jesus from God.

Perhaps then Apollos concerned himself with the (Jewish) scriptures. He would have shown how Jesus was the prophesied Messiah.[132] Though Paul saw Apollos's activity as coordinate with his own, it is quite possible that there were those who saw Paul's approach as incompatible with that of Apollos (I am of Apollos) and vice versa (I am of Paul). Paul would rather make the point that there is a division of function. God has given a labour to each man (vv. 5, 8) for the faithful accomplishment of which each one shall receive his wages. The wages should not be separated from the labour, nor should they be thought of as earned. The analogy only seeks to carry out the idea that each man has a vocation from God which he must perform in conjunction with all those others who are his (and God's) fellow workers. The whole point of the analogy is to show the complementary character of the work of Paul and Apollos.

129. Cf. above.
130. Cf. pp. xxviff.
131. Cf. Gal. 1¹¹,¹²,¹⁵ff..
132. Cf. Acts 8³⁰⁻⁵.

you are God's field, God's building.

   ¹⁰*According to the commission of God given to me, like a skilled master builder I laid a foundation, and another man is building upon it. Let each man take care how he builds upon it. ¹¹For no other foundation can anyone lay than that which is laid, which is Jesus Christ. ¹²Now if any one builds on the foundation with gold, silver, precious stones, wood, hay, stubble – ¹³each man's work will become manifest; for the Day will disclose it, because it will be revealed with fire, and the fire will test what sort of work each one has done. ¹⁴If the work which any man has built on the foundation survives, he will receive a reward. ¹⁵If any man's work is burned up, he will suffer loss, though he himself will be saved, but only as through fire.*

The relation of Christian leaders to one another is probably still fore-most in Paul's thinking. He turns from the agricultural analogy to that of building. In both these analogies Paul refers not so much to the object of their labours, that is the field or the structure, but rather to the work itself, that is husbandry or cultivation, building or construc-tion. Paul refers to God's saving activity in which he graciously co-opts man. What one man does as a fellow worker can be and, it is to be hoped, is complementary to what other fellow workers do. In the first analogy Paul stresses this complementary quality, despite the differences in approach of the men involved. God does not give the same kind of task to different people. This should not lead us to think, however, that, because the approaches of men differ in their response to God's call, they are all equally good, or that some are not contrary to God's purposes. This is the point of the second analogy.

∽

11

no other foundation can anyone lay: Men will respond to God's call in their different ways, but somehow they must all conform to Jesus Christ. He is normative.

24

than that which is laid, which is Jesus Christ: The Greek text has the sense of 'alongside' that which is laid, i.e. there is no way to begin again. The Christ whom Paul preached to the Corinthians is the beginning, the 'pioneer'[133] of their faith. The 'superstructure' of the faith must somehow be appropriate to the foundation.

13

the Day will disclose it: This is a reference to the 'last day', the day of judgement. This was closely associated in Jewish thought with the idea of fire.[134] The divine fire in the last day destroys those things and people who are opposed to God. Paul must be referring here to the work which men do in the church which is subsequent to and different from his work of foundation-laying. As in a serious fire, the entire superstructure of an edifice can be destroyed and leave the foundation walls upon which the structure can be rebuilt.

13ff.

the fire will test what sort of work each one has done: some work will survive, some will not. Those whose work survives will be *rewarded*. Those whose work burns up will *suffer loss*. Again one must not press what is an obvious analogy too far.

reward:[135] The nature of the reward or the loss is not important. What is important is that the work of those who follow Paul may survive and it may not, depending upon how true the workers are to Jesus Christ as Paul has preached him.

15

though he himself will be saved, but only as through fire: This statement stands in sharp contrast to what follows (vv. 16f.). The person himself will not be destroyed, even though his work does not stand the test of the judgement fire.

as through fire: R.-P. suggests that this is a proverbial saying, like 'a brand snatched from the burning'.[136]

133. Cf. Heb. 3[12].
134. Cf. Mal. 3[1f.]; 4[1f.]; other references in Héring.
135. Cf. above on *wages*, v. 8.
136. Cf. Amos 4[11]; Zech. 3[2].

^{16}*Do you not know that you are God's temple and that God's Spirit dwells in you?* ^{17}*If any one destroys God's temple, God will destroy him. For God's temple is holy, and that temple you are.*

If anyone destroys God's temple, God will destroy him: This is similar to the thought of 1 Thess. 3^8. The temple is another analogy for the church. There was only one temple of God, and it was in Jerusalem. Anyone who harmed it in any way could be destroyed. Like the temple, the church was considered holy. Like the temple, the church also has God's presence (the Spirit). Destruction of the temple (church) would thus also involve an affront to the Spirit.[137] To consider the question of whether temple is to be taken individually or collectively is to miss the point of the analogy.[138]

^{18}*Let no one deceive himself. If any one among you thinks that he is wise in this age, let him become a fool that he may become wise.* ^{19}*For the wisdom of this world is folly with God. For it is written, 'He catches the wise in their craftiness,'* ^{20}*and again, 'The Lord knows that the thoughts of the wise are futile.'* ^{21}*So let no one boast of men. For all things are yours,* ^{22}*whether Paul or Apollos or Cephas or the world or life or death or the present or the future, all are yours;* ^{23}*and you are Christ's; and Christ is God's.*

This passage once again demonstrates the paradoxical character of true wisdom.[139] True wisdom has as its content Christ crucified, which the world (Jews and Greeks) consider foolishness (1^{23}). There is a direct parallel here to 1$^{20ff.}$, now applied to the individual.

༄༅

137. Cf. Mark 3^{28}; Acts 5$^{1-11}$.   138. Cf. also 11$^{28ff.}$.
139. Cf. above 1$^{20-25}$.

18

in this age: Should be taken with *wise*.[140]

let him become a fool . . . cp. 4[10] below. The word fool (Greek, *mōros*) was used by one of the philosophical groups (the later Stoics) as a semi-technical term to designate their opponents.

19f.

Now Paul once more substantiates his attitude towards wisdom by appeal to the scriptures.[141]

20

The Lord knows that the thoughts of the wise are futile: For *wise* some manuscripts read 'men'. This is the reading of the Greek text of the Psalm. Paul could have been quoting from memory and substituted 'wise' for 'men' on the analogy of the quotation from Job. A later copyist could have changed 'wise' back to 'men' either because he knew the text of the Psalm or because he was looking ahead to 'men' in v. 21.

21

boast of men: Here Paul picks up his statement about boasting in 1[29,31]. Any boasting should be of God and what God has done for man whom he has placed, according to Jewish thought, over all things.[142] Man's wisdom, Paul has shown, is no cause for boasting[143] and leads him, not to a greater knowledge of God, but to quarrelling with his brethren. True wisdom consists in man's becoming a fool,[144] that is through his faithful response to the foolishness of the preaching of the cross (1[21]). True wisdom consists in knowing that God has placed man in a place of honour within the created order.

For all things are yours: The list which follows is in the style of the diatribe and is a technique used elsewhere by Paul.[145] Paul is really repeating here two slogans of the Corinthians: 'all things are ours'[146] and 'we are Christ's'.[147] Paul is now able to repeat them with approval because he has qualified them. The Christian's boast is not in any human leader in the church because as a 'spiritual' man he is judged by no one (2[15]). It is proper for him to boast 'I am Christ's' only if he is willing to add

140. Cf. N.E.B.: 'wise, I mean, by the standards of this passing age'.
141. Job 5[12f.]; Psalm 94[11].
142. Cf. Gen. 2[19f.], Mishnah, *Aboth*, 6[1] (through the study of the Law).
143. Cf. 1[26-9], 3[19].   144. Cf. v. 19 above.   145. Rom. 8[38f.].
146. Cf. 2[15].   147. Cf. 1[12].

'and Christ is God's'. Paul's reversal of the three initial slogans 'I belong to Paul . . . etc.' to read (in effect) 'Paul etc. belong to me' should probably not be taken as more than rhetorical hyperbole. Paul will later describe, with some care, the relation of the members of the community to one another.[148]

22

life or death: Paul tends to personify death.[149]

the present or the future: The past is not mentioned because this constitutes a part of the created order to which man no longer has access, and which conversely no longer has any control over man.[150]

4^{1-5} LEADERSHIP IN THE CHURCH

   [1]*This is how one should regard us, as servants of Christ and stewards of the mysteries of God.* [2]*Moreover it is required of stewards that they be found trustworthy.* [3]*But with me it is a very small thing that I should be judged by you or by any human court. I do not even judge myself.* [4]*I am not aware of anything against myself, but I am not thereby acquitted. It is the Lord who judges me.* [5]*Therefore do not pronounce judgement before the time, before the Lord comes, who will bring to light the things now hidden in darkness and will disclose the purposes of the heart. Then every man will receive his commendation from God.*

Paul has shown that the leaders within the community may not be played off against one another by those who would form factions around them. In this section he now speaks positively of the function of such church leaders as Apollos and himself.

                        ཙཙ

I

servants of Christ: The Greek word represented here by servant is *hypēretēs.* Originally it referred to those who manned the lower ranks of oars in a Greek trireme, a war galley or sailing ship with banks of

148. Cf. 6^7, 8^{7-13}, 11^{20-2}, 12^{12-31}.   149. Cf. Rom. $5^{12ff.}$.
150. Cf. Rom. 7^{1-6}.

rowers who propelled the ship in a calm. Then by extension it is
applied to all labourers.[151]

stewards: Greek *oikonomos,* a term for the one servant in the household
in charge of the other servants. Paul thus sharpens the perspective with
relation to the subordination of all men in the church to Christ (3[21ff.]).
As Paul has already implied in his statements about laying the foundation,[152] he stands in a position of authority where the Corinthian
Church is concerned.

mysteries of God: Paul refers here to such things as the mystery of the
general resurrection.[153] There is perhaps a distinction between what
Paul has received as the tradition of the church[154] and the divinely
inspired interpretation of the tradition.[155] The wisdom of God comes
in a mystery.[156] There is no evidence in Paul or the rest of the N.T. that
mysteries refers to the church's sacraments, that is Baptism, Eucharist.

2ff.

Paul makes two things clear in these verses: (1) the criterion for stewards
is trustworthiness; (2) the steward is judged by those whose stewards
they are, not those over whom they exercise stewardship.

2

Moreover: Is probably not the correct sense. The Greek is ambiguous.[157]
Hōde loipon probably means something like 'such being the case (i.e.
that we are stewards) it (only) remains that ...'

3

that I should be judged by you: The Corinthians held[158] that the spiritual
man judges all things but is himself to be judged by no one. Is Paul here
once again turning the thought of the Corinthians back upon themselves? Paul is willing to postpone all judgement on his apostolic activity,
including his own, until the coming of the Lord at the end of the world.
But, as the remainder of the epistle indicates, there is plenty of judging
to be done in other areas of the community's life.

151. N.E.B. catches the sense better: 'Christ's underlings'.
152. Cf. above 3[10ff.].   153. Cf. 15[51].
154. Cf. *witness,* 2[1]; *What I received,* 15[3].
155. Cf. *what I received from the Lord,* 11[23]; *I want you to understand,* 12[3];
the distinction between what the Lord charges the married, 7[8], and what Paul
himself says *to the rest,* 7[12].
156. Cf. above on 2[7].   157. Cp. N.E.B.[5] 'Well then ...'
158. Cf. above on 2[15].

or by any human court: The Greek says literally 'human day'. The phrase is copied from 'day of the Lord', the Hebrew phrase meaning end of the world, that is judgement day.[159]

4

I am not aware of anything against myself, but I am not thereby acquitted: Acquitted, that is, of any untrustworthiness in the exercise of his apostolate.[160]

5

before the time: That is, the day of the Lord as opposed to the human day.[161]

things now hidden in darkness ... the purposes of the heart: This is a way of emphasizing that nothing will escape the illumination of the divine judgement.[162]

commendation from God: Here again, as above,[163] the wages or the reward should not be separated from the work itself. As Paul has shown above, the reward is that the work remains and is not destroyed.[164] Paul has used this reward motif three times, twice in Chapter 3 and once here in Chapter 4. We must see the subject as an intra-community one. The work of which Paul speaks is that of the apostles.[165] It is not meant to refer to man's life in general. Paul is rather concerned to establish his position of apostolic authority, as a steward of God's mysteries, before he proceeds, in the next major section, to deal with specific problems. Paul's doctrine of justification by faith is not at issue here.

159. Cf. Isa. 13[6]; Joel 1[15]; Zeph. 1[14].
160. Allo, ad loc. In the Didache, xi. 7f., it is forbidden to put to the test or judge a prophet speaking in the Spirit. However, the passage goes on to state that not everyone who speaks in the spirit is a prophet and that his way of life will be a criterion by which to decide whether or not he really is a prophet. There is thus a distinction at some point in the tradition between the kinds of activity upon which one may or may not pass judgement. The judgement is left to a later time. In the Didache it is left for the immediate future, and in 1 Corinthians it is left for the final day of judgement.
161. Cf. above on v. 3.
162. Cf. Heb. 4[12f.]; Rom. 2[16]; cp. 1 Cor. 14[25].
163. Cf. 3[8,14].
164. 3[14f.].
165. Cf. below v. 9.

⁶*I have applied all this to myself and Apollos for your benefit, brethren, that you may learn by us to live according to scripture, that none of you may be puffed up in favour of one against another.* ⁷*For who sees anything different in you? What have you that you did not receive? If then you received it, why do you boast as if it were not a gift?*

⁸*Already you are filled! Already you have become rich! Without us you have become kings! And would that you did reign, so that we might share the rule with you!* ⁹*For I think that God has exhibited us apostles as last of all, like men sentenced to death; because we have become a spectacle to the world, to angels and to men.* ¹⁰*We are fools for Christ's sake, but you are wise in Christ. We are weak, but you are strong. You are held in honour, but we in disrepute.* ¹¹*To the present hour we hunger and thirst, we are ill-clad and buffeted and homeless,* ¹²*and we labour, working with our own hands. When reviled, we bless; when persecuted, we endure;* ¹³*when slandered, we try to conciliate; we have become, and are now, as the refuse of the world, the offscouring of all things.*

Paul now begins to sum up the results of his opening discussion.

৯৫

6a
I have applied all this: The Greek verb translated here *applied* is *meta-schēmatizein.* It is related in meaning to the verb *metamorphousthai,* from which our word metamorphosis is derived. It means 'to change the form' and then by extension 'to use a figure of speech'. The reference must be to the three figures named above which use the reward motif.

all this: The Greek says literally 'these things' and is to be preferred. A more adequate translation of this verse might be, 'I have used these figures of speech ... with reference to myself and Apollos'.[166]

166. Cf. N.E.B.: 'Into this general picture ... I have brought Apollos and myself.'

6b

learn ... to live according to scripture: The Greek is literally 'learn the not beyond that which is written'. This has the look, because of the article, of a catch-phrase or slogan. The reference 'to that which is written' is clearly to the Old Testament. The phrase could mean a kind of literalism which forbade interpretation. But in that case we are at a loss to understand Paul's many interpretations. The other possibility is that it refers to doctrine or belief which was not based upon the O.T. at all. The Corinthian slogan in 6^{12} and 10^{23} may be related to this. Paul had taught that the gentile man of faith was no longer bound by the Law of the Jewish scriptures. It would have been natural for the gentile to assume then that none of the ethical requirements of the O.T. applied to him, i.e. 'everything is allowed', we are in the 'post-scriptural age'. Paul would say that the Christian must start with the scriptures because there are many examples in them which are meant also for us.[167] The scriptures are holy[168] and spiritual.[169] They point out to us those errors into which the children of Israel fell and which we should try to avoid.

6c

in favour of one against another: The quarrelling which took the form of one saying 'I am of Paul', 'I am of Apollos, etc.' is probably what Paul has in mind here. There is no particular necessity to see 6c as the result of 6b. Even starting with the same text of scripture interpreters can come up with widely diverging interpretations.

7–13

There follows a highly ironic description of the attitude of the Corinthian Christians. It must refer to their attitude rather than their style of life, already described in other terms.[170] Their self-esteem stands in marked contrast to the actual situation of those who have the responsibility for them as apostles.[171]

7

Does this question refer to what immediately precedes it, or does it look ahead to what follows in v. 8? The reference is probably backward, that is, What is the distinction on the basis of which one could be puffed up? But, having asked this question, Paul asks another and makes the transition to a related subject.

receive: From whom did they receive? Probably from God through the apostles. There is no problem here, as some have suggested.[172] Paul was

167. Cf. 10$^{6f.}$.   168. Cf. Rom. 7^{12}.   169. ibid., v. 14.
170. Cf. 1$^{26ff.}$.   171. ibid., vv. 9–13.
172. Cf. Barrett, ad loc.; cp. R.-P., ad loc.

not concerned about the role of the apostles. He was concerned about those who would play one apostle's approach off against another in a divisive manner.[173]

boast: Paul has already demonstrated by an appeal to their general economic, social, and intellectual condition and by a quotation from scripture that their only legitimate boasting could be in God.[174]

8
Already: Could refer back to *before the time.*[175] Their assumption of an extraordinary attitude of self-satisfaction is also somewhat premature.[176] Some[177] see this as evidence of the Gnostic character of Paul's opponents in Corinth. The terms *filled, rich, kings* and *rule,* can be paralleled in later writings by avowed Gnostics. The problem, as I have indicated in the Introduction, is the extent to which a developed Gnostic scheme of thought can be presupposed in the Corinth of Paul's day. One thing is certain, and that is that the Corinthians looked upon wisdom and Spirit as things which were theirs by right. If this is not full-blown Gnosticism, it is certainly the intellectual climate within which Gnosticism could spring up.

filled ... rich ... kings ... reign: The use of these terms must be seen as figurative. Further, as I pointed out above,[178] they refer to the attitude of the Corinthians rather than to any outward style of life. In the 'gnostic' view of things, the terms would mean that those who had *gnosis,* i.e. knowledge of wisdom, were full (of the Spirit) and were therefore rich – treating the spirit as a possession. They reigned as kings because knowledge afforded them power to overcome the heavenly beings hostile to them and desirous to prevent their return to their heavenly abode in the primal man.[179]

9–13
Paul's description of the life of the apostles.[180]

173. Cf. above on 3^6.
174. Cf. 1^{26-31}.
175. Verse 5 above. Cf. Schlatter, ad loc.
176. Cf. Paul's statements in Phil. 3^{12}.
177. Cf. W. Schmithals, *Die Gnosis in Korinth,* 2nd ed. 1965, 169–71. Cp. Wendland, ad loc. Evidence for Stoic influence in Weiss, Moffatt, Barrett.
178. Cf. above on vv. 7–13.
179. Cf. the general Introduction, p. xix.
180. Cp. 15^{30-2}; 2 Cor. 11^{23-33}.

9

exhibited . . . like men sentenced to death . . . a spectacle: These are terms borrowed from the arena, where condemned men were forced to fight beasts and one another for the entertainment of the populace.

10

fools . . . wise; weak . . . strong; honour . . . disrepute: Three contrasts which recall the statements of v. 8 and look ahead to the contrasts of vv. 12bf. The background for the meaning of *fools* is in the general discussion 1$^{18-25}$, 2$^{18-23}$. *Strong* and *honour* refer to v. 8. Some[181] would see here again evidence of the Gnostic character of the Corinthian Christians. Much is made, in this argument for Gnostic influence, of the change in preposition – *for* Christ's sake . . . and . . . *in* Christ. The 'for' presumably characterizes Paul's position, in which he maintains the distinction between the believer and Christ. The 'in' characterizes the position of the Gnostics, who hold that the one who has received *gnosis*, knowledge, will be absorbed into the Christ, the primal man. The change of preposition, could, however, be merely stylistic.

12

we labour, working with our own hands: Paul mentions this several times.[182] Jewish teachers or rabbis quite often supported themselves.[183] Among the Greeks, however, it would have been considered beneath the dignity of a teacher to work.[184]

12bf.

This kind of patient forbearance demonstrated by the apostles is brought in at this point, partly by way of contrast with the Corinthians's own proud attitude, and partly to serve as a basis for Paul's admonition to imitation.[185]

13

refuse . . . offscouring: There was a custom at one time in antiquity to allow derelicts to volunteer as human sacrifices for the welfare of the community in return for a year's luxurious living. The Greek words translated here as *refuse* and *offscouring* were used in connection with these unfortunates.[186] By this time, however, the words may have lost their technical meaning and expressed only great opprobrium.[187]

181. Cf. Schmithals, op. cit. (n. 177), 171–3; cp. Wilckens, op. cit. (n. 10), 212, 216.

182. 9^6; 2 Cor. 11^7; 1 Thess. 2^9; 2 Thess. 3^8.

183. S.-B., II, 745f., 10f.   184. Cf. Moffatt, ad loc.

185. Cf. below, v. 16.   186. Cf. H. Lietzmann, ad loc.

187. Cf. Moffatt, ad loc.

¹⁴*I do not write this to make you ashamed, but to admonish you as my beloved children.* ¹⁵*For though you have countless guides in Christ, you do not have many fathers. For I became your father in Christ Jesus through the gospel.* ¹⁶*I urge you, then, be imitators of me.* ¹⁷*Therefore I sent to you Timothy, my beloved and faithful child in the Lord, to remind you of my ways in Christ, as I teach them everywhere in every church.* ¹⁸*Some are arrogant, as though I were not coming to you.* ¹⁹*But I will come to you soon, if the Lord wills, and I will find out not the talk of these arrogant people but their power.* ²⁰*For the kingdom of God does not consist in talk but in power.* ²¹*What do you wish? Shall I come to you with a rod, or with love in a spirit of gentleness?*

The tone of Paul's address changes abruptly. Paul does not want to 'make them hang their heads', but rather to 'set them straight'. He has a right to do this because he stands in a relation to them analogous to that between father and child. The section takes on a positive note as Paul admonishes the Corinthians to imitate him.

ↀↀ

15

guides ... fathers: The Greek word translated *guides* is *paidagōgos*. This was a domestic slave whose job it was to see that the children of the household got back and forth to school. It was an inferior position, hardly comparable to that of father and head of the family. Paul uses a similar analogy in Gal. 3^{23ff.}: 'Before faith came, we were confined under the Law ... so that the law was our *paidagōgos* until Christ came ...' The law, according to Paul, fulfils a temporary, custodial function in the scheme of salvation. The decisive event is Christ's coming. So Paul characterizes his own role in the economy of the Corinthians' salvation as decisive when compared to what others may have or still may yet do for them.

in Christ ... in Christ Jesus: All this which Paul describes happens within the church.

I became your father . . . through the gospel: The Greek is literally 'I begat you'.[188] It was in response to Paul's preaching that the Corinthians became Christians. As I have said above,[189] it was the peculiar nature of their response which produced the unusual problems with which Paul is faced in this gentile community. It was undoubtedly through Paul's preaching that they received the Spirit. It was therefore he who should admonish them and he whom they should imitate.

17

Timothy, my . . . child: Timothy is mentioned first in Acts 16¹, where he is already a Christian. He might well have become one at the time of Paul's first visit to Lystra and Derbe.[190] Since he is said to have accompanied Paul after Acts 16¹, it is possible that he came with him to Corinth on his initial visit.[191]

my ways in Christ: Paul has already in his letter given the Corinthians an adequate basis for imitation. His *ways* must refer to something else. The reference is perhaps to the Hebrew *halakah*, which means literally a 'way of walking'. It is the technical term in Jewish writings for the interpretation by a particular rabbi of a passage of the Law. The 'ways' of Paul would then refer to Paul's interpretation of Jewish scripture from the Christian point of view.[192]

18–21

Paul's failure to return to Corinth has, in his mind at least, allowed the Corinthians to indulge in their quarrelling with one another. This quarrelling, which has been a matter of talk, is of no interest to Paul in itself. As he has stated previously, he has no intention of 'matching words' with those who oppose him in Corinth.[193] The worth of what they have done will be evident, not as talk but as action.

18

arrogant: See above on v. 6 (puffed up).

soon: According to 16⁸⁻⁹ Paul decided to stay where he was in Ephesus until Pentecost. Either Paul changed his plans or the epistle was written shortly before Pentecost. According to 2 Cor. 1¹⁵ᶠ.,²³ there was a change in plan, assuming that the same visit is meant.

19f.

the talk . . . their power: The contrast is between the verbal bickering which has been going on in Corinth and the power of the Gospel to

188. Cf. N.E.B.: 'You are my offspring.'
189. Cf. the general Introduction.   190. Acts 14⁶ᶠ.   191. ibid., 18¹ᶠ.
192. Cf. above, v. 6.   193. Cf. 2¹ᶠ., 1¹⁷.

turn men to Christ. *Power* here probably does not refer to the performance of miracles as such but may refer generally to manifestations of
the Spirit.[194] Later on in the epistle Paul is not the least bit shy about
comparing his spiritual gifts with those of his opponents.[195]

Power in Paul's thought is closely related to the Spirit.[196] The Spirit
is the source of power for the Christian.[197] The concrete expressions of
the working of the Spirit are manifold.[198] Certainly there were verbal
expressions of the Spirit, as Paul himself implies with regard to his own
preaching[199] and prophecy.[200] Paul is not concerned here to set words
over against deeds. He is rather concerned with the effect of the words
and the deeds. Paul is concerned with the words of the Corinthians
because they have been divisive. In the chapters which follow he will be
quite concerned with some of their ways of expressing their faith.[201]
But he is not interested in their expressions in themselves. He is interested
in the results, that is the power of words and deeds. The difficulty for
the Corinthians was probably in setting too great store by talking, not
seeing it in its proper perspective. Just what that perspective is Paul
makes clear later on.[202]

the kingdom of God ... power: Possibly this refers back to the figurative
statements in v. 8. They think they reign as kings. If so, there is the
strongest of contrasts here between the self-assumed kingship of the
Corinthians and the only kingship of which Paul knows – the kingship
of God.

21

with a rod: Speaking figuratively, Paul refers to chastening.[203] This is
contrasted, not with love, but with *a spirit of gentleness:* the Corinthians
could choose reproof or gentleness by their reaction to Paul's admonitions. Love undergirds all the actions of the Christian. Without it
neither reproof nor gentleness is worth anything.[204]

Paul now turns his attention to some matters which require reproof.
Some commentators see an abrupt transition here.[205] This is primarily
the result of moving from general statements to more specific problems.

194. Cf. 2[4].   195. Cf. 14[18f.].   196. Cf. 2[4].   197. Cf. 12[11].
198. Cf. 12[4ff.]; cp. Rom. 12[3-8].   199. Cf. 2[1ff.].   200. Cf. 14[3,5].
201. Namely 12[31], 15[12].   202. Cf. 12[1ff.].   203. Cf. 2 Sam. 7[14].
204. Cf. Chapter 13.   205. Cf. Lietzmann, ad loc.

Chapters 5-6

In the two chapters which follow Paul takes up three problems: (1) sexual immorality; (2) civil suits between Christians; (3) association with sinners. (1) is covered in 5$^{1-8,13b}$; 6$^{12-20}$. (2) is taken up in 6$^{1-11}$ and (3) is covered rather parenthetically in 5^{9-13a}.

5$^{1-5}$ THE PROPER ATTITUDE TOWARDS
GROSS IMMORALITY

¹*It is actually reported that there is immorality among you, and of a kind that is not found even among pagans; for a man is living with his father's wife.* ²*And you are arrogant! Ought you not rather to mourn? Let him who has done this be removed from among you.*

³*For though absent in body I am present in spirit, and as if present, I have already pronounced judgement* ⁴*in the name of the Lord Jesus on the man who has done such a thing. When you are assembled, and my spirit is present, with the power of our Lord Jesus,* ⁵*you are to deliver this man to Satan for the destruction of the flesh, that his spirit may be saved in the day of the Lord Jesus.*

Paul proceeds to chastise the Corinthians for their lax attitude towards a case of gross sexual immorality. His main concern is not what the man in question has done but the fact that the Corinthians have done nothing about it. He does not hesitate to pass judgement and sentence upon this person. The more general rationale for Paul's position is given in 6$^{12-20}$.

༄

I

immorality: The Greek word is *porneia.* It refers specifically to sexual immorality.[206]

206. Cf. N.E.B.

not found even among pagans: This is misleading. The Greek is literally 'not even among the gentiles'. The verb which must be understood is probably something like 'permitted' in the sense of 'being legal'. Roman law forbade the marriage of a man to a woman who was or even had been his father's wife.[207] The same prohibition was made by the Old Testament.[208] Paul's failure to mention the Old Testament proscription, however, may reflect one of two things:

1. The Rabbis made an exception to the Old Testament rule in the case of proselytes, since in their turning to Judaism all paternal ties were severed.[209]

2. Or Paul may have been concerned, not about an illicit marriage, but fornication or adultery which happened to be with a stepmother. It has been proposed that, since the stepmother comes in for no criticism, she was probably not a Christian. Quite a bit depends on whether or not the father was still alive. If he were, Paul's indignation would be easier to understand. On the other hand, if he were not, it is difficult to see the ground upon which Paul bases his severe judgement.

living with: This has a definite implied meaning in English not conveyed in Greek. The Greek can mean either living together as married or 'living together', i.e. not married, as we say. Did the man marry his father's wife? Was his father still alive? Did the man simply take his stepmother as a paramour? These are all questions left unanswered by the text.

2

arrogant:[210] Literally, 'puffed up'. This is what concerns Paul the most. The context in which this word appears in Chapter 4 suggests a connection with the propensity of the Corinthians to engage in discussions which issue in no concrete actions. All this talk does not interest Paul in the least. When he comes he will be interested in the power (i.e. the actions and their results) of those who are puffed up.[211]

3f.

But Paul is not present. So he must convey to them what he thinks their action should be: they should mourn and they should exclude the offender from the community.

207. Cicero, *Pro Cluentio*, v. 14; Gaius, *Institutes*, i. 63; cf. Barrett.
208. Lev. 18⁸; 20¹¹.
209. Talmud, *Sanhedrin*, 57b f. – a proselyte may marry his father's wife, provided she is not his mother.
210. Cf. above on 4^{6,18,19}.   211. Cf. above on 4^{18f.}

absent in body ... present in spirit: In body refers in Paul to man's natural condition in which he walks by faith, not by sight.[212] The Spirit, i.e. the Holy Spirit, enables man, in the context of faith at least, to overcome some of the limitations imposed upon him by his mortal condition.

4f.

in the name of the Lord Jesus: This actually goes with what follows as a solemn invocation: *In the name of the Lord Jesus . . . When you are assembled . . . deliver this man . . . that his spirit may be saved . . .*

my spirit: Has to be understood (as above vv. 3f.) along with 'his spirit' (v. 5) as man enabled by God's spirit to overcome some of the limitations of his mortal condition.

the destruction of the flesh: Most commentators take this to mean that, once removed from the protection of God's holy community, the man will be subject to the vicissitudes of a world under the domination of Satan and death.[213] Some degree of exclusion from the community is undoubtedly implied in vv. 2 and 13. Whether or not it was complete exclusion is another question. We know for instance from the Qumran writings (the so-called Dead Sea Scrolls) that their discipline called for degrees of exclusion.[214] The use of the phrase 'deliver ... to Satan' in I Tim. I²⁰ carries with it the purposive statement 'that they may learn not to blaspheme'. This implies a disciplining within the church rather than outside it. Paul was not so naïve as to think that Satan did not function perfectly well within the church.[215] To 'deliver to Satan' probably implies a degree of exclusion rather than complete loss of membership.

that his spirit may be saved: One must understand that Paul looked upon man as a totality, as all Jews did.[216] Because he was mortal and weak he was said to be 'flesh'. Because he was alive and could do things he was said to be the recipient of God's spirit. Paul refers to the 'outward' man which is deteriorating and the 'inward' man which is daily renewed.[217]

212. Cf. 2 Cor. 5^{6f.}.
213. Cf. 15^{25f.}; I Tim. I²⁰; Acts 5¹⁻¹¹; cp. Matt. 18¹⁷.
214. 1QS (Serek ha-yahad, one of the Dead Sea Scrolls) ix.1, viii.16b f., 22; cp. v.12; vii.1, 16.
215. Cf. 7⁵.
216. Cf. W. Robinson, 'Hebrew Psychology', *The People and the Book*, ed. A. S. Peake, 1925, 362; J. Pedersen, *Israel*, I-II, 99-181.
217. Cf. 2 Cor. 4¹⁶.

When the end of the world comes, man will be different from what he is now.²¹⁸ Man's spirit must then be understood as 'man as he is becoming and some day will be'.

5⁶⁻⁸ THE CHRISTIAN LIFE IS A TOTALLY NEW LIFE

⁶Your boasting is not good. Do you not know that a little leaven ferments the whole lump of dough? ⁷Cleanse out the old leaven that you may be fresh dough, as you really are unleavened. For Christ, our paschal lamb, has been sacrificed. ⁸Let us, therefore, celebrate the festival, not with the old leaven, the leaven of malice and evil, but with the unleavened bread of sincerity and truth.

It is clear from v. 7b that by this time Christian tradition had identified the death of Christ with the sacrifice of the Passover. This enables Paul to use the prescriptions regarding leaven in the Old Testament as an analogy to the contemporary situation in Corinth.

צצ

6a
Their 'boasting' is Paul's main concern. Their attitude towards themselves, their arrogance,²¹⁹ is not an appropriate expression of their Christian faith. Here in Chapter 5 and again in Chapter 6 Paul analyses two instances which belie any claim by the Corinthians that they are really full, rich or kings.²²⁰ Any outward expression of their faith is inevitably related to the fact and significance of Jesus Christ's death.²²¹

6b
This was evidently a common proverb.²²² It means that a little (leaven) affects a much larger mass (of dough). What Paul has in mind here is not a specific case of immorality. It is the specific case of laxity in dealing with this case of immorality. Their tacit or explicit approval of this particular action contradicts the whole nature of the community.

218. Cf. 1 Cor. 15⁵¹ff·.   219. Cf. above on v. 2.
220. Cf. above on 4⁸.   221. Cf. 11²⁶; Rom. 6³f·.
222. Cf. Gal. 5⁹; Matt. 13³³.

7a

The analogy is drawn from the prescriptions of the Old Testament in Exod. 12^{15f.} and 13⁷. According to Jewish usage all leaven and leavened bread must be removed from the house before the beginning of Passover at sundown on the fourteenth day of Nisan.

you may be fresh dough, as you really are unleavened: Probably for rhetorical purposes, Paul presses his analogy. The basis for the analogy is the nature of the Christian community itself and its relation to the saving acts of God-in-Christ, here more particularly his death. If Christ is *our* Passover, then, like the Jews leaving Egypt, we are assured of God's favour and protection, provided we obey God's commands. So, just as the Jews were commanded to remove all leaven from the household, so we are commanded to remove from our midst all traces of arrogance and boasting which issue in moral laxity.

our paschal lamb: The animals were slain before sundown of 14 Nisan so that they might be prepared for the Passover Meal. This has nothing to do with the date of the crucifixion or the Last Supper. The identification of Jesus's death with the feast of the Passover is first and foremost theological and is not dependent upon chronology.

8

Let us, therefore, celebrate the festival: Does this reference to a festival imply a specific celebration? It is unlikely that a gentile congregation would have been keeping Passover.[223] Some commentators see here a reference to Easter.[224] Others refer it to the general way of life of the Christian.[225] The reference is most probably a general one, but that does not exclude the possibility of specific cultic instances of celebration,[226] for which one would want to be prepared.

old . . . leaven of malice and evil . . .[227] *unleavened bread of sincerity and truth:* Those commentators are probably right who see the reference here to the old way of life of the gentiles (old leaven) as contrasted with the new (unleavened bread). The contrast, however, is not between some moralistic notion of good and bad. Rather the former way of life which was condemned to malice and evil by their adherence to idols, i.e. false gods,[228] is contrasted with the truth and sincerity which come from faith in him who is the truth.

223. Cf. Gal. 4^{9f.}.   224. Cf. Allo, ad loc.   225. Godet, ad loc.
226. Cf. Matt. 5^{23ff.}; Did. 14^{1ff.}.   227. Cf. Matt. 16⁶, 11 par.; Mark 8¹⁵.
228. Cf. 12².

⁹*I wrote to you in my letter not to associate with immoral men;* ¹⁰*not at all meaning the immoral of this world, or the greedy and robbers, or idolaters, since then you would need to go out of the world.* ¹¹*But rather I wrote to you not to associate with any one who bears the name of brother if he is guilty of immorality or greed, or is an idolater, reviler, drunkard, or robber – not even to eat with such a one.* ¹²*For what have I to do with judging outsiders? Is it not those inside the church whom you are to judge?* ¹³*God judges those outside. Drive out the wicked person from among you.*

It is clear from this passage that our 1 Corinthians is not the first letter which Paul wrote to the Corinthians. Many attempts have been made to reconstruct the correspondence of Paul on the basis of such statements as this.²²⁹ Some commentators would identify 2 Cor. 6¹⁴–7¹ mostly on the basis of content as a part of this previous letter. In this previous letter Paul has written, *Do not associate with immoral men.* This has been interpreted by the Corinthians²³⁰ to imply that they give up contacts with all immoral men. If Paul has made this kind of admonition and in the meantime the Corinthians have not looked askance at the case of extreme sexual immorality mentioned in v. 1, it would seem that they have ignored Paul's admonition. In this situation Paul qualifies what he has said: when he wrote *immoral men* he was referring to Christians who were immoral.

ﻬ

9

associate with: This is something of a technical term for the intimate relations which the faithful enjoy within the community.²³¹ Paul qualifies his meaning in v. 11: *not even to eat with such a one.* The problem here, as we have indicated above,²³² is the degree of exclusion im-

229. Cf. also 2 Cor. 2³ᶠ·, 7¹², with possible references to a 'tearful letter'.
230. Perhaps by way of a caricature. Cf. Hurd, 50–52, 149–54.
231. Cf. 2 Thess. 3¹⁴. Also below, n. 233.
232. Cf. above on vv. 4f., *the destruction of the flesh.*

plied.[233] The qualification made by Paul is twofold: (1) when I said immoral men, I was referring to immoral Christians; (2) when I said 'Do not associate with,' I meant, 'Do not eat (i.e. share the cult meal) with this type of person'.

10f.
not at all: The interpretation of Paul's statement was too general, so that he must say 'No, not in any general sense'. Paul's immediate concern is for the community of the faithful.

greedy and robbers, idolaters . . . reviler, drunkard: Paul expands his statement, even while he qualifies it, to include several more kinds of behaviour not appropriate to Christians. Lists of vices such as these were common in the ethical literature of Paul's day[234] and are found extensively in the New Testament.[235]

12
For what have I to do with judging outsiders?: Their interpretation of his statement has put him in an unfavourable light. Judging those outside is up to God. In 4⁵ Paul would seem to be prohibiting any kind of judging which comes before the end of the world. In 2¹⁵ᶠ· he seems to turn his statement of 5¹² upside down. The spiritual man judges everyone but is judged by no one. The context of Chapters 3 and 4 is, however, different from that of 5. In Chapters 3 and 4 the problem is the nature of the believers' relation to the Spirit and the apostolate. These are matters which have to do with one's membership in the community. In Chapter 5, this matter having been settled, Paul turns his attention to the problem of discipline within the community.

233. Cf. 2 Thess. 3¹⁵: 'Do not look on him as an enemy, but warn him as a brother' (cp. 1 Tim. 1²⁰, and cf. above on v. 5). While it is true that the statement in v. 13, *Drive out the wicked person from among you*, is a formula of excommunication borrowed from the Old Testament – cf. Deut. 13⁶, 17⁷, 19¹⁹, 22²¹,²⁴, 24²⁷; Barrett – the instances in the Old Testament refer to the death of the individual. It is unlikely that this is the case in the New Testament, since the likelihood of restoration is always held out.
234. Cf. B. S. Easton, *The Pastoral Epistles*, 1948.
235. For example 6⁹⁻¹⁰; Gal. 5¹⁹ff·; Rom. 13¹³; 2 Cor. 12²⁰; Col. 3⁸; Eph. 4³¹; 1 Tim. 1⁹⁻¹⁰; 2 Tim. 3²⁻⁵.

¹*When one of you has a grievance against a brother, does he dare go to law before the unrighteous instead of the saints?* ²*Do you not know that the saints will judge the world? And if the world is to be judged by you, are you incompetent to try trivial cases?* ³*Do you not know that we are to judge angels? How much more, matters pertaining to this life!* ⁴*If then you have such cases, why do you lay them before those who are least esteemed by the church?* ⁵*I say this to your shame. Can it be that there is no man among you wise enough to decide between members of the brotherhood,* ⁶*but brother goes to law against brother, and that before unbelievers?*

⁷*To have lawsuits at all with one another is defeat for you. Why not rather suffer wrong? Why not rather be defrauded?* ⁸*But you yourselves wrong and defraud, and that even your own brethren.*

⁹*Do you not know that the unrighteous will not inherit the kingdom of God? Do not be deceived; neither the immoral, nor idolaters, nor adulterers, nor homosexuals,* ¹⁰*nor thieves, nor the greedy, nor drunkards, nor revilers, nor robbers will inherit the kingdom of God.* ¹¹*And such were some of you. But you were washed, you were sanctified, you were justified in the name of the Lord Jesus Christ and in the Spirit of our God.*

Paul here continues with the theme of the holy community which he took up in Chapter 5 and which he will continue in 6^{12–20}. The specific subject under consideration is legal or civil disputes, that is grievances between two individuals who are Christians. This section has three divisions. (1) vv. 1–6: It is wrong for Christians to take their civil cases before a non-Christian tribunal. (2) vv. 7–8: The Christian should be willing to renounce his civil rights in favour of his Christian brother. (3) vv. 9–11: The reason for this lies in the holy character of the Christian community. Paul has made it quite clear in Chapter 5 that it is possible for an individual in the holy community to be separated, at least to a degree, for disciplinary reasons. However, as long as he is in full association with the community, he shares that holy character which is God's gift through Christ and which is acted out or symbolized in the sacrament of Baptism. Paul has stated in 5⁹ᶠ· that it is impossible for Christians as individuals to separate themselves completely from their pagan surroundings. Disputes which arise within the community, however, should be handled within the community. Paul's thought here is that of the ghetto dweller who seeks a minimal contact with the outside world as a means of retaining his own identity.

တတ

1
a grievance: A civil suit.

the unrighteous: Pagans, non-Christians. No moral judgement as such is involved here.

2f.
The idea of the holy community judging the world is carried over from Judaism.[236] There is, however, no parallel to the idea of judging angels in Jewish literature. The judgement referred to is the final one at the end of the world.[237]

matters pertaining to this life:[238] The Greek is literally 'things pertaining to life (*biōtika*, i.e. everyday things, as opposed to extraordinary matters).

4
lay them before those who are least esteemed: The rendering of the R.S.V. gives the general sense, but the N.E.B. is more precise and closer to the original: '. . . entrust jurisdiction to (outsiders, men) who count for nothing in our community.'

5
no man . . . wise enough: In the Jewish community the wise men settled this kind of civil dispute. Paul could be hearkening back to Jewish usage here. He could also be engaging in some irony about the possession of wisdom by some of the Corinthians.[239]

236. Cf. Dan. 7²²; Wis. 3⁸; Psalm 149⁶ᶠᶠ·; Enoch 1⁹, 38⁵, 48⁹, etc.
237. But see 1 Cor. 2⁶,⁸, 15²⁴.
238. Cp. N.E.B.: 'mere matters of business'.
239. Cf. above on 1²⁰ᶠᶠ·, 2⁶ᶠᶠ·.

7

The sense here is that by going into the pagan court at all (quite apart from the outcome of the case) the participants have in a larger sense already lost. Speaking rhetorically Paul says that (by comparison) it would be better to suffer the wrong, that is leave the whole issue pending from a legal point of view. The integrity of the believing community is what is at stake here. If Christians cannot handle their mutual problems within the community of faith, then there is something wrong with the community of faith. The believer should put up with what he considers to be an injustice before he admits this defeat. The only future there is lies within the community of faith. The gross immorality which characterizes the world outside the community of faith can be handled by discipline within the community.[240] Outside the community the faithful have no jurisdiction.[241] The fate of those who participate in this gross immorality outside the bounds of the faithful community has already been determined.[242]

11

The faithful have changed their identity. In an act of faith and through the rite of baptism, Christians have identified themselves with Jesus Christ. For them now to take intra-community problems before the tribunal of the non-believers would be to say that this had never happened.

washed . . . sanctified . . . justified: Three different ways of describing the change of status effected by faith in becoming a member of the Christian community. The first two refer to the symbolism of Baptism.

¹²*'All things are lawful for me,' but not all things are helpful. 'All things are lawful for me,' but I will not be enslaved by anything.* ¹³*'Food is meant for the stomach and the stomach for food'* – *and God will destroy both one and the other. The body is not meant for immorality, but for the Lord, and the Lord for the body.* ¹⁴*And God raised the Lord and will also raise us up by his power.* ¹⁵*Do you not know that your bodies are members of Christ? Shall I therefore take the members of Christ and make them members of a*

240. Cf. above on 5¹ff.   241. Cf. above on 5¹².
242. Cp. above 5¹¹ff.

prostitute? Never! ^{16}*Do you not know that he who joins himself to a prostitute becomes one body with her? For, as it is written, 'The two shall become one.'* ^{17}*But he who is united to the Lord becomes one spirit with him.* ^{18}*Shun immorality. Every other sin which a man commits is outside the body; but the immoral man sins against his own body.* ^{19} *Do you not know that your body is a temple of the Holy Spirit within you, which you have from God? You are not your own;* ^{20}*you were bought with a price. So glorify God in your body.*

Paul now returns to the general subject of fornication, a specific instance of which he discussed in Chapter 5. Some commentators find the abrupt reintroduction of this subject here after the discussion in 6$^{1-11}$ evidence of an interpolation.[243] It seems more likely that Paul is here continuing his theme of identification with Christ through the faithful community.[244] Sexual relations with a prostitute, as Paul will show, are not a purely individual matter, as are one's eating habits. Rather what one does, in so intimate a fashion, with another human being, has an effect upon the *body*.[245] Food, which is so much a matter of indifference in itself, becomes important in Chapters 8 and 10. It assumes importance, however, only because of its connection with intra- and extra-community relations on the one hand,[246] or its connection with the relation of the faithful to Christ[247] on the other. So here the sexual relation in itself is not the problem. The difficulty consists in the attachment of the body by means of the sexual act to the body of a prostitute. In this way the bodies of the faithful fulfil, not the will of Christ, but the intention of the prostitute. Thus, not only is the meaning of the sexual act perverted, but the meaning of faithful membership in the body of Christ as well.

ಬಬ

12

All things are lawful for me: This probably represents a slogan of the Corinthians. Paul is in the embarrassing position of having to agree with

243. Cf. Weiss, et al.   244. Cf. above on v. 11.

245. Here *body* means the individual in relation to other individuals in the faithful community (Rom. 12^{3ff}), as well as the individual in relation to Christ (v.13b).

246. 8$^{9-13}$, 10$^{23-33}$.   247. 10$^{14-22}$.

it. Paul himself had most likely insisted, in his presentation of the Christian Gospel, that the gentile was not bound by the letter of the Jewish scriptures. As he says in Gal. 5^{18}: *if you are led by the spirit, you are not under the law.* It is no great mental leap from this idea to the one that all things are lawful. Paul must therefore qualify this misleading interpretation of his own words about the law. He accordingly counters with two qualifying statements: (1) *not all things are helpful . . .*; (2) *I will not be enslaved by anything.* Both these statements are only introductions to what follows: the second qualifies the first. The second statement involves a play on the words *exesti, are lawful,* and *exousias thēsomai, I will be enslaved.* Paul's point is: I will not have my freedom taken away in the very act of (supposedly) exercising it. Man must learn ever anew that freedom is relative to his goals in life. Man may no more have freedom as his goal than he can choose to make no decisions.

13
Food is meant for the stomach and the stomach for food: Paul is probably quoting another Corinthian slogan. The Corinthians may have used this line of reasoning to justify their continuance of the sexual morality they had known as gentiles.[248] Paul cannot disagree. He himself will argue for a spiritual body in the resurrection.[249] He also says quite specifically in Rom. 14^{17}: *. . . the Kingdom of God does not mean food and drink . . .* But the conclusion which the Corinthians have drawn from the transitory character of some bodily functions does not follow. The *body,* i.e. the self-in-community,[250] cannot proceed on the basis of any principle other than its adherence to the Lord. It is true that the Jewish law no longer provides the basis for right action. But this is not to say that any action is right. Now it is the individual self-in-community who must look to the Lord, the head of the community, for some kind of direction, i.e. *the Lord for the body.*

14
A parenthetical statement of the church's resurrection faith. The connection with what precedes is purely verbal, i.e. *the Lord.*

15f.
Picks up the thread of the argument in v. 13. The Lord speaks (through Paul) in the very make-up of *the body.* They are intimately related to Christ as 'members' of a body. Sexual intercourse as an intimate union is attested to also in the Jewish scriptures, in the context of marriage.[251]

248. Cf. above on v. 9.   249. $15^{43ff.}$.
250. Cf. above in the introduction to this section.   251. Gen. 2^{24}.

49

The degree of intimacy involved in sexual relations with a prostitute is inconsistent with the relation of the members of the body to Christ. Paul amplifies what he means in what follows.

17

he who is united to the Lord becomes one spirit with him: The word for united, *kollōmenos,* means in v. 16 the quite physical joining of male and female in intercourse. It is used here only analogically and for effect. Paul's point is that something happens to the individual in sexual intercourse, even with a prostitute, which is not indifferent, which is not on a level with eating and drinking, but which is analogous to the faith commitment which a Christian makes to his Lord. Therefore these two acts are mutually exclusive. Because this is so Paul can categorically tell the Corinthians to *shun immorality.*[252]

18

Every other sin which a man commits is outside the body: There is no justification in the Greek text for the word *other.* Its introduction is interpretative and assumes that the word *body* means the same thing as 'his own body'. It would seem probable, however, that by using the phrase *his own body* Paul means to distinguish this from his previous use of the word *body.* We have suggested above that *body* in this passage at least refers to the self-in-community. Paul has already indicated a number of sins which excluded one from participation in the kingdom of God.[253] He has also, by implication, characterized those outside the community by a similar list of sins.[254] He also counsels that when such sins are committed by members of the Christian group such offending members should be disciplined by some degree of ostracism.[255]

It would be in this sense then that for Paul every sin is *outside the body,* that is leads to a degree of ostracism and identifies the offender with those outside the community. Furthermore, what happens to the individual in sexual intercourse with a prostitute is even a sin against his own body.[256]

252. The Greek is quite a bit stronger; it is literally 'flee', or 'run away from'.
253. Cf. vv. 9, 10.
254. 5⁹ff.
255. Cf. above on 5⁵.
256. Héring, ad loc., suggests that Paul's great emphasis on the dangers of intercourse with a prostitute arises from the fact that many of these were temple prostitutes and intercourse with them would then constitute idolatry. Paul gives no clear indication of this practice, unless it is his use of the term *temple* in v. 19.

19f.
Paul uses the analogy of temple to describe the community as a whole in 3¹⁶, and here the individual believer (cp. 2 Cor. 6¹⁶).

You are not your own; you were bought with a price: Most commentators attempt to relate this 'purchase' motif to the 'ransom' motif used elsewhere by Paul (Rom. 3²⁴) and the Gospel tradition (Mark 10⁴⁵), or the 'substitution' idea of Gal. 3¹³. Neither one of these ideas is present here, however, where the analogy is simply that of an outright purchase. Paul is saying, you were bought and paid for, i.e. you belong to God.

The reference is a rather crass one. Paul probably has in mind the price paid to the prostitute in return for her services. This would still be the case if one were to accept Héring's thesis of the temple prostitute. The price then would be worship of the temple deity.²⁵⁷ 'You are the one,' says Paul, 'who has been bought (by God), therefore you owe your body to him and the service which he requires is his glorification.' This is not a very delicate way of putting it, but the Corinthians were probably not very delicate people.

257. Cf. preceding note.

Chapter 7

MARRIAGE

Paul is concerned in this chapter with the question of marriage. It is clear that he himself is unmarried and that he feels this to be a distinct advantage for anyone who can remain so. Paul does not, however, either denigrate marriage or put a premium on celibacy. Rather he operates on the general principle that one should remain in that status in which one was converted to Christ. The time, says Paul, is short (v. 29). One should not make any more commitments than one has to, so as better to attend to the business of salvation. But each person has received a call from God to live in a particular manner.

Within the world of Paul's day there were sharply divergent tendencies in the moral and ethical sphere, both within Judaism and in the Hellenistic world. Some tended towards a libertine, 'anything goes' kind of attitude, as we have seen in Chapter 6. Others tended towards a world-denying kind of puritanism. This hyper-ascetical expression of Christianity is reflected in Paul's treatment of marriage in this chapter.

7¹⁻⁷   ASCETICISM IN MARRIAGE

¹*Now concerning the matters about which you wrote. It is well for a man not to touch a woman.* ²*But because of the temptation to immorality, each man should have his own wife and each woman her own husband.* ³*The husband should give to his wife her conjugal rights, and likewise the wife to her husband.* ⁴*For the wife does not rule over her own body, but the husband does; likewise the husband does not rule over his own body, but the wife does.* ⁵*Do not refuse one another except perhaps by agreement for a season, that you may devote yourselves to prayer; but then come together again, lest Satan tempt you through lack of self-control.* ⁶*I say this by way of concession, not of command.* ⁷*I wish that all were as I myself am. But each has his own special gift from God, one of one kind and one of another.*

1

Now concerning: A formula which recurs five times[258] between this point and the end of the letter. The occurrence of the formula probably indicates the beginning of a new question raised by the Corinthians.

which you wrote: Paul now turns to those questions put to him in the letter from the Corinthians.

It is well for a man not to touch a woman: This, like the statement in 6^{12} and 10^{23}, is probably a slogan current among the Corinthian Christians.

well: Commentators disagree sharply on the moral force to be given this word. It represents the Greek word *kalon*, which generally means 'good' in an unqualified sense. This was probably the force which it had for the Corinthians.

a man ... a woman: Since Paul does not say here 'husband ... wife', some commentators have concluded that his reference is solely to sexual intercourse apart from a specific reference to the married state. One must remember, however, that Paul is here quoting a Corinthian slogan. If sexual intercourse were their sole reference, Paul puts it immediately within the context of the marriage relation in vv. 2–5 below.

to touch: This is a euphemism for sexual relations. Paul understands this specific reference in vv. 2–5 below.

2

because of the temptation to immorality: This is often cited as proof that Paul put a low value on marriage. The word 'immorality' here refers specifically to sexual immorality as above.[259] If Paul were here trying to justify marriage as an institution, one might be right in thinking he put a low value on it. But this is not his point. Marriage is here assumed by Paul. He deliberately changes the wording from *man ... woman* as in v. 1 to *husband ... wife*.[260] It is not his aim to show that marriage is necessary to avoid immorality, but rather that, given the marriage relation, asceticism has only a limited place, if any, where the conjugal relation is concerned. There is for Paul no undefined middle ground between celibacy and the married state. One must choose between marriage and celibacy. There is room in Paul's thinking only for a full

---

258. 7^{25}, 8^1, 12^1, 16^1, 16^{12}.   259. Cf. above on 5^1.
260. Cf. above on v. 1.

commitment to one state or the other. There is little place if any for asceticism in marriage, and obviously no place for anything but asceticism in sexual matters for the celibate.

2ff.

The mutuality of marriage as it is symbolized and consummated in the intimacy of sexual expression has never been more forcefully expressed. This pattern of mutuality runs throughout this chapter.[261] It is difficult to see how, in the face of this, commentators have been able to characterize Paul's attitude toward marriage as negative.[262]

each man should have his own wife: The Greek says literally 'let each man'. This is obviously not referring to marriage, since Paul recognizes the validity of celibacy. The point must be, therefore, 'let each man (who is married) have (sexual relations with) etc.'. This is a counsel against adultery (i.e. having sexual relations with someone else's wife) and a general statement against asceticism in marriage, which Paul proceeds to spell out in vv. 3–5.

3–4

The statement of mutuality in the marriage relation which differentiates sex as an expression of marriage from sex as an expression of sex, i.e. one's own masculinity or femininity.[263]

5

Paul allows married couples to practise asceticism in the marital relation only for a specific length of time and only by mutual consent. This suggests he had known of married couples or individuals with a desire to remain married in some sense but without having sexual intercourse.[264]

lest Satan tempt you through lack of self-control: Tempt here represents the Greek *peirazein.* The force of this word is 'to put to the test', 'make trial of', or 'prove'. The purpose of the period of abstinence is a more active engagement in prayer. If it becomes a 'trial' by Satan, then Paul thinks it less than worthwhile. The main purpose of marriage is marriage including the mutual sharing of sexual intercourse. This is preferable

261. E. Kähler, *Die Frau in den paulinischen Briefen,* 1960, 22f.
262. Cf. G. Delling, *Paulus Stellung zu Frau und Ehe,* 1931.
263. Cf. n. 261.
264. Cf. Hurd. On the relation of this to so-called 'spiritual' marriages or betrothals, cf. below on vv. 36–8.

to a period of abstinence which becomes a bout with Satan, rather than a time of prayer.

6

I say this by way of concession, not of command: This refers to the immediately preceding v. 5. The force of this would be: practise asceticism in marriage, if you feel you must, but don't feel it is a necessity of the married state.[265]

7

It would have simplified things greatly for Paul if he hadn't had to deal with this problem at all. But there are *varieties of gifts* (12[4]) in the area of marriage as in all others.

one of one kind and one of another: This sweeping statement shows that Paul had not just the subject of marriage in view, but that he placed marriage at this point within the broad context of God's manifold gifts.

7^{8–16}   TRIAL SEPARATION AND DIVORCE

[8]*To the unmarried and the widows I say that it is well for them to remain single as I do.* [9]*But if they cannot exercise self-control, they should marry. For it is better to marry than to be aflame with passion.*

[10]*To the married I give charge, not I but the Lord, that the wife should not separate from her husband* [11]*(but if she does, let her remain single or else be reconciled to her husband) – and that the husband should not divorce his wife.*

[12]*To the rest I say, not the Lord, that if any brother has a wife who is an unbeliever, and she consents to live with him, he should not divorce her.* [13]*If any woman has a husband who is an unbeliever, and he consents to live with her, she should not divorce him.* [14]*For the unbelieving husband is consecrated through his wife, and the unbelieving wife is consecrated through her husband. Otherwise, your children would be unclean, but as it is they are holy.* [15]*But if the unbelieving partner desires to separate, let it be so; in such a case the brother or sister is not bound. For God has called us to peace.* [16]*Wife, how do you know whether you will save your husband? Husband, how do you know whether you will save your wife?*

265. Cf. J.B.: 'This is a suggestion, not a rule.'

Paul now takes up the matters of marriage (in the case of those who are as yet unmarried or widows) and divorce (in cases where both parties are Christian and in cases where only one party is Christian). Here again Paul's counsel is the same as above (vv. 2–5). There is no middle ground between celibacy and marriage.

ഇരു

9
to be aflame with passion: This is perhaps as good an expression as any to describe the form of Satan's temptation in v. 5b above.

10f.
The prohibition of divorce is unconditional here, as in Mark 10^{9f.}.[266]
I give charge, not I but the Lord: This is obviously a command of Jesus. The question is whether it represents a saying attributed to Jesus in the tradition, as we have it in Mark 10^{9f.}, or whether it is a word of the (risen) Lord given to some Christian prophet such as Paul.[267]

divorce: Paul does not preclude the possibility of separation. Separation, however, may not result in marriage to another but may be overcome only by reconciliation to one's former spouse.[268] It has been suggested that these divorces were being instigated out of the same ascetical concern as we saw reflected above in v. 5. V. 10 might then be understood as representing an extreme case of that which underlies v. 5.

separate . . . divorce: These represent two different words in Greek, but are both used in this period for divorce in our sense of the word. Under gentile (Roman) law, either the husband or (under certain circumstances) the wife could institute a divorce suit. Under Jewish law, except in rare cases, only the husband could initiate a divorce suit.[269]

12–16
The cases of marriages in which only one partner is a Christian are now considered. Divorce is to be permitted only if the unbelieving partner desires it. The unbelieving husband (wife) is consecrated through his wife (her husband). This is probably best understood by analogy to what Paul says about fornication in 6^{15f.}: *shall I . . . take the members of*

266. Cp. Matt. 19^{6, 9}.
267. Cf. 1 Cor. 9¹⁴; 1 Thess. 4¹⁵. E. Käsemann, 'Sätze heiligen Rechtes im Neuen Testament', *Exegetische Versuche und Besinnungen*, 1960–64, II, 69–82.
268. Cf. Mark 10¹¹ parr.
269. Cf. D. Daube, *The New Testament and Rabbinic Judaism*, 1956, 363f.

Christ and make them members of a prostitute? . . . he who joins himself to a prostitute becomes one body with her. Somehow the unbelieving partner participates in the holiness of the Christian community through participation in the marriage relation – this at least is what Paul says. He may simply intend, however, to assure believers that their marriage to a non-believer does not defile them or the church. Paul is probably considering only marriages contracted prior to conversion to Christianity. There is some evidence that he discouraged marriage with non-believers subsequent to conversion.[270]

14b

Otherwise, your children would be unclean, but as it is they are holy: This is an argument supporting Paul's statement in v. 14a. He says *your children* referring to the children of all believers. Many of these children would have been born before the conversion of their parents. Obviously their sanctification was effected through the conversion of their parents. By analogy, the sanctification of the unbelieving partner takes place through the faith of the believing partner. The Jews held a similar notion about the unborn children of proselyte women.[271]

This passage says nothing one way or the other about the church's practice of the Baptism of infants.

15

in such a case the brother or sister is not bound: The problem is: *not bound* to what? The Greek word rendered *bound* is *dedoulōtai* and means literally 'to be enslaved'. Some contend that this refers to the status of the believing party during his marriage to an unbeliever and also afterwards, that is he is free to remarry. The problem of remarriage, however, is not specifically mentioned by Paul. It is best to take *bound* as referring only to the possibility of divorce with a non-believing and non-consenting partner.

For God has called us to peace: Peace describes a situation in which the Christian now stands by virtue of his calling. It is a characteristic of the church and refers to the proper relation of the gifts of each of the members.[272] The marriage of a believer to a non-believer affords sanctification to the non-believer and could be considered a part of one's calling or gift from God, provided the non-believer is consenting.

270. Cf. 2 Cor. 6¹⁴.
271. Cf. Talmud, *Jebamoth*, 78a.
272. Cf. E. Neuhäusler, 'Ruf Gottes und Stand des Christen beim 1 Kor. 7', *BZ*, 3 (1959), 43ff.

In a situation, however, in which the non-believing partner wishes a divorce, it may be assumed that this union is not a part of one's calling and gift and the believer is not bound to maintain it. It would not constitute part of the *peace* of the community. The believing partner should not maintain the union with an unconsenting non-believer in the fond hope of eventually saving him.²⁷³

7¹⁷⁻²⁴   STAY AS YOU WERE WHEN YOU
BECAME A CHRISTIAN

¹⁷*Only, let every one lead the life which the Lord has assigned to him, and in which God has called him. This is my rule in all the churches.* ¹⁸*Was any one at the time of his call already circumcised? Let him not seek to remove the marks of circumcision. Was any one at the time of his call uncircumcised? Let him not seek circumcision.* ¹⁹*For neither circumcision counts for anything nor uncircumcision, but keeping the commandments of God.* ²⁰*Every one should remain in the state in which he was called.* ²¹*Were you a slave when called? Never mind. But if you can gain your freedom, avail yourself of the opportunity.* ²²*For he who was called in the Lord as a slave is a freedman of the Lord. Likewise he who was free when called is a slave of Christ.* ²³*You were bought with a price; do not become slaves of men.* ²⁴*So, brethren, in whatever state each was called, there let him remain with God.*

In these verses Paul digresses from the subject of marriage in order to illustrate, in a wider context, his basic idea that one should remain in that status in which one was called. If one had been a Jew one should not try to hide that fact. Nor should it concern a man if he has been (or perhaps still is) a slave. In Christ, slaves are freemen and freemen are slaves. The details (cf. below) of this passage are easy enough to understand. It is difficult, however, to get at Paul's main point. *Don't*

273. Cp. above on v. 5. A case can be made on grammatical grounds for quite the opposite meaning for v. 16, i.e. How do you know you will be the salvation . . .? The implication would then be that one cannot be sure. Cf. Héring, ad loc. The translation of the R.S.V. is dictated by the general sense of the passage. Cf. also J. Jeremias, 'Die missionarische Aufgabe in der Mischehe (I Kor. 7, 16)', *Neutestamentliche Studien für R. Bultmann*, 1957, 255–60.

efface the mark of circumcision, if taken literally, is hardly comparable to the counsel regarding marriage and divorce on the one hand or slavery on the other. The question is: why would anyone want to efface this mark? Would it not be because one wished to hide the fact that one was a Jew?

Now this is a subject comparable with those of slavery and marriage. The status in life – married–single, slave–free, Jew–gentile – of the man who is converted to Christianity is not something which he leaves behind when he enters the church. He brings it with him. It is part of his calling, his gift, his way of life.[274] One who had been a Jew could keep the commandments of God in a way in which one who has not been a Jew cannot. One who has been a slave will know more of what freedom in Christ means than one who has been born a freeman. Each one has his gift.

ಬಲ

17
Only, let everyone lead the life which the Lord has assigned to him. . . . This is my rule in all the churches: This is the general principle under which Paul has formulated his thoughts on marriage. He now seeks to illustrate it further by the examples of (1) a person converted to Christianity while a Jew and (2) one converted while a slave.

18
to remove the marks of circumcision: This was a practice already among Jews who wished to participate in the athletic games even before the time of Jesus.[275]

19
keeping the commandments of God: This has come to be, by Paul's day, a technical term (Greek, *tērēsis entolōn theou*). It meant following the prescriptions of the Jewish scriptures.[276] The sense of this is that those who were Jews and those who were not lived together now as Christians. Neither Jew nor gentile hid what he was, but found a new identity in Christ.

---

274. Neuhäusler, op. cit. (n. 272), 44ff.
275. Cf. 1 Macc. 1¹⁵; Josephus, *Antiquities*, XII, v. 1, *Assumption of Moses* 8.3; Mishnah, *Aboth*, iii.15. The custom among the Greeks was to participate in the nude.
276. Cf. LXX Ecclesiasticus 32²³; Wis. 6¹⁸.

21

if you can gain your freedom, avail yourself of the opportunity: The Greek also permits the reading: 'even if a chance of liberty should come, choose rather to make good use of your servitude.'[277] Commentators disagree sharply here on whether Paul counsels for or against manumission. This is not Paul's point at all. His point is that, once a Christian, what you are or have been remains a part of your calling in Christ. One brings one's slavery with one into the community of faith even if one has taken advantage of an opportunity to be free – just as the Jew brings his Jewishness with him. Paul is saying: make good use of your servitude whether you remain a slave or not.

23

You were bought with a price; do not become slaves of men: The idea is similar to that in 6^{20}, except that here the analogy is slavery rather than prostitution. You belong to Christ, says Paul, you cannot have another owner. Our ultimate loyalty and devotion must be to him who bought us with his own life once offered. Therefore all our actions for man, even in the intimacy of marriage, are done according to God's will expressed in Christ.

7^{25-38} THE PRACTICE OF CELIBACY

25*Now concerning the unmarried, I have no command of the Lord, but I give my opinion as one who by the Lord's mercy is trustworthy.* 26*I think that in view of the impending distress it is well for a person to remain as he is.* 27*Are you bound to a wife? Do not seek to be free. Are you free from a wife? Do not seek marriage.* 28*But if you marry, you do not sin, and if a girl marries she does not sin. Yet those who marry will have worldly troubles, and I would spare you that.* 29*I mean, brethren, the appointed time has grown very short; from now on, let those who have wives live as though they had none,* 30*and those who mourn as though they were not mourning, and those who rejoice as though they were not rejoicing, and those who buy as though they had no goods,* 31*and those who deal with the world as though they had no dealings with it. For the form of this world is passing away.*

277. N.E.B. alternative rendering.

³²*I want you to be free from anxieties. The unmarried man is anxious about the affairs of the Lord, how to please the Lord;* ³³*but the married man is anxious about worldly affairs, how to please his wife,* ³⁴*and his interests are divided. And the unmarried woman or girl is anxious about the affairs of the Lord, how to be holy in body and spirit; but the married woman is anxious about worldly affairs, how to please her husband.* ³⁵*I say this for your own benefit, not to lay any restraint upon you, but to promote good order and secure your undivided devotion to the Lord.*

³⁶*If anyone thinks that he is not behaving properly towards his betrothed, if his passions are strong, and it has to be, let him do as he wishes: let them marry – it is no sin.* ³⁷*But whoever is firmly established in his heart, being under no necessity but having his desire under control, and has determined this in his heart, to keep her as his betrothed, he will do well.* ³⁸*So that he who marries his betrothed does well; and he who refrains from marriage will do better.*

೧೮೮

25
Now concerning the unmarried: We recognize here one of the main division points in subject matter referred to above.²⁷⁸ Paul has already addressed himself to the group of *unmarried* in Corinth along with the *widows* (v. 8). He is therefore here referring more specifically to 'virgins' or 'celibates' (Greek, *parthenoi*). Up to this point Paul has discussed instances of marriage and/or divorce in which the individual was somewhat limited by force of circumstances. Now he deals with those who have chosen celibacy as a way of life. Differences of opinion on this particular section are many. They turn, however, mainly upon the interpretation given vv. 36–8. We shall take them up therefore at that point.

25
I give my opinion as one who by the Lord's mercy is trustworthy: Paul is here referring to his particular way of life, which would include the manner in which he was called by God to faith in Christ,²⁷⁹ as well as his way of life since then, which was presumably as a celibate. That is he is qualified to address himself to those who are as he is.

278. Cf. above on 7¹.
279. Cf. Gal. 1¹⁵ᶠ·; cp. Acts 9¹⁻⁹, 22³⁻²¹, 26⁹⁻²⁰.

26

in view of the impending distress: The *impending distress* refers to the end of the world, which in the eyes of the early church was imminent.[280]

it is well for a person to remain as he is: The literal rendering of the text here is: it is well for a man to be so. If 'so' here refers ahead, then, the R.S.V. rendering is correct. If, however, 'so' (Greek, *houtōs*) refers to the preceding verse, the meaning would be 'remain a virgin' (or celibate). Paul has just stated and illustrated his general principle that a man should abide in the status he had at the time of his conversion.[281] There have, however, already been exceptions stated to the rigorous interpretation of this principle: the person married to a non-believer may allow the non-believer to sue for divorce (v. 15). The slave may take advantage of an opportunity for manumission (v. 21). The most reasonable interpretation of this section would be that 'so' refers back to the matter of celibacy. Paul gives as his opinion that it is a good thing for one who is a celibate to remain so. He also makes it clear in v. 27 that, if one is married, one should remain so. Yet there remains a qualification to Paul's opinion: the celibate who decides to marry may do so and the virgin who decides to marry may do so. These exceptions must be seen in the light of what Paul says about the various gifts: each person has his own gift from God (v. 7) which is related to the status in which he was converted.[282] It is Paul's counsel to retain that status. If one does not retain it, it can only be because it was not meant by God as a permanent part of one's gift. Nevertheless it is part of one's past which one brings along in faith to Christ. The Jew remains a Jew (though Christian). The slave remains a slave (though free). The single man remains single though married. A man sorrows but does not sorrow, he rejoices but does not rejoice, he buys things and possesses nothing and uses things and does not really use them. These ambiguous statements refer to man's life in the community of faith, which, though not unlike the life he knew before he was converted, is also radically different.[283] Within the community of faith Paul knows that *the form of this world is passing away* (v. 31). Paul knows it because in marriage believers are asking themselves if they should maintain their normal marital relations (vv. 1ff.) or whether they should perhaps even be divorced (vv. 10f.). Paul knows the form of this world is passing away

280. Cf. Mark 13 parr. On distress in this sense, cf. Luke 21²³; cp. LXX Psalm 118¹⁴³; Sol. 5⁶; T. Jos. 2⁴.

281. Cf. above on vv. 19ff.   282. Cf. vv. 17, 24.

283. Cf. 2 Cor. 5¹⁷.

because there are those who choose to live as celibates.[284] Paul's preference for the celibate life is clearly stated. He also emphasizes the parity of the celibate and the married life. But the fact that the form of this world is even now changing has its effect upon all aspects and expressions of the community's life. This is what underlies Paul's paradoxical statements about marriage, joy, sorrow, and business. The man who is engaged in all these activities and has come to faith in Christ will not 'take his cue' from anything or anyone less than Christ himself (v. 35).

In the case of the ascetic, it is easier to see how this loyalty to the Lord works out. The less there is to concern oneself with, such as spouse, feelings, and possessions, the simpler it is *to please the Lord*.[285] On the other hand, to serve the Lord is incumbent upon all men of faith. So for those who have families, feelings, possessions, etc. there will be a radical effect upon all these aspects of their lives.

What precisely this means perhaps even Paul was not in a position to say. In attempting to describe it he uses a phrase of the Stoic philosophers, 'to do something as if not doing it'.[286] Paul's thought, however, is not Stoic. What he wishes to convey here is the radical change which takes place in human activities as they become a part of the life of faith. It is not therefore marriage or feelings *per se* which are passing away, but the form which is being radically altered and therefore passing away. Paul's considerations move from the profound to the pragmatic. In the final verses of this section he restates his reasons for preferring celibacy.

28

those who marry will have worldly troubles: The text is literally: trouble in the flesh. The reference to flesh is to that aspect of the world in which change manifests itself. This does not take place without *trouble*. 'Flesh' in Paul refers to man in his weakness and in his mortality.[287] It is not the stuff of which we are made, but the totality of the limitations under which we live. It is man seen apart from his creator. Once one has chosen the celibate life, one has eliminated the possibility of participating in the radical changes affecting family life, by making what is in itself a radical choice, i.e. not to marry.

---

284. This in itself would seem to have been a sign to Paul of the New Age. Cf. Gal. 3²⁸.

285. Cf. below on v. 32.

286. Cf. Epictetus, iii. 24.60; iv. 1.159f.; Seneca, *Ep. Mor.* 74.18; cp. Acts of Paul and Thecla, 5.

287. Cf. J. A. T. Robinson, *The Body, a Study in Pauline Theology*, 1952, 17ff.

29

I mean: Paul uses the same phrase in 15⁵⁰ He means 'Let me explain'. What he will explain is the rationale for his own position on marriage and celibacy.

the appointed time has grown very short: The Greek text would also allow one to render this: the appointed time has been shortened. This latter idea is also found in Mark 13²⁰: *if the Lord had not shortened the days...*[288] This is part of the *impending distress.*[289] The timetable of the world has been somehow altered. The things which Paul sees going on in the community of faith are indications of radical change at all levels of existence.[290] This is all part of the *passing away* of *the form of this world.*

30–31

Most commentators try to distinguish Paul's counsel from Stoicism. This is certainly correct. Paul affirms the world, he does not deny it. However, most commentators end up with an interpretation which might as well be Stoic. Christians are far more influenced by their classical past than they realize. Paul means something far more radical than a kind of detachment or independence of man from the world. There is a great deal of the medieval spiritual counsel in what most commentators have said about this passage. Paul specifically does not say: this world is passing away. He says: *the form of this world is passing away*, that is, the outward appearance. The world, as Paul sees it from his vantage point of the faithful community, is changing. Paul does not call therefore for some kind of inward change in man in an unchanging world. He rather calls man to a radical adaptation of the *form* of his life in the face of radical change in the form of the world. One form which this radical adaptation might take is that of celibacy. But Paul also envisages drastic changes in the form of married life as well as in other areas of man's life which we have discussed above.[291]

32

free from anxieties: If we take this statement seriously, what do we do about the unmarried woman in v. 34 who is *anxious about the affairs of the Lord?* Most commentators think that Paul approves of this latter type of anxiety. In order to overcome this contradiction many commentators take v. 34 seriously and ignore v. 32, or they take both seriously and assign a different connotation to anxiety in each case. But Paul is quite emphatic.

288. Cp. 2 Pet. 3¹²; Barn. 4³.   289. Cf. above on v. 26.
290. Cf. the introductory section on vv. 27–35.
291. Cf. above on vv. 27–35, and also below on vv. 36–8.

I want you to be free from anxieties: One could infer logically that the anxieties which he enumerates are those from which he would have the Corinthians free. The Gospel tradition also has evidence of a negative attitude toward anxieties.[292] The anxieties enumerated include both those of the unmarried, including celibates, and those who are married. The anxieties of the unmarried are concerned with pleasing the Lord. The anxieties of the married are concerned with pleasing the spouse. Paul clearly approves of both these considerations.[293] What he does not approve of are the anxieties. As we suggested above, all phases of man's life are, according to Paul, in the process of radical alteration. The very form of life is being altered. Some have taken the radical step of celibacy. Others are practising a limited kind of asceticism within the bounds of marriage. Paul sees the inevitability of radical change extending to all phases of the life of the faithful. In this radical change in married life, then, the concern or anxiety for the things of the world has no place. Surprisingly enough, the concern or anxiety for the things of the Lord is not the way to please him.

We have already some indication of the shape which these concerns took. For those who were unmarried there was more opportunity to engage in the prayer mentioned in v. 5 than there was for those who were married. For those who were married there was more opportunity to engage in the joy and sorrow of the members of the family as well as to provide for them (cf. vv. 30f.) than there was for the celibate. But neither prayer (for the celibate or part-time ascetic) nor family life (for the married man) is in itself as an object of concern the way to fulfil the will of God. Paul would insist that one is better off without these concerns or anxieties. If the married man is anxious for the welfare of his family he is divided, because there will also be a corresponding anxiety for the things of the Lord.[294] If the celibate or unmarried person is concerned about holiness in flesh and spirit, he may end up in a bout with Satan and/or his flaming passions.[295]

In the knowledge of who one is, there is the assurance of what one must do. Through the gift of God one knows, according to Paul, one's true identity, one's calling. In the fulfilment of this calling Paul wants the Corinthian Christians to be without anxiety. It is not a matter of being anxious for *worldly affairs*[296] because one is married, or anxious for

292. Cf. Matt. 5^{25, 27, 28, 31, 34}; Luke 19⁴¹.
293. On 'to please the Lord', cf. Rom. 8⁸; 1 Thess. 2¹⁵, 4¹; 2 Cor. 5⁹. On 'to please the husband (wife)', cf. above on vv. 3–5.
294. Cf. vv. 2ff.   295. Cf. above on vv. 5, 9.
296. Vv. 33, 34b.

*the affairs of the Lord*²⁹⁷ if one is not. Paul would say rather that the main thing is to abide in that status in which one was called into the faith of Christ. Paul would probably have conceded to the celibate that his involvement in the *affairs of the Lord*, such as prayer, was a good thing. He even concedes that involvement with prayer is good for the married person, if the abstinence involved can be fitted into the pattern of married life. But whatever one does in faith must be according to one's gift from God²⁹⁸ and also must contribute to that wholeness and integrity of the community of faith to which Paul refers in v. 15: *For God has called us to peace.*

So in the radically changed life of faith the distinction between *the affairs of the Lord* and *worldly affairs* has no place. This is probably the kind of distinction which the Corinthians made to their own confusion.²⁹⁹ There is no need for the anxiety which was evidently being demonstrated by some of the Corinthian Christians. Some were saying: I'm married, but if I were a celibate, I could serve the Lord better. Others were saying: I'm a celibate, but the natural passions are difficult to control. Others were saying: Celibacy is a superior way of life, while still others claimed superiority for marriage. In this confusion they addressed themselves to Paul. He counsels them that the best way to know what their way of life should be is consider what they were when they were converted. This, however, is not infallible as a test. There are a number of exceptions. But God will show the man of faith what it is he must do. There is no need for anxiety. When the married person can be as though he had no spouse, when the one who cries can be as though he did not cry, when he who is joyful can be, etc., then there will be no anxiety, but only the ready acceptance of God's will in the peace of the faithful community.

35

not to lay any restraint upon you: The Greek text may be rendered literally: 'not in order to put a noose around you.' To tell a person that he is where God wants him to be should, in most cases, be liberating rather than imprisoning. It frees one from the anxiety of wanting always to be somewhere else. The modern church is particularly prone to this anxiety: the priest should not be in church but in the world. The lay person should not be in the world but in the church. The student should not be in the classroom but in the streets protesting. The Corinthians had, in the name of freedom, put the noose around their

297. Vv. 32b, 34a.   298. Cf. above on vv. 7, 17, 20, 24.
299. Cf. above on 6¹²ᶠ·.

necks when they failed to relate positively their status in life to their conversion to Christ.

to promote good order: The reference here is back to the *peace* to which God has called us (v. 15).

secure your undivided devotion to the Lord: This is addressed to everyone. To do away with the anxieties, the frustrations, the false division between the affairs of the Lord and those of the world is Paul's intention. But this takes place only within the radically changing life of the community of faith.

36–8
Many scholars have attempted to unravel the tangled threads of this section. The difficulties in the passage are as follows:

36
(a) *If anyone thinks that he is not behaving properly towards his betrothed:* The Greek word rendered by R.S.V. *betrothed* is *parthenos*, the singular of the word in v. 25 rendered by R.S.V. *unmarried.* The word *parthenos* in Greek means 'virgin'. Therefore the passage starts by referring to *his virgin.* The question is: who behaves improperly towards his virgin?
(b) *if his passions are strong:* Can also be rendered 'if she is ripe for marriage',[300] so the phrase may not refer to 'anyone', but to the 'virgin' (R.S.V. betrothed).
(c) *let them marry: Them* here would refer to *anyone* and 'virgin' (R.S.V. *betrothed*).

37
(a) *being under no necessity, but having his desire under control:* This may also be rendered: 'being under no compulsion and having complete control of his own choice.'
(b) *to keep her as his betrothed:* Again, *betrothed* renders Greek *parthenos*, 'virgin'.

38
(a) *he who marries his betrothed:*[301] The Greek word rendered here *marries* usually means 'gives in marriage'.
(b) *he who refrains from marriage:* This contains the word which in Greek means 'gives in marriage', as above.

300. N.E.B. alternative reading.
301. Cf. above on vv. 36, 37.

Three basic interpretations have been made of this passage:

1. *Anyone* refers to a father or guardian who wonders whether he ought to allow his daughter to be married. This interpretation relies chiefly upon solving problems 38(a) and (b) in which the normal rendering would be 'give in marriage'. It leaves, however, difficulties 36(a) and (c) and 37(b). 36(b) and 37(a) are explicable. This is the solution of J.B.

2. The reference is to a man and his fiancée. This is the solution of R.S.V. The unsolved difficulties here are 36(a), 37(b), and 38(a) and (b).

3. The situation envisaged is one in which a man and woman have agreed to live together but without sexual intercourse. This solution is favoured by N.E.B. It solves all the problems except 38 (a) and(b). I favour this solution over the other two for the following reasons.

i. It is impossible to make 'virgin', *parthenos*, mean either 'unmarried daughter' or 'betrothed' without making the passage ludicrous.

ii. Problem 36(c) rules out solution 1 unless a male subject can be understood.

iii. The Greek word *gamizein*, which normally means 'give in marriage', could in this later period of language have taken on the meaning 'marry'. There are analogous cases of other Greek words with the causative ending *izein* which took on the other root meaning.[302]

iv. This solution seems to fit best into my analysis of the passage as a whole. Paul has been discussing the problems connected with marriage and celibacy among the Christians at Corinth. He has stated that radical changes in all phases of man's life come through membership in the community of faith: some men take the step of voluntary celibacy, some married folk practise abstinence. No one's life remains the same. Now Paul describes what is without a doubt the most radical change in a married way of life. Men and women live together as brother and sister, but, again, not without problems.

36

not behaving properly: Should be taken with *if his passions are strong.* The thought is similar to that in v. 9 above, *if they cannot exercise self-control* . . . The advice is also the same – *let them marry.* Paul conceives of such arrangements as these and the temporary abstinence discussed in v. 5 as being directed towards a specific purpose within the life of the community. They are not ends in themselves. When it becomes obvious that this kind of life is not a part of God's gift to a man, then he should

302. Cf. F. Blass and A. Debrunner, *A Greek Grammar of the New Testament and Other Early Christian Literature* (E.T. and ed., R. W. Funk), 1961, Section 101.

marry. Neither temporary nor permanent abstinence from sexual relations should become a situation in which a man is put to the test.[303]

38
well . . . better: Paul does not mean this in any absolute sense.[304]

39A wife is bound to her husband as long as he lives. If the husband dies, she is free to be married to whom she wishes, only in the Lord. 40But in my judgement she is happier if she remains as she is. And I think that I have the Spirit of God.

ೞೞ

39
free to be married to whom she wishes:[305] It has been suggested that this is an intentional abrogation of the custom prescribed in Deut. 25^{5–10}, so-called Levirite marriage. Why this should have been of concern to a gentile community is difficult to say. The statement would seem to be simply the context of freedom within which Paul wishes his one proviso to be understood, *only in the Lord.* Most commentators take this to mean 'only to a man who is a Christian'. Paul has already described certain problems which had arisen in the cases of marriage between believers and non-believers. He would perhaps spare the widows those problems at least.

40
He would prefer to spare them all the problems connected with marriage[306]

in my judgement: Cf. above on v. 12; cp. vv. 8, 10.

I have the Spirit of God: With this last statement the sense of strife and self-defence which we noted in Chapters 1–4 seems to have returned.[307]

303. Cf. above on v. 5.
304. Cf. above on v. 28.
305. Cf. above on v. 34.
306. Cf. above on vv. 27–35.
307. Cf. 1¹⁷, 2^{1ff.}, 4^{3f.},^{9ff.},^{14f.}; cp. 2¹⁶.

Chapter 8

There have been many attempts to demonstrate that neither 1 nor 2 Corinthians are unities. The principal evidence for this is usually drawn from 1 Cor. 8–10. More particularly, it is usually demonstrated that, compared with the rest of 8–11^1, 10$^{1-22}$ has the appearance of an interpolation. This section is then assigned to an earlier letter.[308]

However, there is considerable evidence within these chapters themselves of an inner consistency of purpose on the part of the author, as I shall try to show. Paul begins this section with his now familiar formula, *Now concerning*, indicating as in 7^{1,25} above a major change of subject. This is then the third question put to Paul in the letter from the Corinthians.

The question concerns meat which has been part of an animal sacrifice to a pagan god. Is it proper for a Christian to eat meat which has been part of a pagan sacrifice? This is a question which could well have been asked by the Christians in Corinth. There were after all occasions when one would be invited to share in the feast which followed such a sacrifice.[309] To what extent was one bound to decline such an invitation? Further, any meat which one might be served in another's home or buy for oneself in the public market could easily have come from one of the pagan sacrifices.[310] The Corinthians probably put the question in the form suggested above. Their concern was with eating.

Paul, however, sees deeper issues involved. First there was the question of idolatry, of which, as a Jew, Paul was keenly aware.[311] Secondly, there was the problem of one's fellow who may witness one's participation in a pagan banquet. He may be a believer who is relatively unsophisticated (8^9), or he may be one of the unbelievers (10^{29}). The former Paul would keep from idolatry, the latter he would win away from it. We will discuss Paul's digression, on Christian freedom, in Chapter 9 below.

308. Hurd, 43ff.
309. Cf. 8^{10}, 10^{18b-21}.
310. Cf. 10^{25,27}.
311. Cf. 8$^{1-13}$, 10$^{1-22}$.

¹*Now concerning food offered to idols: we know that 'all of us possess knowledge'. 'Knowledge' puffs up, but love builds up. ²If anyone imagines that he knows something, he does not yet know as he ought to know. ³But if one loves God, one is known by him.*

⁴*Hence, as to the eating of food, offered to idols, we know that 'an idol has no real existence', and that 'there is no God but one'. ⁵For although there may be so-called gods in heaven or on earth – as indeed there are many 'gods' and many 'lords' – ⁶yet for us there is one God, the Father, from whom are all things and for whom we exist, and one Lord, Jesus Christ, through whom are all things and through whom we exist.*

⁷*However, not all possess this knowledge. But some, through being hitherto accustomed to idols, eat food as really offered to an idol; and their conscience, being weak, is defiled. ⁸Food will not commend us to God. We are no worse off if we do not eat, and no better off if we do. ⁹Only take care lest this liberty of yours somehow become a stumbling-block to the weak. ¹⁰For if anyone sees you, a man of knowledge, at table in an idol's temple, might he not be encouraged, if his conscience is weak, to eat food offered to idols? ¹¹And so by your knowledge this weak man is destroyed, the brother for whom Christ died. ¹²Thus, sinning against your brethren and wounding their conscience when it is weak, you sin against Christ. ¹³Therefore, if food is a cause of my brother's falling, I will never eat meat, lest I cause my brother to fall.*

1

all of us possess knowledge: Another slogan of the Corinthian Christians.[312] The knowledge which they[313] have is that given them by their acceptance of the Gospel of Christ; the idols are nothing because there is only one God (v. 4), and the so-called gods and lords, i.e. the various cult deities who are represented by the idols, play no vital role in salvation, since there is only one God and one Lord involved in creation and redemption (v. 5). Knowing this, the Corinthians' problem is: in how many of their old customs, which they have known as pagans, can they still participate? After all, if the idols are nothing and the

312. Cf. above on 6¹². 313. Or some of them – cf. below on v. 7.

so-called gods are powerless, what harm can there be in participating in meals which follow pagan sacrifices or in eating meat which has been part of those sacrifices?

1b f.

Paul contrasts *knowledge* with *love* and *being known by him* (God). The force of this contrast is, as Moffat points out,[314] in the idea which is common both to Paul as a Jew[315] and to the Corinthians acquainted with the religions of the Hellenistic world:[316] to know anything is not necessarily of any value if it does not rest ultimately upon a vital relation between the 'knower' and God. Just what this implies becomes now Paul's task to explain. The subject of the vital relation between the 'knower' and God Paul will handle at length in Chapter 13.

4

As to the eating of food, offered to idols: The addition of the word *eating* here by Paul to his original statement *concerning food . . .* (1) points up two things: (1) the Greek word translated *food offered to idols* (*eidōlothuta*) does not, of itself, imply *food*; (2) Paul adds the word *food* (Greek, *brōsis*) to indicate the level at which he will attack the problem. It is fair to say that throughout this discussion Paul does not waver from his position that, from God's point of view, eating in itself is a matter of indifference.[317]

an idol has no real existence: Paul here must be understood as describing sympathetically the sophisticated attitude of the Corinthian Christians (at least some of them). They understand that an *idol* is just a piece of wood or stone.[318] They also understand that the so-called *gods* and *lords* of pagan religions are not that at all, because there is only one God and one Lord. Now all Christians have been freed (as Schlatter says) from the power of the false gods and their idols (12²). But not all Christians have arrived at the degree of sophistication displayed in vv. 4b–6.

7

some . . . eat food as really offered to an idol: They really believe in the existence and the efficacy of these images and the deities whom they represent. Paul has already alluded to this phenomenon in what must

314. Ad loc.
315. Cf. Psalm 1⁶; Nah. 1⁷; Jer. 1⁵; cp. Isa. 49¹; Exod. 33¹²,¹⁷.
316. Cf. Lietzmann, ad loc.
317. Cf. v. 8 and 10²⁵,²⁷,³¹.
318. R.S.V. takes *idol* to refer to the pagan deities themselves, but cf. below on 12².

be a reference to Deut. 10[17] in v. 5 above, *many 'gods' and many 'lords'*. Not only is the world of such people full of *gods* and *lords*, but the sacrifices offered to them are real, and the meat left over represents what is left of that sacrifice. Further, eating that food constitutes participation in that sacrifice.

being hitherto accustomed to idols . . . their conscience being weak: The worship which the Corinthian Christians had known was real. They had been won over to the Gospel, but the basic view of reality of some of them had not been changed: pagan worship was still real. The usual interpretation of the words *weak conscience* would give this passage a moralistic character which the Greek does not really convey. The word *conscience* translates the Greek word *suneidēsis*. The usual argument is that this is a concept derived by Paul from the Greeks among whom it sometimes had the sense of the English word *conscience*. However, the Greek can also mean 'awareness' or 'consciousness', without any moralistic overtones. This would seem to be a more apt meaning here. The distinction Paul makes is between those who are knowledgeable or sophisticated and those who are not. When he comes to characterize the effect of the action of the sophisticated upon the unsophisticated, he uses the word *oikodomein*, to 'edify' (rendered misleadingly in the R.S.V. *encouraged*).[319]

Paul says nothing in this passage about the inner disposition of the *weak* or the person whose *conscience* is weak. Paul is concerned with the possible destruction of the weak person, who may be led by the example of the more knowledgeable brother to participate in the banquet following a pagan sacrifice. But Paul is not concerned because the weak person's conscience is going to hurt or bother him, but because the unsophisticated person cannot distinguish between mere participation in a meal and participation in the pagan worship which was the occasion for the meal. The more sophisticated Christian knows that he has been freed from the power of the pagan idols. He also knows that the pagan idols and their gods have no claim on him even if he partakes of the sacrificed meat. The not-so-sophisticated Christian knows that Christ has claimed his allegiance. He knows that he is Lord in a way that the pagan gods are not. But he does not understand

319. The instances of the word *suneidēsis* usually cited by commentators in connection with this passage are from the Pastoral Epistles: 1 Tim. 3[9]; 2 Tim. 1[3]; cp. Tit. 1[15]. Of these three instances only one can be construed as meaning an inner awareness of one's shortcomings (2 Tim. 1[3]). The other two have clearly to do with a correct perception of Christian doctrine.

that the idols and the pagan gods are as nothing. For him to return, even part way, towards pagan worship, would result, in Paul's mind, only in his destruction.

8
Paul emphasizes his point: eating *per se* is not what is at issue here.

commend us to God: The sense is rendered better by N.E.B., 'bring us into God's presence', or by J.B., 'bring us in touch with God'. It is not the unrestrained exercise of their newly-found freedom which constitutes any necessary part of their Christian faith. They haven't missed anything if they do refrain from exercising it – *if we do not eat* – nor are they at any advantage if they *do*.

9
liberty: Translates Greek *exousia*, which means literally 'right' or 'authority'.[320] The irony here is that the unrestrained exercise of their rights could lead to the destruction of another Christian.[321]

a stumbling-block: The occasion for a relapse into paganism.

10
in an idol's temple: As von Soden[322] points out, this shows that Paul's interest is in the possibility of idolatry, not in the inner disposition of the *weak* person.

11
is destroyed: That is, lapses back into paganism.[323]

12
sinning against your brethren . . . you sin against Christ: cf. Matt. 25[40,45]; Acts 9[4,5].[324]

wounding their conscience: The Greek is more literally rendered 'cudgelling their awareness'. This is opposed to what Paul ironically refers to in v. 10 as *be encouraged*.[325] The sophisticated Corinthians were, instead of building up, further perverting their brethren's self-understanding and their religious outlook. To make them think that one could still

320. Cf. 6[12] and 10[23], where the verbal form *exesti*, 'it is lawful', occurs.
321. Cp. Rom. 14[13f.].
322. H. von Soden, 'Sakrament und Ethik bei Paulus', *Urchristentum und Geschichte*, I, 1951, 243.
323. Cp. 5[5], 11[29f.]; Acts 5[5,19].
324. Cp. 1 Thess. 4[8].
325. Cf. above on v. 7, *oikodomein*.

participate (to any degree) in idolatrous worship was anything but edifying. One might compare this in our day with giving an alcoholic a drink. Just as there is no such thing as one drink for the alcoholic, so there cannot be, according to Paul, a harmless degree of association with pagan worship for some gentile Christians. Naturally an individual lost to the community is something which affects the *brethren*, but it also affects Christ, into whose intimate fellowship their faith has admitted them.

13

This is purely hypothetical. It is simply Paul's way of restating his opinion about the unrestrained exercise of freedom in a most radical way. In v. 8 Paul has said that food is not really the crux of his argument. It is not the food *per se*, but the effect which this may have on the less sophisticated Christian[326] which is the crux of the problem. However, Paul implies, if food *per se* were the principal issue he would give up meat forever. If one wishes to draw any general conclusions from this *ad hoc* argument, one ought to take full stock of what follows in Chapter 9. This verse can best be taken as a transition to Paul's autobiographical treatment in this next chapter.

326. Cf. above on v. 12.

Chapter 9

The most obvious question about this whole chapter is: Why does it appear here? It is difficult to see why, after introducing the subject of meat offered in pagan sacrifices, Paul should suddenly turn to this highly personal account of his own self-support. Those who find continuity in this section 8^1–11^1 usually do so by making Chapter 9 a subdivision of Paul's essay on the handling of the tender conscience. The point of the chapter is then seen as exemplary: Paul sets himself up as a model of self-denial. He will not use any of his rights as an apostle (vv. 2–18), but rather strives to give no offence to anyone, Jewish-Christian or gentile, in order more effectively to preach the Gospel. Other commentators would see this chapter as originally part of another letter. In this case the chapter constitutes a defence by Paul against those who are denying his right to be an apostle. According to this view, the fact that Paul accepts no support from the Corinthian Church indicates doubt on his part about his apostleship.

Paul, however, is not primarily concerned in the section 9^{1-11} with his own image or with his authority as an apostle. As we have indicated in the introduction to Chapters 8–10 (page 70), Paul is interested in two things:

1. How to win the gentile Corinthians over to the new faith and away from pagan worship (10^{14}).

2. How to keep those Christians in Corinth who are less sophisticated from lapsing back into pagan worship.

Thus Paul's main concern is with idolatry. In dealing with this problem he draws two separate sets of distinctions between people:

1. (a) those who are under the law (9^{20}), that is the Jews (or possibly Jewish-Christians) (cf. below on vv. 19–23); (b) those who are without the law (9^{21}) that is the Greeks (cf. below on vv. 19–23) (or possibly the gentile-Christians).

2. (a) those who have knowledge, that is a sophisticated group (8^1; cp. 8^{10}); (b) those who do not have knowledge, that is the not-so-sophisticated (8^7) to whom Paul also refers as *the weak* (8^9, 9^{22}).

Paul would try and win over from paganism group 1(b). He also

76

wants to keep group 2(b) from lapsing back into paganism. Though he is the apostle to the gentiles, Paul also feels it necessary to keep the channels open between himself and the Jews. This is part of his peculiar vocation. It is one which he cannot force upon anyone else, just as in his discussion of celibacy,[327] though it is clear where his inclinations tend (11^1).

Chapter 9 must be seen in the context of Paul's general discussion of his strategy against idolatry.[328] His main theme in this chapter is freedom. This freedom which Paul has is an intrinsic part of his Christian calling. It is not, however, a freedom which he gives up for the sake of the Gospel, but the condition afforded by his refusal to take support from the Corinthian congregation.

Paul is not saying in Chapter 9 that because he is free (i.e. he can have the support of the church if he so desires it) and because he forgoes this freedom his preaching is that much more effective. He says, rather, that he is free because he will not accept the support of the church. It is this freedom, in turn, which affords him the possibility to be *all things to all men*. Only in this way can Paul preach the Gospel to both Jews and Greeks. Only in this way can he hold together the disparate factions which threaten the unity of the congregation.

9^{1-18} PAUL'S USE OF HIS FREEDOM

¹Am I not free? Am I not an apostle? Have I not seen Jesus our Lord? Are not you my workmanship in the Lord? ²If to others I am not an apostle, at least I am to you; for you are the seal of my apostleship in the Lord.

³This is my defence to those who would examine me. ⁴Do we not have the right to our food and drink? ⁵Do we not have the right to be accompanied by a wife, as the other apostles and the brothers of the Lord and Cephas? ⁶Or is it only Barnabas and I who have no right to refrain from

327. Cf. above on Chapter 7.
328. It is difficult to follow the reasoning of one recent writer who sees Paul's careful delineation of the groups involved as indicating that he was not primarily interested in describing his missionary strategy; cf. G. Bornkamm, 'The Missionary Stance of Paul in 1 Corinthians 9 and in Acts', *Studies in Luke–Acts*, ed. L. E. Keck, J. L. Martyn, 1966, 195.

working for a living? ⁷Who serves as a soldier at his own expense? who plants a vineyard without eating any of its fruit? Who tends a flock without getting some of the milk?

⁸Do I say this on human authority? Does not the law say the same? ⁹For it is written in the law of Moses, 'You shall not muzzle an ox when it is treading the grain'. Is it for oxen that God is concerned? ¹⁰Does he not speak entirely for our sake? It was written for our sake, because the ploughman should plough in hope and the thresher thresh in hope of a share in the crop. ¹¹If we have sown spiritual good among you, is it too much if we reap your material benefits? ¹²If others share this rightful claim upon you, do not we still more?

Nevertheless, we have not made use of this right, but we endure anything rather than put an obstacle in the way of the gospel of Christ. ¹³Do you not know that those who are employed in the temple service get their food from the temple, and those who serve at the altar share in the sacrificial offerings? ¹⁴In the same way, the Lord commanded that those who proclaim the gospel should get their living by the gospel.

¹⁵But I have made no use of any of these rights, nor am I writing this to secure any such provision. For I would rather die than have any one deprive me of my ground for boasting. ¹⁶For if I preach the gospel, that gives me no ground for boasting. For necessity is laid upon me. Woe to me if I do not preach the gospel! ¹⁷For if I do this of my own will, I have a reward; but if not of my own will, I am entrusted with a commission. ¹⁸What then is my reward? Just this: that in my preaching I may make the gospel free of charge, not making full use of my right in the gospel.

The division of this chapter is indicated by the occurrence of the word *free* (vv. 1 and 19). After some preliminary statements about his apostleship (vv. 1, 2), Paul sets about to show how (not why) he is free. It is possible that Paul has been accused by the hyper-enthusiasts, who are exercising their freedom in an unrestricted manner, of going back on his own message of freedom. They have perhaps accused him of inconsistency, particularly over this subject of participation in pagan banquets and eating meat which has been part of a pagan sacrifice. So Paul must first establish his credentials. In a series of rhetorical questions Paul states them: he is *free*; he is an *apostle*. It is his apostleship which he defends on the grounds that he has *seen Jesus our Lord*,[329] and that he has founded a church of which they (the Corinthian Christians) are the living proof or *seal of . . . apostleship*.[330]

കൗ

3
Having established his credentials as an apostle, Paul then proceeds to explain how it is that he is free.

This is my defence: This refers to the whole of vv. 1–18, though we would see the reference as primarily backwards to the preceding vv. 1b–2.[331] In sheer bulk, what follows in vv. 4–18 outweighs vv. 1b–2, but in importance it does not. Vv. 4–18 constitute only an explanation of Paul's method of being free. The profound part of his argument is in vv. 1b–2 and 19–23.

4f.
Paul states his *rights*.

the right to our food and drink: Most commentators see in this statement the added implication, 'at the expense of the community'. There is no doubt that the matter of support by the community is treated in vv. 6–23. However, as most commentators admit, the sequence of thought from vv. 4–6 is broken at the end of v. 5. The usual explanation for this break in sequence is that v. 6 interprets vv. 4 and 5. Another, perhaps more probable, explanation is that vv. 4 and 6 represent rights and prerogatives already acknowledged by the community, whereas v. 5 represents a part of Paul's life which is a problem for them. We have already seen that Paul chooses the celibate life and even recommends it for others.[332] Furthermore, Paul has suggested in 8^{13} at least one motive for total abstinence from flesh meat. Paul will go on in vv. 24–7 to give further reasons for such self-denial. It would not be unreasonable to conclude therefore that in vv. 4f. Paul defends his right to food and marriage, even though he practises fasting and celibacy. In this way he provides a transition from Chapters 7–8, in which these two subjects have been treated from another perspective.

to be accompanied by a wife: Attempts have been made to show that what is implied here is a non-conjugal arrangement in which the woman is a kind of travelling assistant for the missionary.[333] This is unlikely. The Greek can simply mean 'have a wife'.

329. Cf. below on 15$^{3\text{ff}}$.   330. Cf. 2 Cor. 3$^{2\text{f.}}$; 4 Macc. 7.^{15}
331. Cf. R.-P., ad loc.   332. Cf. 7^{1,7,8,26}.
333. Cf. J. B. Bauer, 'Uxores circumducere', *BZ*, 3 (1959), 94–102. Cf. Luke 8$^{2\text{ff.}}$; and above on 7$^{36-8}$.

as the other apostles and the brothers of the Lord and Cephas: Most commentators would see here a reference to the *right* of support exercised by the *other apostles,* etc. If, however, this was a recognized right or prerogative of the apostles, it is difficult to understand the necessity for Paul's argument in vv. 7–14. The other possibility is to take the word *as* (Greek, *hōs*) to mean 'in the manner of',334 i.e. supported by the community. We must then understand that the *right to . . food and drink* and the *right to . . . a wife* refer quite simply to food and to marriage, two practices already established in the community and interpreted by Paul in Chapters 7 and 8. But Paul is different, and he must defend his uniqueness. He has already defended his celibate state. He has also given one ground of defence for abstinence from flesh meat (8¹³). But the *other apostles* etc. were already receiving and accepting support while, at least in Corinth, Paul was not. As Hurd suggests,335 the reason may well have been that no support was offered to Paul by the Corinthian community. This being the case, Paul had first to establish the *right* of the missionary to support, so that he could make a point of refusing it. Paul's argument in vv. 7–14 is academic, as is his argument in 8^{10ff.}.

the other apostles: The problem here is the relation between the *apostles* and the *twelve.* The tradition cited by Paul in 15^{5,7} would seem to distinguish between the *apostles* as a group and the *twelve* as a group, though it leaves open the possibility that they may have overlapped. A comparison of the lists336 of those who were presumably members of the *twelve* shows that no two of them are in complete agreement. Thus there is also the possibility that the *twelve* is a later idealization on the basis of some such idea as Matthew 19²⁸. One cannot seriously doubt, however, that there was an inner group around Jesus during his lifetime, that Cephas held a definite pre-eminence within that group,337 and that *the brothers of the Lord* were not a part of it.338

7–14

Paul argues his case for the right of support on four different levels:

 1. Experience: the soldier, the vine-grower, and the herdsman (v. 7).
 2. Scripture: Deut. 25⁴; cp. 1 Tim. 5¹⁸ (vv. 8–11).
 3. The current practice of (a) the Church (v. 12) and (b) the other cults (v. 13).
 4. Teaching of Jesus (v. 14).

334. W. Bauer, op. cit. (n. 67), *s.v.* Ib.
335. Cf. p. 204.
336. Mark 3¹³⁻¹⁹; Matt. 10¹⁻⁴; Luke 6¹²⁻¹⁶; Acts 1¹³.
337. Cf. Mark 8^{27ff.} parr.
338. Cf. Mark 3^{31ff.} parr.; cp. John 7^{3ff.}.

10f.

This argument depends upon an allegorical or mystical understanding of the text which is not in violation of, but not dependent on, the literal sense of the scripture.[339]

It was written for our sake, because . . .: The R.S.V. rightly avoids the notion that this introduces another quotation. It does not, however, adequately convey the sense that this is what the citation from Deut. 25⁴ really means.[340] What we have here is an interpretation of an interpretation, i.e. from oxen to farmer to missionary. The process of interpretation proceeds somewhat as follows:

One first has to understand that there is a meaning implicit as well as explicit in the scriptural text. This meaning applies to men rather than to animals. This implicit meaning gives hope to the one who *ploughs* and *threshes*. But these ideas are in turn applied to the business at hand of preaching (sowing spiritual good) and receiving support (reaping . . . material benefits).

13

This allusion to temple cult practice could apply equally to either Jewish or pagan usage at this time. There can be no doubt that the Corinthians would have thought mainly of the pagan practice with which they were already acquainted.

14

This command from Jesus himself is the clinching argument.[341] It is possible that this is not part of a tradition handed down from Jesus, but represents Christian prophecy speaking for Jesus.[342] Paul has now established his *right* to support from the local congregation by establishing the *right* of all missionaries to this support.

12

others share this rightful claim upon you: Paul alludes to the fact that support is already given to missionaries. This does not necessarily have to come from the Corinthians, i.e. *others share this* (in other places which is a) *rightful claim upon you*. Paul could not argue that he never received support from the church,[343] though this self-denial was not a policy which he followed only in Corinth.[344]

339. Cf. W. Arndt, 'The Meaning of I Cor. 9:9, 10', *CTM*, 3 (1932), 329–35.
340. Cf. N.E.B.: 'Of course it refers to us in the sense that . . .'
341. Cf. I Cor. 7¹⁰; I Thess. 4¹⁵.   342. Cf. above, n. 267.
343. Cf. 2 Cor. 11⁷,⁹; Phil. 4¹⁶.   344. Cf. I Thess. 2⁹; 2 Thess. 3⁸.

15-18

In vv. 15-18 Paul explains what it means to him not to receive support from the Corinthian congregation, and why under no circumstances would he consent to receive any support. He has already given a strong indication in v. 12 that his receiving support from the Corinthians might constitute an *obstacle in the way of the gospel of Christ*. Just what this obstacle might be he does not make clear at this point. It may well have been, as Moffat suggests, that for a teacher like Paul to accept payment for teaching the Christian religion would have been objectionable to Jews. There is some ambiguity in the Talmud on this subject.[345] If Paul were being criticized in Corinth, as some have suggested,[346] for not receiving support (perhaps because none was offered),[347] and if the gentiles would have opposed this in principle,[348] there would have been strong motivation, in this set of circumstances alone, for Paul to make a point of refusing support. At this point Paul introduces into his explanation the idea of *boasting*. The text is further complicated by the manner in which this idea is introduced: the sentence which constitutes v. 15c is apparently broken off in the middle. The idea of boasting is introduced in the clause which resumes the sentence.

For I would rather die than have any one deprive me of my ground for boasting: This break is completely glossed over in the R.S.V. translation. Literally the Greek must be rendered: 'I would rather die than ... no one shall take away something that I can boast of.' The question of course is: *than* what? The thrust of the previous clause, *nor am I writing this to secure any such provision*, would suggest that 15c might have been, as N.E.B. conjectures, an expostulation: I'd rather die, i.e. than accept support. Such a strong statement would be especially understandable if no support had even been offered.

16f.

Whatever this *ground for boasting* may have been, it was not Paul's preaching. This is excluded because Paul has no choice but to preach. His preaching is a matter of *necessity*. Like the prophets, Paul had to speak what God commanded him.[349] This explains v. 17.

345. Cf. in Mishnah, *Aboth*, where there are conflicting statements. Some seem to advocate that one who occupies himself in the study of the Torah should be supported (*Aboth* III, 5; IV, 5). Others speak quite strongly against this idea (ibid., II, 2; IV, 5; VI (Bar.), 4, 9).

346. Cf. Lietzmann, ad loc.

347. Cf. above n. 335.   348. Cf. above on 4¹².

349. Cf. Amos 3⁸; Jer. 17, 20⁹; Ezek. 3¹⁷ᶠ·; cp. Gal. 1¹⁵ᶠ·.

17f.

Again Paul's analysis is somewhat academic. Paul assumes two possibilities: (1) he preaches by choice, or (2) he does so by necessity. The
first is ruled out by v. 16, and, along with it, the idea of a *reward*. The
second possibility represents the actual condition and carries with it
the idea of a *commission*. Obviously Paul has removed the possibility
of a reward in the usual sense of a 'recompense' by indicating that he
only did what he had been commissioned to do.[350] However, he asks
the question again: *What then is my reward?* By so doing Paul shows
that he does not use *reward* in its usual sense. His reward is that there is
no reward. Paul expends his efforts as a missionary of the Gospel in the
same manner as God, *free of charge*. Like God's bestowal of the grace of
salvation, there are no conditions attached to what Paul does as a
missionary.[351] He does it because it is his calling.[352]

9[19-23]

[19]For though I am free from all men, I have made myself a slave to all,
that I might win the more. [20]To the Jews I became as a Jew, in order to win
Jews; to those under the law I became as one under the law – though not
being myself under the law – that I might win those under the law. [21]To
those outside the law I became as one outside the law–not being without law
toward God but under the law of Christ – that I might win those outside
the law. [22]To the weak I became weak, that I might win the weak. I have
become all things to all men, that I might by all means save some. [23]I do
it all for the sake of the gospel, that I may share in its blessings.

ଉଉ

19

I am free from all men: The fact that he receives no support from them
means Paul is not in any way dependent upon them. He is free to do as
he chooses because he chooses not to be supported. His attachment can
therefore be, not just to some, but to all. In a time when the church

350. Cf. Luke 17[7-10].
351. Cf. E. Käsemann, 'Eine paulinische Variation des "amor fati"',
Exegetische Aufsätze und Besinnungen, II, 223–39.
352. Cf. Gal. 1[15]; Rom. 1[1]; cp. 1 Cor. 7[17,7].

was changing from a predominantly Jewish to a predominantly gentile constitution, Paul stands in a unique position. He can speak to both Jews and gentiles because he is bound to neither group. We know how deeply Paul felt about his 'kinsmen by race' (cf. Rom. 9$^{1-5}$). Certainly it was to keep the door open for them that he adopted this peculiar stance with regard to support by the church. Commentators tend to forget, in the general discussion of this passage, the advice given by Paul in 7$^{18-22}$. The Jew does not cease being a Jew, because he accepts Jesus as the promised Messiah of the Jews. In the same way the gentile cannot become a Jew and should not try. He becomes a child of Abraham by faith in Jesus the Messiah.[353] Both together, Jew and Greek, bring their gifts into the Christian community, where they are pooled for the common good and a new synthesis is achieved – a new creature.[354]

a slave to all: This describes the way in which Paul takes upon himself voluntarily the various usages or customs of Jew and non-Jew. He could not do this if he were not free. There are four separate groups mentioned in vv. 20–22:

1. *Jews:* would indicate those Jews who had not accepted Jesus as the Messiah.

2. *Those under the law:* these are Jewish Christians who still observe the prescriptions of the law, even though they have accepted Jesus as the Messiah.

3. *Those outside the law:* those who do not now or never did keep the prescriptions of the Jewish law. These would be gentiles for the most part.

4. *The weak:* we have already seen that they are those gentiles who still hold a strong and somewhat naïve pagan world view, even though they have accepted Jesus as the Messiah.[355]

In this period of the church's history the break with Judaism was far from complete. There was, as we know from Paul's writings on the destiny of the Jews in Rom. 9–11, a genuine open-endedness in his thinking about his 'kinsmen by race'. This is not balanced by an openness towards paganism. While his remarks about Judaism are probably somewhat academic, his real purpose in Chapters 8–10 is to keep his pagan converts from lapsing back into pagan ways.

20–22

not being myself under the law . . . not being without law toward God but under the law of Christ: This is one of Paul's all-too-familiar paradoxes.

353. Cf. Gal. 3^{29}.   354. Cf. 2 Cor. 5^{17}; cp. Gal. 6^{15}.
355. Cf. above on vv. 7ff.

It is usually explained by giving a different meaning to the word *law* in each case: in v. 20 *the law* is the law of Moses; in v. 21 *law* is understood in a much more general sense. *Law of Christ* is usually interpreted rather vaguely as the 'law of love'.[356] Dodd suggests that *under the law of Christ* refers to a body of precepts (such as is reflected in 7[10] and 9[14]) much more concrete in nature than a general commandment to love one another.[357] This growing body of Christian law would of course take precedence over and serve to interpret the Jewish law. Paul's point would be then that he submits voluntarily to the prescriptions of Jewish law when he is with Jews. When he is with non-Jews, however, he is still under the law of Christ, whether they are Christians or pagans. The fact that Paul is *under the law of Christ* means, however, only that he will do nothing to contradict his faith in Christ. It does not prevent him from taking seriously the beliefs of those who still practise or are not far removed from practising pagan rites, i.e. *the weak.*

23

I do it all for the sake of the gospel: Everything Paul has mentioned here in this section has as its goal the proclamation of what God has done through Jesus. Paul feels that by not receiving support from this community he is in a better position to reach both Jews and Greeks, sophisticated and unsophisticated, believers and non-believers with this message.

that I may share in its blessings: This can be interpreted in two ways.
  1. Paul now thinks mainly of himself and his own salvation, which is by no means guaranteed.
  2. Paul thinks of his partnership in the proclamation of the Gospel – the mission of the church.
The interpretation turns, not so much on the idea of *sharing*, as on the nature and character of the *blessings* in which Paul shares. If we have rightly understood Paul's description of and his rationale for his own particular way of life, and if this life carried with it certain conditions, namely supporting one's self, then might we not see the serious fulfilment of these conditions as underlying what Paul says in v. 23, and what he explicates in his athletic metaphor of vv. 24–7?

356. Cf. Gal. 5[13ff.]
357. 'ENNOMOS CHRISTOU', *Studia Paulina in honorem J. de Zwann,* ed. J. N. Sevenster and W. C. van Unnik, 1953, 96–110.

²⁴ *Do you not know that in a race all the runners compete, but only one receives the prize? So run that you may obtain it.* ²⁵*Every athlete exercises self-control in all things. They do it to receive a perishable wreath, but we an imperishable.* ²⁶*Well, I do not run aimlessly, I do not box as one beating the air;* ²⁷*but I pommel my body and subdue it, lest after preaching to others I myself should be disqualified.*

On the surface it is difficult to see the precise application of this metaphor. It is obviously not the prize. Only one person wins a contest. There is no real comparison between what the Christian strives for and the pine wreath given to the winner of an athletic event (v. 25). The basis of comparison is rather that in a contest *all ... compete*, that is everyone tries as hard as he can to win. It is taken seriously by all, even though only one person will triumph. This is true, not only in the contest itself, but in the preparation, the training for the event (vv. 26f.).

25

self-control in all things: The athlete must exercise a discipline which affects all aspects of his life, such as food, sleep, recreation, etc. The Christian is involved in nothing less than a witness to the meaning of life itself as this has been and continues to be revealed in Christ. No part of his life is exempted.

26

I do not run aimlessly. I do not box as one beating the air: The athlete does not practise for his event without some idea of what he is doing. I can remember running as a schoolboy, 330-yard sprints to get conditioned for running 220-yard races. There was a method and reason behind all the exertion.

27

but I pommel ³⁵⁸ *my body:* Paul refers directly back to v. 26.

358. Two Greek words are attested as variants at this point: *hypopiazein*, which means buffet or pommel, and *hypōpiazein*, which means to deliver a blow beneath the eye. If one accepts the second variant, the imagery is that of the boxer. Cf. Moxley, 'I Buffet my Body', *ET*, 34 (1922–3), 235.

and subdue it: The whole point of athletic training is to acquire both endurance and skill. There is little value in brute force if one has not acquired coordination, so that the body does what it is told when it is told.

disqualified: Victory in competition also includes observance of the rules of the game.[359] This must also be a part of one's training. It does one little good in tennis, for instance, to have a smashing service if one constantly faults by stepping over the base line.

The business of proclaiming the Gospel of Jesus Christ to a group of newly converted gentiles requires, according to Paul, at least as much application and effort as learning to run or box with an eye to the little green wreath of victory. And in the end, when one's work is done, of what value is it if by a stupid oversight one has forfeited one's right to victory?

359. Cf. 2 Tim 2^5.

Chapter 10

In Chapter 9 Paul described his strategy for dealing with the problem of idolatry. It is one which enables him to deal effectively with all groups within and without the church. It permits him to perform his unique function as a bridge either between Jews and Greeks or between wise and simple Christians. Paul now returns to the subject of idolatry and its attendant evils, with which he has dealt in a preliminary way in Chapter 8. In that chapter he warned of the dangers inherent in the sophisticated point of view in eating meat which has been part of a pagan sacrifice. These dangers were spelled out in terms of the damage which could be done to the unsophisticated or *weak* brother who could easily lapse back into paganism. In Chapter 10 Paul brings to bear upon this problem both the scriptures and the worship of the church (vv. 1-22). He concludes this major section with a re-examination of the sophisticated point of view, but now with an eye to its effect upon the pagan.

10$^{1-13}$ THE CHRISTIAN SACRAMENTS

^{1}*I want you to know, brethren, that our fathers were all under the cloud, and all passed through the sea, ^{2}and all were baptized into Moses in the cloud and in the sea, ^{3}and all ate the same supernatural food ^{4}and all drank the same supernatural drink. For they drank from the supernatural Rock which followed them, and the Rock was Christ. ^{5}Nevertheless with most of them God was not pleased; for they were overthrown in the wilderness.*

^{6}*Now these things are warnings for us, not to desire evil as they did. ^{7}Do not be idolaters as some of them were; as it is written, 'The people sat down to eat and drink and rose up to dance.' ^{8}We must not indulge in immorality as some of them did, and twenty-three thousand fell in a single day. ^{9}We must not put the Lord to the test, as some of them did and were destroyed by serpents; ^{10}nor grumble, as some of them did and were destroyed by the*

Destroyer. [11]*Now these things happened to them as a warning, but they were written down for our instruction, upon whom the end of the ages has come.* [12]*Therefore let any one who thinks that he stands take heed lest he fall.* [13]*No temptation has overtaken you that is not common to man. God is faithful, and he will not let you be tempted beyond your strength, but with the temptation will also provide the way of escape, that you may be able to endure it.*

As I pointed out above, many commentators see Chapter 9 as an extended discourse on the subject of Christian freedom in which Paul uses himself as a case in point. I have suggested that what Paul really does in this chapter is to outline his personal strategy against idolatry. I cannot therefore agree with those who analyse Chapter 10 in terms of an attack on hyper-sacramentalism. Many analysts of this chapter would insist that the Corinthians had espoused the notion that participation in the Christian sacraments of Baptism and Eucharist was proof against any dangers which might befall them from participation in meals associated with pagan worship.

This is an assumption which follows logically from others, such as the presence of a full-blown Gnosticism[360] in Corinth and Paul's preoccupation with the problem of the tender conscience.[361] I have, however, questioned both these assumptions. It would seem to me that, if hyper-sacramentalism were the problem in Corinth, Paul's argument was singularly ill designed. I shall try and indicate, on the contrary, that it is probably more reasonable to assume that Paul is combating an established pagan form of sacramental worship (cult meals) with a nascent Christian sacramentalism which the Corinthians are not taking half seriously enough.

೫೫

1–2

Paul compares the crossing of the Red Sea by the Israelites with Christian Baptism. The difficulty is his basis of comparison. What is it? The whole point of the crossing legend in the Old Testament is that the Israelites didn't even get wet, while the Egyptians who pursued them were drowned.[362] If Paul is attempting to play down the extent to

---

360. Cf. my general Introduction, pp. xviiiff., also above on p. 88.
361. Cf. above on 8[7].   362. Cf. Exod. 14^{22-9}.

which Christian Baptism is a protection, then he chose the wrong scriptural allusion. Actually, as commentators have recognized, the phrase *baptized into Moses* is constructed by Paul on the analogy of *baptized into Christ*.[363] There is no Jewish parallel to this construction. This has even led some to conjecture that Paul never intended to make a reference to Baptism at this point.[364]

The basis of the analogy is best seen, not in the act itself, i.e. going through the sea or getting in the baptismal water, but in the result of the act. In both cases the result is freedom: freedom from Pharaoh and freedom from sin. This is what in both cases God provides for his people.

under the cloud: A curious allusion to the cloud which went before the Israelites by day to lead them in their departure from Egypt[365] and which served to separate them from the Egyptian forces while they prepared to cross the Red Sea.[366]

2

were baptized: Some ancient witnesses read the middle, *ebaptisanto*, 'received Baptism' or even 'baptized themselves', rather than the passive, *ebaptisthēsan*, accepted by R.S.V.

in the cloud and in the sea: These were the elements in their deliverance. Paul is having enough trouble with these 'free-wheeling' Corinthians without bringing in the pillar of fire which was what led the Israelites by night. This would have brought up the matter of the spirit in the wrong context. Paul will use the concept now with respect to his eucharistic typology but with a very special meaning.

3-4

Paul compares the feeding of the Israelites with manna[367] and water[368] with the Eucharist. It is reasonable to suppose that Paul had the Eucharist in mind because of his explicit reference to Baptism in v. 2. However, once again it is not the act itself which provides the basis for comparison. The point of comparison can best be seen in the use of the word *supernatural*. In Paul's usage that which is *supernatural* (literally 'spiritual') conveys the spirit. In this case the elements involved conveyed a mean-

363. Rom. 6³; Gal. 3²⁷.

364. Cf. G. Gander, 'I Cor. 10.2, parle-t-il du Baptême?', *Rhpr*, 37 (1957), 97–102.

365. Cf. Exod. 13²¹ᶠ·.   366. Cf. ibid., 14¹⁹ᶠ·.
367. Cf. ibid., 16⁴⁻³⁵; Deut. 8³.   368. Cf. Exod. 17⁶; Num. 20⁷⁻¹¹.

ing over and above their obvious function as nourishment. In the case of the manna, the legend makes it quite clear that the manna was given by God as an answer to their murmurings against Moses and Aaron. The Israelites accused Moses and Aaron of bringing them out into the wilderness *to kill this whole assembly with hunger* (Exod. 16³). God then provides the manna to *prove them whether they will walk in my law or not* (Exod. 16⁴) and so that *you shall know that it was the Lord who brought you out of the land of Egypt* (Exod. 16⁶; cp. v. 12). The water also was given by God in answer to the people's complaints and murmurings against Moses (Exod. 17²,³). This is interpreted in the O.T. story as putting God to the proof (Exod. 17²,⁷). What is crucial therefore in Paul's allusion to the manna and the water from the rock is the (spiritual, supernatural) meaning these events had received in the O.T. *I am the Lord, who brought you out of the land of Egypt, and not in order to kill you with hunger or thirst.*

That this is the basis of comparison of these legends with the two Christian sacraments can be seen from the conclusion which Paul draws to this particular section in v. 13: *God is faithful, and he will not let you be tempted beyond your strength.* God has not brought you into the community of the faithful only to allow you to return to paganism or to be a kind of religious will-o'-the-wisp.

the supernatural Rock which followed them . . . was Christ: The one who is known in the manna and in the water miraculously provided in the wilderness is the God who brought Israel out of Egypt. But who is the one who brings man out of sin? It is Jesus Christ. He is the present deliverer and leader, not Moses. He is the present source of revelation and nourishment, not the rock in the wilderness. When we read of Moses and what the children of Israel did in the wilderness they are but pointers to what is coming in Christ and the church. But this foreshadowing has both a positive and a negative side. Positively, Paul indicates how God's self-revelation to the Israelites in the Exodus and in the desert wandering foreshadows the Christian sacraments of Baptism and Eucharist. But this is only part of the point which he wishes to make. Negatively, Paul must also show how Israel's failure to respond to these self-disclosures of God brought down his punishment upon Israel. Instead of acknowledging God in his self-revelation, the Israelites indulged in *idolatry* (v. 7) and *immorality* (v. 8). Because of this *most of* the Israelites *were overthrown in the wilderness* (v. 5). The Israelites' failure to acknowledge properly the true God who disclosed himself to them in the 'sacraments' of the wilderness resulted in their destruction. And this, Paul makes very clear, is what will happen to you, if you don't *shun the worship of idols* (v. 14), with all its attendant immoralities.[369]

5
This verse is transitional. What Paul has said up to this point is positive. Now he turns to the negative side of his argument.

God was not pleased: The English word *pleased* is a little misleading.[370] The word *pleased* translates the Greek *eudokein*. This is the word which occurs in the story of Jesus's Baptism, *Thou art my beloved Son, with thee I am well pleased.*[371] It expresses God's choice of those by whom he would reveal his will.[372] But that choice is not irrevocable, as Paul shows in this passage.[373]

they were overthrown in the wilderness: Cf. Num. 14^{16}; cp. ibid., v. 29.

6
these things are warnings for us: The Greek word translated here *warnings* is *typoi* or our English word *types*.[374] This implies the notion of foreshadowing to which we have referred above.[375]

7–10
Paul now proceeds to list those things which the Israelites did in the wilderness which caused God to override his choice of them[376] and brought his punishment. One can assume that Paul's choice of these particular acts is somewhat governed by his knowledge of what is going on in Corinth.

7
Idolatry has a specific reference in a quotation from Exod. 32^6 . . . *eat and drink . . . dance.* These were all elements in the pagan worship referred to in the Exodus story.[377]

8
immorality: Fornication is what is meant.[378]

369. Cf. below, 11$^{29f.}$.
370. N.E.B. is better: 'were not accepted by God'.
371. Mark 1^{11} parr.
372. Cf. 1 Cor. 1^{21}; Gal. 1^{15}; Col. 1^{19}; Luke 12^{32}.
373. Cp. Heb. 10^{6,8,38}.
374. N.E.B. is better here: 'symbols' (to warn).
375. Cf. above on v. 4. Also an excellent note on types in J.B., ad loc. Cf. also Rom. 15^4.
376. Cf. above on v. 5.   377. Cf. R.-P., ad loc.
378. Cf. above in 5^1; also Num. 25^{1,9}.

twenty-three thousand: The Old Testament reads twenty-four thousand.

9

put the Lord to the test:[379] This is something which, in the Bible, God does to man,[380] but man may not do to God.[381] The connection between the *serpents* (Num. 21[6]) and putting the Lord to the test is made in Psalm 78[17ff.]. The proof or testing of God is always a demand for him to authenticate further his claim to be the God of his people. The problem is idolatry and the attendant sins. Modern commentators tend to forget that we are further removed in outlook from Paul than he was from the Israelites of the O.T. We can be sure that when he saw 'idolatry' in the Jewish scriptures he equated that with pagan cults of Corinth. For the gentile Christians of Corinth to participate at all in pagan cultic activities was the equivalent of what the Israelites had done in the wilderness and would receive the same punishment from God.

10

grumble:[382] It is significant that all the sins catalogued in vv. 7–10 are grouped around the theme of acknowledging or not acknowledging God's self-revelation. They form part of a total picture of God's activity in covenanting with the Israelites and the response of Israel to that divine activity. None of the events is important in itself, but only the total picture of God's self-disclosure to the Israelites and their response either positively in obedience or negatively in idolatry or denial, grumbling, putting God to the test and fornication (closely connected with idolatry).

Paul can therefore refer to *these things* both as a *warning*[383] and a *warning* which is *for our instruction*. The positive point of the 'types' is to show the prefiguring of the Christian sacraments; to show in other words that they were 'meant to be'. The negative, i.e. the *warning* part of the 'types', lies in the punishments which befell the Israelites when they did not respond properly to God's self-disclosure.

11

upon whom the end of the ages has come: The Greek text is literally *ends* (pl.) . . . *have reached*. The plural *ends of the ages* could refer to the end of the age to come and the end of the present age. The Christian lives

379. Cf. Num. 14[22].
380. Cf. Exod. 16[4]; Deut. 8[2,16].
381. Cf. Acts 5[9]; cp. Heb. 3[9].
382. This particular sin is noted in Num. 14[36-8], 16[11-35,41-9], 16[11-35,41-9]. It is punished by death, however, only as a result of the events in Num. 16.
383. Cf. above on v. 6.

at the end of each age, i.e. at the completion of one and the beginning of the other.[384] Or the reference could be to the culmination of the ages, as in Heb. 9[26] ,or the fullness of time, as in Gal. 4[4]. It is also possible that the plural, *ends*, was the result of attraction to the plural, *ages*. On the other hand the Greek word which is rendered by R.S.V. as *end* can also mean 'revenue', as it does elsewhere in the New Testament.[385] Whether or not we can pin down Paul's precise reference here in this phrase, his general meaning is clear: The church stands in the time of fulfilment; this fulfilment has come in the person of Jesus Christ. It continues to actualize itself in the sacraments of the church, which Paul can now show are the fulfilment of promises or foreshadowings in the Jewish scriptures. But the time of fulfilment is also the time of judgement. Those who do not respond in faith to the acts of God do not accept this judgement. Destruction awaits them as surely as it did the Israelites in the wilderness. This is what the Jewish scriptures can now teach us, i.e. both the God-given character of the Christian sacraments and the punishment awaiting those who are not whole-hearted in their commitment to God through those sacraments. There is no way for the gentile Christian, the ex-pagan, to bring any of his paganism with him into his new-found faith. That is as much behind him as Egypt was behind Israel. There is no way back. The gentile Christian can no more return to paganism than the Jewish Christian can require of him a legalistic observance of the law as the basis of salvation. But as in the wilderness, so in the church; God reveals himself to man, not in arbitrary symbols, but in the stuff of man's life, in water and in bread, in the mystery of man's initiation (Baptism) into the people and in the sustenance (Eucharist) of the abiding fellowship of the faithful. Even while God puts man to the test, he provides the means whereby man can express his single-minded faith.

IO[14-22]   THE CHRISTIAN EUCHARIST

[14]*Therefore, my beloved, shun the worship of idols.* [15]*I speak as to sensible men; judge for yourselves what I saw.* [16]*The cup of blessing which we bless, is it not a participation in the blood of Christ? The bread which we*

384. Cf. Weiss, ad loc.
385. Cf. Matt. 17[25]; Rom. 13[7]. R. MacPherson, '*Ta telē tōn aiōnōn*, I Corinthians 10:11', *ET*, 55 (1943–4), 222.

break, is it not a participation in the body of Christ? ¹⁷Because there is one loaf, we who are many are one body, for we all partake of the same loaf. ¹⁸Consider the practice of Israel; are not those who eat the sacrifices partners in the altar? ¹⁹What do I imply then? That food offered to idols is anything, or that an idol is anything? ²⁰No, I imply that what pagans sacrifice they offer to demons and not to God. I do not want you to be partners with demons. ²¹You cannot drink the cup of the Lord and the cup of demons. You cannot partake of the table of the Lord and the table of demons. ²²Shall we provoke the Lord to jealousy? Are we stronger than he?

In these verses Paul compares and contrasts the worship or cultus of the Christians in Corinth first with that of the Jews and then with that of the pagans. His primary concern is still to prevent the Corinthian Christians from lapsing back into pagan worship. As he says quite explicitly in v. 20: *I do not want you to be partners* (i.e. in worship) *with demons.* Paul has shown in vv. 1–13 that God gave Israel all kinds of supernatural[386] nourishment while they were in the desert and also punished them for their idolatrous conduct. Now Paul brings this matter to focus upon the present activity of the Corinthians, which is at least bordering upon idolatry. To participate in the meal which follows the sacrifice in the temple is to participate in the worship of the deity to whom the sacrifice was offered (v. 18), whether it be the God of the Jews or the gods of the pagans (vv. 18, 20). And it makes no difference how sophisticated a monotheism one holds (v. 19). One is reminded of the old adage, 'One might as well eat of the devil as drink of his broth'.

Now into this discussion of idolatry Paul injects some comments upon the worship-practices of the Corinthians. These comments in vv. 16 and 17, along with Paul's further statements in 11¹⁷⁻³⁴, have provoked over the years a series of lengthy discussions, and they still go on today. This is due to the fact that these passages, along with the so-called Institution Narratives in the synoptic Gospels,[387] form the biblical basis for most discussions of the origin of the Christian Eucharist. The basic questions involved in understanding what Paul is saying here about the worship of the Corinthian Church are three: (1) What do we conceive to have been the nature of the worship-practice of the Corinthian Church between the time Paul first

386. Cf. above on v. 3f.   387. Mark 14²²⁻⁵; Matt. 26²⁶⁻⁹; Luke 22¹⁵⁻²⁰.

preached to them and the time in which he wrote his first epistle to them? (2) What if any difference was there between this practice and that of churches closer to or even in Palestine? (3) What was the relation between the action of Jesus at the Last Supper and the subsequent worship-practices of the Christian Church, in Palestine, Corinth, or elsewhere?

In the discussion of this problem, several sets of evidence should be more clearly presented than they usually are.

1. In regard to the Corinthians' practice of worship: (a) Paul does not approve of what they are doing at all (11^{17}). (b) He does have a reversed order of the elements in $10^{16f.}$ from what he recounts as tradition in $11^{23ff.}$: i.e. cup-bread/bread-cup. (c) It is not at all clear whether Paul is rehearsing an already-assimilated and put-into-practice form of worship or placing his own interpretation upon the worship gatherings of the Corinthians.[388] (d) Finally, it has been seldom, if ever, pointed out that, even in $11^{23ff.}$ where everyone assumes that Paul is rehearsing a worship-tradition already passed on and established in the Corinthian community, the immediate context is not that of a worship-tradition, but the tradition of what Jesus did *on the night when he was betrayed.*

2. There have been over the years several attempts to show that, within the early church, one can trace at least two different strains of worship-practice[388a]. One of these involved the use of the formulae known from I Cor. $11^{23ff.}$ as well as the synoptic accounts and emphasized strongly the fact and significance of Jesus's death. The other strain emphasized the joyful meeting of believers together with the present risen Lord Jesus and did not use the above-mentioned formulae.[389] This would suggest that there was some variety in the worship-practice of the early congregations of the church. The emphasis placed by the Corinthians on the gift of the Spirit, and more particularly upon the ecstatic manifestations of this, would tend to

388. K. Wegenast, *Das Verständnis der Tradition bei Paulus und in den Deutero-Paulinen*, 1962, 93ff.

388a. F. Spitta, 'Die urchristlichen Traditionen über Ursprung und Sinn des Abendmahls', *Zur Geschichte und Literatur des Urchristentums*, 1893, I, 207–337. H. Lietzmann, *Messe und Herrenmahl*, 1926.

389. Cf. O. Cullmann, 'The Meaning of the Lord's Supper in Primitive Christianity', *Essays on the Lord's Supper*, O. Cullmann and F. J. Leenhardt, 1958, 9.

place them in the latter rather than the former type of worship-tradition.

3. It is almost universally assumed that the eucharistic practice of the Christian Church goes back to what Jesus did at the Last Supper. That is, he instituted the church's eucharistic practice. This, however, is not necessarily true, if there was such a variety of usage as we noted above in (2). This notion is not borne out in the Marcan version of the Last Supper, which is held by Jeremias[390] to be the oldest account. Mark places the account in the same context as does Paul, it is the night of his betrayal.[391] However, the following differences must be noted: (a) Mark does not speak of Jesus's *body which is for you* but only Jesus's *body*. (b) Mark does not speak of the *new covenant* in connection with the cup, but only of *the covenant*. (c) Mark does not say at all *do this . . . in remembrance of me*. (d) Finally Mark does not give any interpretation to this act as a whole, such as Paul's *you proclaim the Lord's death until he comes*. Rather he recounts that Jesus prophesies that he will not drink wine again *until that day when I drink it new in the kingdom of God*.

The context within the Marcan Gospel and the specific wording of the tradition preserved in Mark both point away from the idea of an institution of a worship form by Jesus. They point rather to a graphic, dramatic act, not unfamiliar in the prophetic tradition[392] or in the life of Jesus,[393] which conveyed, in a unique way, the prophet's message.

I have set this evidence down at some length to justify a radical departure from the usual interpretation of these two 'eucharist' passages in 1 Corinthians. I would contend that there were at least two different strains of eucharistic tradition within the early church. Neither one of these is to be traced directly back to Jesus's action at the Last Supper, though one tradition adopts these words and actions and makes them central to its rite. What we see in 1 Cor. 10^{16,17} and 11$^{17ff.}$ is one way in which this adaptation of the Last Supper tradition took place.

390. *Die Abendmahlsworte Jesu*, 3rd ed. 1954.
391. Cf. Mark 14^{10,18}; cp. 1 Cor. 11^{23}.
392. Cf. Isa. 20$^{1ff.}$; Jer. 13$^{1ff.}$, 19$^{1ff.}$, 27$^{1ff.}$, 32$^{1ff.}$, 51$^{59ff.}$; Ezek. 4$^{1ff.}$, 12$^{1ff.}$, 24$^{15ff.}$, 37$^{15ff.}$; cp. ibid., 28$^{8ff.}$; Rev. 10$^{8ff.}$.
393. Mark 11$^{15-17}$ par. Cp. John 2$^{13-17}$; Mark 14$^{13-16}$ parr., 11$^{12-14}$ par.

The worship of the Corinthian Church contained at least two elements. It was first of all a meal which each one provided for himself, his own family, or perhaps his own group.[394] It was also an occasion for certain ecstatic phenomena, such as speaking in tongues and prophecy.[395] There is nothing to suggest that their worship included, as a regular part, the narrative of the Lord's Supper. It is true that Paul states that he had already handed over this narrative to them. But it is also true that the narrative itself is set in the context of the Passion narrative both in Mark and in 1 Corinthians. Further it receives its character as a part of worship only from the command 'Do this in remembrance of me', which does not appear in the older Marcan version.

Paul is therefore calling upon the Corinthians to modify their current worship-practice by the addition of the narrative of what Jesus did at the Last Supper. He begins with a situation in which the Corinthians have approached dangerously close to a return to idolatrous pagan worship. In order to prevent this, Paul attempts to force the Corinthians to take their own worship more seriously. To do this he centres their cultus around the significance of Jesus's death, just as he does for the church of Rome in the case of Baptism.[396]

14
shun the worship of idols:[397] The Greek is literally 'flee from'.[398]

15
sensible men: Greek *phronimoi* means 'capable of discernment'. This would seem to contradict Paul's estimate of the Corinthians in 1^{26} or 3^{1}.[399] He is here, however, operating on terrain familiar to all of them, pagan worship.

16
The cup of blessing, which we bless: The term *cup of blessing* in itself is well known from Jewish usage as the final cup of wine with which any meal ended,[400] or the third cup of wine of the four drunk at the Passover meal.[401] However, the worshipper does not bless the cup according to Jewish usage, but blesses (i.e. thanks) God who gives it.[402] There was

---

394. Cf. 11^{21}.   395. Cf. 14$^{22ff.}$.   396. Cf. Rom. 6$^{3ff.}$.
397. Cf. below on v. 20b.   398. Cf. J.B. 'keep clear of'.
399. Cp. 4^{10}; 2 Cor. 11^{19}.   400. Talmud *Berakoth*, 51a–b, 52a.
401. Talmud, *Pesahim*, 117b–118a.   402. Cf. S.-B., iv, 621, 628.

therefore as part of their meal, which was in turn part of the Corinthians' worship, a cup of wine called *the cup of blessing*, but which was hallowed or blessed in gentile fashion. The meaning which this cup had for the Corinthians is not stated. Perhaps it had no special meaning. Paul, however, interprets the cup as *a participation in the blood of Christ*. The Corinthians would have understood that in a pagan sacrifice the participants partook in a banquet following the ceremonial immolation of the victim. In this banquet the participants were guests of the particular deity to whom the sacrifice had been made. Through participation in this banquet the worshippers were brought into close union with the particular deity.[403] There is no suggestion here, however, of theophagy, i.e. eating the deity, as some commentators have suggested.[404] The worshippers ate of what was left of the offerings. It is in this sense that Paul can speak of *those who eat the sacrifices* as *partners in the altar* (v. 18) and of pagan worshippers as *partners with demons* (v. 20).

Paul tries to explain the significance of the worship of the Corinthians in the terms of the banquet which follows a sacrifice. The host at the banquet is the risen Lord, who is present in the Spirit. The victim offered on the 'altar' of the cross is Jesus, in whose blood and body they now share. The place, however, where they share in these things is within the congregation of the faithful at *the table of the Lord* (v. 21). Whatever meaning the Corinthians may have attached to their worship meal, Paul wants them to understand it in strong cultic terminology which knows what eating of the holy offering means. What remains of course from the sacrifice of Jesus Christ is not anything of the earthly Jesus, but the risen Lord, the Spirit, and the church. These come into being only as a result of Jesus's death and resurrection. The Corinthians seem to have some grasp of the resurrection,[405] as well as the possession of the Spirit. What they do not grasp is the significance and importance of Jesus's death.[406] It is comparable, implies Paul, to a sacrifice in which the worshippers share in the banquet which follows. So in the meal which constitutes part at least of the worship of the Corinthians the wine and bread are truly what is left over from the sacrifice of Christ. But what is 'left over' from the sacrifice of Christ is the church, the Spirit, the Risen Lord. The meal of the Corinthian worshippers already was full of this realization. What needed to be

403. S. Aalen, 'Das Abendmahl als Opfermahl im Neuen Testament', *Nov Test* (1963), 128ff.
404. ibid., loc. cit.
405. Cf. $15^{12, 20}$.
406. Cf. general Introduction, pp. xxivf.

spelled out was the part played in all this by the death of Jesus. Paul will make this even clearer in Chapter 11. What Paul seems to be saying here is, is the meal in which you partake as part of your worship not a participation in the sacrifice of Christ on the cross? This is your true worship and excludes participation in any other.

17

Because there is one loaf, we who are many are one body, for we all partake of the same loaf: As I have tried to show, Paul does not accept the cultus of the Corinthians as it is, but is attempting to modify it. The R.S.V. translation assumes that Paul is merely interpreting the present cultic practice of the Corinthian Church and is therefore misleading. Paul is trying to show the reality of the church's participation in Christ's sacrifice. He uses the common elements of the meal to make his point: the wine which we bless is our participation in the blood of Christ; the bread which we break is our participation in the body of Christ. Verse 17 constitutes Paul's final substantiation of his interpretation. The givens in this worship situation are the actions in which the worshippers share: *we bless* (the cup), *we break* (the bread). The symbolism of pouring the wine doesn't work here to express sharing, though it is used elsewhere to express the idea of sacrifice.[407] The symbolism of sharing in *one loaf* does work, however, and Paul uses it to show how we all participate in the *one loaf* which is really a participation in the *body of Christ.* Paul can take for granted only that the Corinthians do drink wine and do eat bread during their cultic meal-gatherings. Furthermore, he must rely on their sense of doing this as a group, even though this sense has been seriously weakened.[408]

18

partners in the altar: In both Jewish and pagan worship the worshippers participated in the sacrifice by sharing in a meal which followed the sacrifice.[409] The food was what remained of the sacrificial victim. The worshippers considered themselves guests of the deity to whom the sacrifice was made. But the banquet was held at a *table* which was in the temple but separated from the altar. It is to this table that Paul refers below in v. 21.

407. Cf. Mark 14^{24} par.
408. Cf. 11$^{18ff.}$. The parallel from the Did. 9$^{1-5}$ often cited in connection with this passage is not relevant. The whole basis for the analogy in Did. is the process by which bread is made, not the way in which it is eaten. See also S. Aalen, op. cit. (n. 403), 139.
409. ibid., 142ff.

19f.

The beings to whom sacrifices are made are not divine, but they are real. Both of these points are neatly made by the quotation from Deut. 32^{17}.

21

the cup of demons: The cup from which libations were poured in honour of the deity[410] is contrasted with the *cup of the Lord* as Paul has interpreted it above.[411]

the table of the Lord: This is not the altar, as has been so often suggested. The altar is separate, and is the place of blood-letting. The Christian altar then, properly speaking, is the cross of Calvary.[412]

22

provoke the Lord to jealousy: The reference is to Deut. 32^{21}, a psalm just quoted by Paul in v. 20. Paul draws upon the material from the O.T. cited above in vv. 1–11. The children of Israel were *overthrown in the wilderness* because of their idolatry and related sins (v. 5). There was no way back for them once they left Egypt. There is no way back for the gentile Christian once he has entered the Christian community. It is not the *demons* who will cause trouble for those who participate in their worship. It is the Lord himself, the divine provider for Israel's needs in the wilderness (v. 4), and the dispenser here and now to the Church's need, who will mete out God's punishment.[413]

$10^{23}-11^1$ THE CHRISTIAN AND NON-BELIEVERS

²³*'All things are lawful,'* but not all things are helpful. *'All things are lawful,'* but not all things build up. ²⁴*Let no one seek his own good, but the good of his neighbour.* ²⁵*Eat whatever is sold in the meat market without raising any question on the ground of conscience.* ²⁶*For 'the earth is the Lord's, and everything in it.'* ²⁷*If one of the unbelievers invites you to dinner and you are disposed to go, eat whatever is set before you without raising any question on the ground of conscience.* ²⁸*(But if some one says to you, 'This has been offered in sacrifice,' then out of consideration for the man who informed you, and for conscience' sake —* ²⁹*I mean his conscience,*

410. Cf. Allo, ad loc.   411. Cf. above on v. 16, and Isa. 65^{11}.
412. Cf. S. Aalen, op. cit. (n. 403), 142ff.   413. Cf. below, $11^{29f.}$.

not yours – do not eat it.) For why should my liberty be determined by another man's scruples? ³⁰*If I partake with thankfulness, why am I denounced because of that for which I give thanks?*

³¹*So, whether you eat or drink, or whatever you do, do all to the glory of God.* ³²*Give no offence to Jews or to Greeks or to the church of God,* ³³*just as I try to please all men in everything I do, not seeking my own advantage, but that of many, that they may be saved.* 11 ¹*Be imitators of me, as I am of Christ.*

The majority of commentators see this section as a resumption of the discussion in 8^{1-13}. With this assumption they are quick to point out and/or gloss over the apparent sudden shift in tone between 10^{14-22} and 10^{23-33}. This has moved some to suggest that 10^{14-22} comes from a different letter from 8^{1-13} and 10^{23-33}.[414] The problem is that most commentators have conceived Paul's purpose in this whole section (Chapters 8–10) too narrowly. He is not, as von Soden has shown,[415] interested primarily in the proper attitude to be adopted by the stronger brother to the weaker. This concern arises only in passing (8^7,$^{9ff.}$). Paul's main interest is in the attitude one adopts as a Christian towards the problem of idolatry. But his interest is not narrowly confined to those already within the church. He is also concerned with the effect upon the non-believers, both Jews and Greeks.[416] He suggests that, since the posture which he has adopted in the matter (9^{22b}) is one which he recognizes in Christ and imitates, they should imitate him as well (11^1).

Paul is concerned with building up the church, not with the exercise of personal freedom.[417] This building-up process represents for Paul both the establishment of the church through the preaching of the Gospel and the constructive, on-going life of the community.[418] It has to do therefore with those outside as well as those inside the church.

The subject of those inside the church is discussed by Paul in 8^{1-13}.

414. Cf. above, introduction to Chapters 8–11¹, and n. 308.
415. op. cit. (n. 322), 243.
416. Cf. 9^{19-21}, $10^{32f.}$.
417. Cf. above on 8^{11}.
418. P. Vielhauer, *OIKODOME, Das Bild vom Bau in der christlichen Literatur vom Neuen Testament bis Clemens Alexandrinus*, 1939. 77ff.

The tone upon which he ends this discussion is rather final. There is nothing specific in 10^{23-33} to indicate that he has resumed this particular discussion. Rather, everything points to a discussion of the problem of idolatry with respect to those outside the church.

ຂວ

24

neighbour: is a highly conjectural translation of the Greek *heteros*, which means 'other'. When Paul speaks of the object of his concern in Chapter 8 it is specifically the *weak man* who is the *brother* (vv. 11, 13). In Chapter 10 it is not a fellow-Christian, but *one of the unbelievers* who *invites you to dinner* (v. 27). It is *someone* or *the man* who informs *you* that *This has been offered in sacrifice* (v. 28). Furthermore the Greek word translated in R.S.V. *offered in sacrifice* is *hierothuton*, the word used by gentile pagans to describe the sacrificial offering.[419] It is not the derisive word coined and used by Jews to describe pagan sacrificial offerings – *eidōlothuton*, 'something offered to an idol'.[420] But this latter is the term employed by Paul in $8^{1,4,7}$ and 10^{19}. Why not here in 10^{28}?

Everything in this section points to a pagan context for Paul's remarks. One is invited to dinner by a pagan. At table one is informed by 'another' (guest, the host?) 'This we are eating was the sacrifice to such-and-such a god'. Paul is discussing the posture which a believer should adopt in such a case. What constitutes, for these pagans, the most effective witness to Christ? In Chapter 8 Paul was concerned about the weaker brother seeing the stronger eating at the banquet which followed the sacrifice in a pagan temple (v. 19). Why? Because it might lead him back to idolatrous worship. In Chapter 10 Paul is concerned with eating the remains of a sacrificial victim in the presence of pagans. Why? Because it constitutes tacit approval of the pagan worship and will not lead men away from that worship.

23

All things are lawful: One of the Corinthians' slogans.[421] Here as in 6^{12} Paul must qualify what is probably a misinterpretation of his teaching on the Jewish law. All things do not serve for the *building-up* of the community. In this case Paul is concerned with the witness to non-believers, i.e. the neighbour.[422]

419. Cf. G. Schrenk, 'Hieros ... hierothuta', *ThWbNT*, III, 252f.
420. Cf. Barrett, ad loc.
421. Cf. above on 6^{12}.
422. Cf. above on vv. 23–33.

25

As far as buying meat in the *meat market* is concerned, there is, according to Paul, no problem. *Meat market* here translates the Greek *makellon* (Latin, *macellum*) – a series of shops or stalls run in connection with the pagan temple, from which the meat was received and sold.[423]

26

the earth is the Lord's and everything in it: Psalm 24[1], which Paul quotes here, was a verse used to support the custom of Jews to bless God for their food.[424] It is also noted in one place as a form of table prayer before a meal.[425] Perhaps it was a custom of the Christians taken over from Jewish usage.

27

Paul's judgement here is the same as above (v. 25) as long as nothing is said about the origin of the meat being served: there should be no *question on the ground of (one's own) conscience* (v. 25).

28f.

The problem arises with the *some one (who) says*.[426] It is *his conscience, not yours* about which Paul is concerned. The *conscience* referred to in 8[7,10,12] is *weak*. Here it is simply *his conscience*.[427] There is nothing specific here to link these references to conscience with those of Chapter 8. Further, nothing is said here about the effect which eating or not eating the food will have upon the other person in question. In Chapter 8, however, Paul is quite specific: *their conscience is defiled* (v. 7); ... *this weak man is destroyed* (v. 11). Paul's intention in 10^{23-33} is quite clearly stated in v. 33: we should work for the *advantage ... of many, that they may be saved; many* here refers to those outside the church.

29

why should my liberty be determined by another man's scruples?: *Scruples* here renders Greek *suneidēsis*, rendered above (v. 28) *conscience*.

30

If I partake with thankfulness:[428] Paul is undoubtedly here anticipating a counter-argument.[429]

Why am I denounced because of that for which I give thanks?: The difficulties of these verses are numerous. Not the least of them is the fact that

423. Cf. floor-plan of a *makellon* in Pompeii in Lietzmann, ad loc.
424. Talmud, *Berakoth*, 35a.   425. Talmud, *Shabbat*, 119a.
426. Cf. above on vv. 23–33.
427. Greek, *syneidesis*; cp. v. 29, *another man's*.
428. Cf. above on v. 26.   429. Cf. above on 6[13f.].

these questions in vv. 29b and 30 receive no answer. However, most of the difficulty results from an insistence that the subject here is exactly that of 8^{1-13}: the weaker and the stronger brother. The issue is only further confused by comparing this passage with Rom. 14^{13-23}, where the subject is similar to that of 1 Cor. 8^{1-13}. When we realize that the subject here is not the weaker and the stronger brother, but the Christian and the non-Christian, certain things become clearer: what Paul enunciates in v. 24 is not just an intra-community policy of brotherly concern, but a policy to be adopted in the church's mission to the non-believers. This statement of policy, then, is picked up rhetorically by Paul in the questions of vv. 29b and 30. The force of the questions now can be better felt: (Do you now ask) *why should my liberty* . . . ? (Is it not clear now) *why I am denounced* . . . ?

The Greek word translated here *denounced* is *blasphēmousthai*, literally 'to be blasphemed'. The meaning here is similar to the use of the word in Rom. 3^8: R.S.V., 'slanderously charge'; N.E.B., 'libellously report'. The point is that a Christian who partook of the remains of a sacrificial victim in the presence of pagans, having been informed that it had been a sacrificial offering, might expect to have stories told about his participating in idolatrous, heathen worship. This would be the case in spite of his Christian freedom and in spite of his Christian intentions in partaking of food offered in a meal-setting.

So there is no answer to these rhetorical questions. Nor are there any sure rules in this matter of witnessing to Christ either inside or outside the church. Rather all must be done . . .

31

to the glory of God: Paul has already told the Corinthians how he goes about this in 9^{22}: *I have become all things to all men.* This is the positive way of saying what he now puts in negative fashion:

32

Give no offence to Jews or to Greeks or to the church of God: This takes in everyone.[430]

The Greek word *aproskopos*, translated here *Give no offence*, comes from the verb *proskoptein*, literally 'to stumble' or 'to cause to stumble'. It is true that in a number of places Paul warns about causing a brother or fellow-Christian to stumble.[431] Here in this passage Paul includes, beside the church, both *Jews* and *Greeks*, i.e. he has in mind those inside and those outside the church.

430. On the peculiarity of Paul's stance towards all men, cf. above on 9^{21}.
431. Cf. Rom. 9^{32}, $14^{13,20f.}$; 1 Cor. 8^9; 2 Cor. 6^3.

33

A restatement of Paul's own position, combining what he says above in 9^{21} and 10^{24}. Paul is not really concerned here with personal piety but with faithful and effective witness to Christ. He picks up the notion of what is an *advantage*. The Greek word here is *sumpheron*, translated above in v. 23 from the verbal form *sumpherei* as *helpful*. What is of *advantage* or *helpful* is relative to the situation.[432]

11^1

This is usually taken as the conclusion of the preceding section, rather than the beginning of the next.

imitators of me . . . of Christ: If we have understood Paul correctly in Chapters 8–10, we must assume that Paul finds a confirmation of his policy towards the problem of idolatry in Christ himself. Usually cited in connection with this verse is Rom. 15^3: *For Christ did not please himself.* This refers to Christ's passion, as is shown by the quotation from Psalm 69^9 which follows: *The reproaches of those who reproached thee fell on me.* This is used to substantiate the intra-community behaviour urged by Paul in Rom. 15^{1-7}. What is not noted is that Paul goes on in Rom. 15^{8-12} to show why *Christ became a servant to the circumcised* (v. 8). It was *in order to confirm the promises given to the patriarchs and in order that the Gentiles might glorify God for his mercy* (v. 9). Paul proceeds to substantiate his statement about the gentiles with no fewer than three separate scriptural quotations.

Paul finds in Christ, therefore, not only a pattern of human behaviour (concern for the brother), but also a pattern of evangelism. Christ became a minister of the circumcision, i.e. a Jew, one born under the Law (Gal. 4^4) of the seed of David (Rom. 1^3). He became poor (2 Cor. 8^9). He became human (Phil. 2^7). But not just to save the Jews. Paul has learned through the very rejection by the Jews of his message that God intends to save the gentiles as well (Rom. 11^{1-11}).

His mission to the gentiles is therefore an imitation of Jesus's mission to the Jews. Paul suffers as Jesus did (1 Cor. 4^{9-13}; 2 Cor. 4^{7-10}; 6^{4-10}), and like Jesus's ministry to the circumcision, his is a ministry to the uncircumcision (Gal. 2^7). Though he was born a Jew (Phil. 3^5; 2 Cor. 11^{22}), he does not seek to retain that status, but becomes all things to all men (1 Cor. 9^{21}). Presumably in their own way Christians are asked to imitate Paul *as* he imitates Christ. So there must be both concern for the brother and a strategy for the conversion of the non-believer.

432. Cf. above on v. 29f.

Chapter 11

²*I commend you because you remember me in everything and maintain the traditions even as I have delivered them to you.* ³*But I want you to understand that the head of every man is Christ, the head of a woman is her husband, and the head of Christ is God.* ⁴*Any man who prays or prophesies with his head covered dishonours his head,* ⁵*but any woman who prays or prophesies with her head unveiled dishonours her head – it is the same as if her head were shaven.* ⁶*For if a woman will not veil herself, then she should cut off her hair; but if it is disgraceful for a woman to be shorn or shaven, let her wear a veil.* ⁷*For a man ought not to cover his head, since he is the image and glory of God; but woman is the glory of man.* ⁸*(For man was not made from woman, but woman from man.* ⁹*Neither was man created for woman, but woman for man.)* ¹⁰*That is why a woman ought to have a veil on her head, because of the angels.* ¹¹*(Nevertheless, in the Lord woman is not independent of man nor man of woman;* ¹²*for as woman was made from man, so man is now born of woman. And all things are from God.)* ¹³*Judge for yourselves; is it proper for a woman to pray to God with her head uncovered?* ¹⁴*Does not nature itself teach you that for a man to wear long hair is degrading to him,* ¹⁵*but if a woman has long hair, it is her pride? For her hair is given to her for a covering.* ¹⁶*If any one is disposed to be contentious, we recognize no other practice, nor do the churches of God.*

In Chapters 8–10 Paul has been discussing the attitude which he has taken and which he hopes the Corinthians will adopt towards pagan worship. He has addressed himself to the problem as it was presented to him by the Corinthians' question concerning food which has been part of a pagan sacrifice. Paul, however, as I have tried to show, places this question in the wider context of pagan worship and the proper Christian attitude toward it.

Now Paul turns to the question of Christian worship. He begins his discussion of the worship of the church by taking up the subject of the proper appearance of women in the worshipping group. There are at least three serious difficulties in the interpretation of this passage:

1. What is the article with which a man would (improperly) cover his head (v. 4) or a woman (properly) cover hers? In the Greek text, this article is not mentioned.

2. What is the meaning of the Greek word *exousia*, translated *veil* in v. 10? In Greek this word means 'power' or 'authority'. And what can this possibly have to do with angels?

3. What is the relation of this section, 11^{2–16}, which seems to take prophecy by females for granted, with 14^{35,36}, in which Paul says women in the congregation should remain silent?

ཚ

2

I commend you: This must be seen as a rhetorical preparation for the reproof which he is about to administer. It also serves to contrast sharply with v. 17, *I do not commend you.*

traditions even as I have delivered them to you:[433] Paul considered both the content and the form in which the *traditions* were preserved important.[434]

3

head: This must be taken in a metaphorical sense such as 'head of the house' or 'head of the firm'. Paul establishes here an order of precedence: God, Christ, man, woman. What he seems to be mainly concerned with, however, is the difference in the outward appearance of men and women in the worshipping group.

4

head . . . head: The second appearance of *head* in this verse is again metaphorical and refers to Christ. The first occurrence, however, must mean the man's head in the literal sense.

with his head covered: This translation of the R.S.V. discreetly glosses over the difficulty in the text. The Greek literally says, 'having down from his head'. The participle 'having' has no object. Naturally one would like to know what the man has 'down from his head'. Most commentators have assumed some sort of veil or covering.

433. Cp. below vv. 23ff. and 15³ff. for the substance of some of these traditions.

434. Cf. below on 15¹.

prays or prophesies: The context is clearly that of the worshipping congregation.

5

Paul now arrives at what seems to be his main concern in this section, the appearance of the woman. He probably takes for granted the customs regarding men's appearance in the worship of the Church. They are 'uncovered' when they pray or prophesy, as is proper. One can only surmise that some women in the congregation have followed the custom of the men and pray and prophesy with heads uncovered. In doing this, these women are ignoring their sex. They may have heard what we know Paul suggested elsewhere,[435] that the difference between male and female in Christ was not important. However, he says the same thing about slaves and free men.[436] We have tried to show that this did not lead him to advocate manumission.[437] In the same way, here Paul does not advocate obliterating the difference between the sexes. Those things which distinguish the sexes, even in the matter of outward appearance, should be maintained. Paul has very deep feelings about this confusion of the the sexes, as is shown in Rom. $1^{26\mathrm{ff}}$.

The evidence with regard to the wearing of veils and the arrangement of hair by women in this period is not altogether conclusive. Since it refers largely to the customs which obtained in public, it may not even be relevant.

5f.

The remarks about shaving and shearing may best be taken as a bit of rhetorical overstatement.

7ff.

Paul now shifts the ground of his argument to the biblical notion of man's creation in the image of God[438] and the creation of woman *from* man,[439] and *for* man.[440] Again what is emphasized is the difference between the sexes. This difference is in the very order of creation. It is clear enough that *a man ought not to cover his head, since he is the image and glory of God.* It is not at all clear why a woman's head should be covered simply because she is the *glory of man.*

It is not evident here that Paul intends his readers to understand by *man* 'husband' and by *woman* 'wife', as some commentators assert, though this is a possibility. If, however, 'man' and 'woman' are taken generically and not as husband and wife, Paul's point remains obscure. It is most satisfactory to understand Paul's argument as one by analogy.

435. Cf. Gal. 3^{28}.   436. ibid., 3^2.   437. Cf. above on 7^{21}.
438. Cf. Gen. 1^{27}; 5^1.   439. ibid., $2^{21\mathrm{ff}}$.   440. ibid., 2^{18}.

That is, just as man is the *glory of God* because he was created *for* God and not vice versa, so woman is the *glory of man* because she was created *for* man and not vice versa.

10

That is why: That refers to the preceding argument, in vv. 7ff.

a veil on her head: This verse is by far the most difficult in this section. The Greek word translated here as *veil* is *exousia*. It means 'power' or 'authority'. It does not mean *veil*. However, there is a Semitic root *SLT* which can mean either 'authority' or 'veil'. It has been suggested[441] that Paul is using a Greek word which means 'power' to render a Semitic word which means either 'veil' or 'authority'. It has also been suggested that *exousia* means symbol of authority[442] or symbol of subordination, i.e. under authority.[443]

because of the angels: We can dismiss outright the suggestion that this refers to the lustful angels of Genesis 6[1ff.]. If the ladies in question were hiding their charms it was probably from the men in the congregation. It has been suggested that *angel* here refers to the human leaders of the congregation's worship.[444] It is more likely that *angels* were considered as part of the worshipping group. Because they were present, a certain decorum in line with the created order of things had to be maintained.[445] That is another way of saying that Paul was unwilling to see the difference between the sexes obliterated even in the special case of a woman prophet.[446]

11f.

In his argument in vv. 7ff., Paul shows how woman was created differently from man. Paul wishes to preserve the difference in sex which he here shows to be the basis of procreation.[447]

441. Cf. Dr Jirku, 'Die Macht auf dem Haupte (I Kor. 11.10)', *NKZ*, 32 (1921), 710–11. M. Ginsburger, 'Le gloire et l'autorité de la femme dans 1 Cor. 11.1–10', *Rhpr*, 12 (1932), 245–8.

442. A. Isaksson, *Marriage and Ministry in the New Temple, A Study with Special Reference to Mt. 19.13–12 and 1 Cor. 11.13–16*, 1965, 178f.

443. Cf. Moffat, ad loc.

444. Cf. R.-P. (the idea comes from the Church Fathers).

445. Cf. J. A. Fitzmeyer, 'A Feature of Qumran Angelology and the Angels of I Cor. xi. 10', *NTS*, 4 (1957), 48–58; M. D. Hooker, 'Authority on Her Head', *NTS*, 10 (1963–4), 410–16.

446. Cf. Hooker, op. cit. (n. 445).

447. Cf. Midrash, *Genesis Rabbah*, VIII, 8.

13f.

Judge for yourselves: i.e. by your own standards.[448] Paul now turns from an argument based on scripture to one based upon *nature*. The appearance of men and the appearance of women in general must be Paul's frame of reference here. We may assume that women's hair was longer than men's. For men to imitate women's appearance was considered by Paul part of the gentile's life without God (cf. Rom 1[26]). It is not clear, however, how long hair more than short hair constitutes a 'cover' for man's head. Here once again we must see that Paul argues for a difference between the sexes which should not be obliterated. The difference lies in the fact that what is considered a part of a woman's beauty is considered shameful for a man. The question of hair style *per se* is not the main point here. It is the difference between male and female which is Paul's main concern.

15

a covering: The Greek work translated here as *covering* is *peribolaion*, which is a *covering* for the whole body, not just the head. If Paul were really primarily concerned with the proper head attire for women prophets, this observation contributes nothing to his argument.

16

we recognize no other practice, nor do the churches of God: Perhaps Paul realizes the weakness of his argument and has to fall back upon custom or usage.

One hesitates to say anything too precise about this section. Paul did want to preserve the difference between the sexes. His reasoning here may be similar to that in Chapter 7, in which he gives great importance to the status one had when converted. Paul makes every attempt to show that one should remain in that status, if that is feasible. Perhaps Paul is saying to the women prophets of Corinth: Do not forget that you are lady prophets, not gentleman prophets! You were ladies when you were converted, and ladies you should remain![449]

II[17–34]

¹⁷*But in the following instructions I do not commend you, because when you come together it is not for the better but for the worse.* ¹⁸*For in the first place, when you assemble as a church, I hear that there are divisions among*

448. Cp. 10[15].   449. Cf. 7[24].

you; and I partly believe it, ¹⁹for there must be factions among you in order that those who are genuine among you may be recognized. ²⁰When you meet together, it is not the Lord's supper that you eat. ²¹For in eating, each one goes ahead with his own meal, and one is hungry and another is drunk. ²²What! Do you not have houses to eat and drink in? Or do you despise the church of God and humiliate those who have nothing? What shall I say to you? Shall I commend you in this? No, I will not.

²³For I received from the Lord what I also delivered to you, that the Lord Jesus on the night when he was betrayed took bread, ²⁴and when he had given thanks, he broke it, and said 'This is my body which is for you. Do this in remembrance of me.' ²⁵In the same way also the cup, after supper, saying, 'This cup is the new covenant in my blood. Do this, as often as you drink it, in remembrance of me.' ²⁶For as often as you eat this bread and drink the cup, you proclaim the Lord's death until he comes.

²⁷Whoever, therefore, eats the bread or drinks the cup of the Lord in an unworthy manner will be guilty of profaning the body and blood of the Lord. ²⁸Let a man examine himself, and so eat of the bread and drink of the cup. ²⁹For any one who eats and drinks without discerning the body eats and drinks judgement upon himself. ³⁰That is why many of you are weak and ill, and some have died. ³¹But if we judged ourselves truly, we should not be judged. ³²But when we are judged by the Lord, we are chastened so that we may not be condemned along with the world.

³³So then, my brethren, when you come together to eat, wait for one another – ³⁴if any one is hungry, let him eat at home – lest you come together to be condemned. About the other things I will give directions when I come.

Paul continues to treat the subject of Christian worship with some sharp criticism of the present practice of the Corinthian Church. How one understands Paul's criticism, however, depends largely upon what one thinks the Corinthians were doing (or thought they were doing) when they came together for worship. Were they joining in some kind of meal? The answer would seem to be, Yes. Was it an ordinary or an extraordinary kind of meal? The evidence seems to point to a meal which was ordinary in the minds of the Corinthians but which Paul tries to show is extraordinary. Accordingly, Paul disapproves of two forms of behaviour occasioned by their gatherings:

1. They have quarrels in the worship assembly.
2. They have not made proper provision for the poor to join in the meal on an equal basis with the well-to-do.[450]

We should not be misled by the fact that Paul has already made, in another connection, some profound remarks about the food eaten at these meals. When Paul says that the *cup* from which they (presumably) drank is *a participation in the blood of Christ* and the *bread* which they (presumably) ate is *a participation in the body of Christ*,[451] he is referring to the bread of the meal and the wine of the meal. This, he says, is the meaning of their gathering together. There is nothing to indicate that there was something already special about any one cup which they blessed as over against cups which they did not bless, or that any bread which they broke had a significance not present in some other bread which they did not break.[452] It is best to say that what was specifically Christian about the worship of the Corinthian Church centred round some form of a meal which was probably called 'the supper in honour of the Lord'.[453] This need not have been anything more than a meal in which the risen Lord was believed to be present. Such a meal is implied in the tradition of

---

450. At this point, many commentators resort to the hypothesis that in the early church there were two aspects to the 'meal' which the Christians shared as a part of their gathering: (1) some kind of a 'fellowship meal', which was in fact a real meal for the purpose of satisfying hunger, and (2) a cultic 'meal' which had as its sole purpose the mystical participation in the 'Body and Blood of Christ'. This is sheer conjecture. There is no evidence that in this period such a church as that in Corinth gathered together for anything other than a meal. That this meal had a 'religious' aspect to it is beyond dispute. But there is no evidence from this period for a non-religious or non-eucharistic *agape* or 'Love feast' such as we find in a later period. (Cf. M. Goguel, 'La relation du dernier repas de Jésu dans I Cor. 11 et la tradition historique chez l'apôtre Paul', *Rhpr*, 10 (1930), 61–89.)

It is common to assume at this point that Paul is removing the eucharistic celebration from its setting within the communal meal. The evidence does not point to a dual function for this gathering. It does not point to two different sets of activities, i.e. a common meal of fellowship and some kind of special cultic activity to express communion with Christ.

451. Cf. above on 10[14-22].

452. A. Ehrhardt, 'Holy Sacrament and Suffering', *The Framework of the New Testament Stories*, 1964, 260.

453. Cf. Barrett on 11[20].

Luke–Acts regarding the earliest practice of the church in Jerusalem.[454] Meals such as this were a part of the pagan gentile culture of the time. There were numerous voluntary associations organized for various religious purposes, which had such meals as these.[455] There were also associations of pious Jews which held fellowship meals as a part of their life together.[456] It is therefore entirely possible that such a custom of a communal meal would pass easily from its original setting in the Palestinian Jewish Church to its setting in the extra-Palestinian church of the Gentiles.[457] However, for some reason, the communal gatherings of the Corinthians had got out of hand, and Paul tries in this section to show the Corinthians the true meaning of their worship assembly.

מאא

17–22

Paul begins by telling the Corinthians what they are doing which is wrong: they are treating this gathering as if it were just an ordinary meal, eaten to satisfy hunger. As a consequence the 'have-nots' go hungry while the 'haves' not only have plenty to eat but get drunk into the bargain. This, Paul says, is not a 'supper in honour of the Lord'.

18

in the first place: There never is a 'second place'. One must conjecture whether or where Paul ended his first point and began his second. The most logical break comes between vv. 22 and 23, at which point Paul passes from negative to positive criticism.

assemble as a church: Church here translates the Greek *ekklēsia*. It is the word used in the O.T. to refer to the congregation or community of Israel.[458] It is the community assembled together for worship, as opposed to the people of God (Greek, *laos theou*), the descendants of Abraham, the children of promise.[459]

---

454. Cf. O. Cullmann, op. cit. (n. 389), and also the prevalence of the eating motif in the Gospels; cf. E. Lohmeyer, 'Das Abendmahl in der Urgemeinde', *JBL*, 56 (1937), 217–52.

455. Cf. Lietzmann, ad loc. (excursus).

456. Cf. 1QS (Serek ha-yahad, one of the Dead Sea Scrolls) vi. 4ff.; also references in G. Dix, *The Shape of the Liturgy*, 1945, 50ff.

457. Cf. N. Dahl, 'Anamnesis', *Studia Theologica*, 1 (1947), 89f.

458. Cf. K. L. Schmidt, '*Kalein ... ekklesia*', *ThWbNT*, III, 505ff.

459. Cf. Gal. 4²⁸.

I hear: This seems to agree with what is said about the quarrels and strife in Chapters 1–3. This was not information contained in the letter from the Corinthians.

divisions . . . factions: These are not quite the same words or ideas as we saw in 1$^{10-17}$. Here in Chapter 11 Paul speaks of *divisions* (Greek, *schismata*) and *factions* (Greek, *haireseis*). In 1$^{10-17}$ he spoke of *quarrels* (Greek, *erides*), which could lead to *dissensions* (Greek, *schismata*).[460] In 1$^{10-17}$ the *quarrels* were reported to Paul, while the *dissensions* were only a possibility which Paul wants the Corinthians to avoid. Here in 11$^{18f.}$ the *divisions* (*schismata*) are reported, and the *factions* are attributed by Paul to the divine will as a means of testing the community.[461]

The problem is evident: if Paul speaks here in Chapter 11 of the same *dissensions* or *divisions* (Greek, *schismata*) to which he refers in 1^{10}, then they are actual here but only potential in 1^{10}. On the other hand, if *divisions* and *factions* here in 11$^{18f.}$ refer only to the matter of the cult-gathering, then *faction* (Greek, *hairesis*) must be ascribed a meaning here it does not normally have. It is perhaps best to take the latter alternative, since the whole train of thought here seems to be governed by the clause *when you assemble as a church.*[462] Whatever Paul means here by *divisions* and *factions* it has something to do with the communal meal-gathering.

19

there must be factions: There must be translates the Greek *dei*. This word in the N.T. usually means a necessity decreed by God.[463] One possible parallel to this situation is in Gal. 2$^{11ff.}$. There Paul criticizes Peter for separating himself from the gentile Christians. This would have constituted a *division* or *faction* within the worshipping group, thereby making it possible to distinguish the genuine (members) from those who are not genuine.[464] Just what this could have implied in terms of concrete actions may perhaps be seen best in v. 22 below.

20

When you meet together: This phrase translates the Greek *sunerchesthai epi to auto*, a technical term meaning a gathering for the specific purpose of worship.[465]

460. R.S.V. is misleading here.
461. Cf. below on v. 19.
462. Cf. above on v. 18.
463. Cf. E. Fascher, 'Theologische Beobachtungen zu *dei*', *Neutestamentliche Studien für Rudolph Bultmann*, ed. W. Eltester, 1957, 228–54.
464. Cp. 1 John 2^{19}.   465. Cf. 14^{23}; cp. Acts 1^{15}, 2^{1,44}; etc.

it is not: The R.S.V. here renders the Greek *ouk esti* as purely descriptive. There may be other overtones, however, somewhat clumsy to translate into English: namely, 'it is impossible – for the following reasons –' (N.E.B.) or 'it is not in order to –', i.e. with the intention – (Barrett). Paul's description indicates that perhaps all these overtones are implied. What he does not imply is that he had two different, separate and distinct activities in mind.[466] What the Corinthians were doing was having a *supper* (Greek, *deipnon*). Paul's criticism is not of the *supper* aspect, but that it could not be called *the Lord's supper* – literally a supper in honour of the Lord.[467] The problem, as I have indicated,[468] is the historical connection between the Corinthians' version of the supper in honour of the Lord and what we commonly call the Lord's Supper, the tradition of which Paul recounts below in vv. 23–5.

21

each one goes ahead with his own meal, and one is hungry and another is drunk: Some have wished to bring out a strong contrast between *his own meal* (Greek, *idion deipnon*) and supper in honour of the Lord or *Lord's supper* (Greek, *kyriakon deipnon*). That is Paul is urging the Corinthians in their communal gathering to concentrate upon a rite known as the supper in honour of the Lord as opposed to their regular meal. I have indicated at some length[469] why I think that these are false presuppositions at work in many commentaries. Suffice it to say here that the Corinthians were aware of the religious character of their gathering. It is hard to see the force of Paul's statement regarding the *church*[470] and his explicit statement regarding *the Lord's supper*,[471] if the Corinthians were not already gathering as a church to participate in something called the *Lord's supper*.

Paul's criticism is not of what the Corinthians do but of the manner in which they do it.... *His own meal* ... must therefore be in contrast with someone else's *meal* in the congregation. This is the someone else who *is hungry* (because he does not have enough) or who has to sit next to someone who is drunk (because he has had too much).

In the congregation one must have regard for one's brethren. Paul has already made this abundantly clear in the preceding section on idolatry.[472] He will emphasize this point further in Chapters 12–14. In Chapter 8 Paul shows how the strong brother can destroy the weak –

466. Cf. above on vv. 17–22.
467. Greek, *kyriakon deipnon*; cf. Barrett.
468. Cf. above on 10$^{14-22}$.   469. Cf. above on 10$^{14-22}$.
470. Cf. above on v. 18.   471. Cf. above on v. 20.
472. Cf. above on 8^{13}, 9^{22}.

the brother for whom Christ died (8¹¹). So here Paul points out that a supper in which there is so little regard for the brethren is not and cannot be a supper in honour of the Lord. Rather such action constitutes *despising the church*[473] and humiliating *the brother.*

22

This verse begins with a facetious remark, particularly since it is the 'haves' who are being addressed rather than the 'have-nots'.[474]

What Paul does next is to spell out what he meant in 8¹¹ by *the brother for whom Christ died.* Now, however, Paul is dealing with the subject of Christian worship and the meaning of that worship. We have already indicated that there is good evidence for a cultic celebration in the early church which centred round a meal in which the presence of the risen Lord was known.[475] We have suggested that this was the kind of cult-meal in which the Corinthians participated. The general tenor of the Corinthian assembly was evidently one of hyper-enthusiasm and hyper-individualism.[476] The gift of the Spirit was highly prized as evidence of the presence of the risen Lord. But Paul does not approve of the turn which this kind of piety has taken in Corinth. He wants to bring this congregation back to an awareness of one another. In order to do this Paul cites the one item of the tradition which is appropriate to the meal setting of the Corinthians' worship and which constitutes the Lord's own interpretation of his life and death.

23

For I received . . . what I also delivered: On this as a formula, cf. above on vv. 17–34.

from the Lord: This phrase does not preclude the possibility of a tradition passed along by human agents. Some have argued, on the basis of Paul's statements in Gal. 2¹¹ᶠ·, that he received his knowledge of the Christian Gospel directly from Jesus at the time of his conversion.[477] Recent study by others has tended to confirm the more common-sense attitude that Paul's original experience of conversion was supplemented by a grounding in the traditions of the church.[478]

---

473. Cf. above on v. 18.   474. But see Ehrhardt, op. cit. (n. 452), 263f.
475. Cf. above on 10¹⁴⁻²². 476. Cf. general Introduction, p. xxviiiff.
477. K. Wegenast, *Das Verständnis der Tradition bei Paulus und in den Deutero-paulinien*, 1962, 95, 1.
478. Cf. G. Bornkamm, 'Herrenmahl und Kirche bei Paulus', *Studien zu Antike und Christentum*, 1959, 141ff.; J. T. Sanders, 'Paul's "Autobiographical" Statements in Gal. 1–2', *JBL*, 85 (1966), 338f.; K. Wegenast, op. cit. (n. 477), 93ff.

on the night when he was betrayed:[479] It is important to note that this is the context within which Paul now recounts and previously recounted the tradition. These are words and acts of Jesus which explain why he died.[480]

23f.

he . . . took bread, and when he had given thanks, he broke it: This ceremony of blessing or thanking God for the bread and then breaking it up and distributing it to those present was the usual way in which a Jewish meal began.[481] Jesus here is in the role of head of the family or host whose prerogative it was to perform this ceremony.

24

This is my body which is for you: In a manner reminiscent of the graphic gestures used by some of the prophets,[482] Jesus expresses the meaning of his life of self-giving:[483] *It is for you.* In the tradition of these particular words, the only stable element is the clause *This is my body.*[484]

25

In the same way: This means that Jesus also took the cup and said the appropriate blessing or thanksgiving over it. In the course of an ordinary Jewish meal the first cup of wine is 'blessed' by the host. This is the arrangement of the Marcan account, in which the bread and cup follow one another immediately.[485]

after supper: In Paul's version of the tradition, the meal is said to have intervened. *The cup* then would refer to the cup of blessing with which it was customary for a Jewish meal to end. In this case, however, it was proper for the host to ask one of the guests to say the accompanying prayer over the cup.[486]

This cup is the new covenant in my blood: In the tradition of Jesus's interpretation of the cup of wine, there is even more variation. Unlike the bread-saying, there is no completely stable element in the tradition. Mark, Matthew: 'This is my blood of the covenant which is poured

479. Cf. Mark 14$^{18-21}$ parr.

480. Cf. above on vv. 17–34.   481. Cf. S.-B., IV, 621.

482. Cf. above n. 392; also K. G. Kuhn, 'The Lord's Supper and the Communal Meal at Qumran', *The Scrolls and the New Testament*, ed. K. Stendahl, 1957, 88; K. Stürmer, 'Das Abendmahl bei Paulus' *Ev.Theol.*, 7 (1947–8).

483. Cf. Mark 10$^{42-5}$.

484. Cf. Mark 14^{22}; Matt. 26^{26}; Luke 22^{19}; Justin, *Apologia*, I, 66. The rest of the interpretation of this gesture varies considerably: Mark and Matthew, none; Luke, 'given for you'; Justin, none.

485. Cf. Mark 14$^{22-4}$.   486. S.-B., IV, 628.

out for many'. Matthew adds 'for the forgiveness of sins'. Luke: 'This cup which is poured out for you is the new covenant in my blood'.

The most important distinction is *covenant* (Mark, Matthew) as contrasted with *new covenant* (Paul, Luke). Most commentators agree that *covenant* in Mark and Matthew refers to Exodus 24[8]. In this story in Exodus we have one of the accounts of the ratification of the covenant between God and Israel: half the blood was thrown against the altar. Then the book of the covenant was read to the people, and they swore their obedience to the prescriptions of the covenant. Then the other half of the blood was thrown upon the people.

In the Marcan version of the cult-gesture of Jesus he portrays his radical obedience to the God of the covenant. But Paul knows that this covenant has been fulfilled. For the gentile who comes to faith it is passé. So for Paul it is not a gesture of obedience to the God of the old covenant which Jesus makes, but a ceremony in which the new covenant is established. The cup is the covenanting pledge. The blood of the covenant is poured out on the cross. The traditions of Mark-Matthew and Paul-Luke, represent two versions of an incident in the life of Jesus. That of Mark-Matthew has retained its original setting, i.e. in Jesus's life. This was the setting in which Paul had first passed it on to the Corinthian Church.

24b, 25b

Do this in remembrance of me: This command, repeated here in vv. 24 and 25, does not appear in Mark or Matthew and occurs only once in Luke, at 22[19]. Paul clearly intends that it be understood as a word of the Lord Jesus. The question is, does he understand it as part of the tradition which he received or is this 'a word of the Lord'[487] to him which further interprets the gestures and words of Jesus?

I am inclined to think that Paul, faced with the abuses of the communal meal in Corinth, sought help from the traditions of the community. He fastened upon those enigmatic gestures of Jesus which the tradition had by now placed *in the night when he was betrayed*. He could presuppose that the Corinthians would readily associate their communal meal with an intimate association with Jesus, as he intimates in 10[15f.]. Now in Chapter 11 he makes his message explicit: it is Jesus's intention that when they gather for worship they are to *do this*. They already know his presence in their assembly. *This* will be the form of his remembrance. The idea of *remembrance* (Greek, *anamnēsis*) in the Bible has a fund of meaning peculiar to the biblical tradition. This meaning,

487. Cf. above, n. 267 on 7[10].

however, is not in the word *anamnēsis* itself, but in the nature of the things remembered.[488] What Israel remembered was what God had done for them – his mighty acts such as the deliverance from Egypt, his guidance of them through the wilderness into the promised land, etc. What the church remembered was what God had done in the person of Jesus.[489]

The Corinthians already had a lively sense of Jesus's presence in the Spirit,[490] as well as their liberation from the forces of sin and death.[491] What they lacked was a sense that all this had anything to do with their life together.[492] So Paul presents them with a picture of Jesus's words and gestures at his last meal with the disciples before his death. *This* is what you *do*[493] for a *remembrance* of God's salvation to you in Jesus. This is what God has done for you and also how he has done it. When you gather for worship *this remembrance*, which is not only your past, but also your present and your future, is what you place at the very centre of your life together – this living presence of Jesus who gave himself, who gives himself, who will give himself *for you*.[494]

26

you proclaim the Lord's death: Proclaim here means tell the saving significance of. The significance is already quite explicit in the words which accompany the gestures. It is in their participation in the bread and in the cup that they *proclaim* the meaning. The meal takes on some of the aspects of a cultic drama.[495] Whether *proclaim* implies a verbal explication in the form of a sermon or homily, as some have asserted,[496] is less clear.

until he comes: This establishes the *terminus ad quem* for this activity. It will continue until the end of this age and the return of Christ.[497] It

488. Cf. D. Jones, '*Anamnesis* in the LXX and the Interpretation of I Cor. xi. 25', *JTS*, 6 (1955), 183–91.

489. Cf. N. Dahl, op. cit. (n. 457 above), 82.

490. Cf. 2^{10ff.}, 3¹⁶, 4⁸.   491. 15^{12b,17b}.

492. Cf. H. Kosmala, 'Das tut zu meinem Gedächtnis', *NovTest*, 4 (1960), 81–94.

493. Cf. Lietzmann, ad loc.

494. Cp. Phil. 2⁵⁻¹¹; cf. G. Bornkamm, op. cit. (n. 478); E. Käsemann, 'Anliegen und Eigenart der paulinischen Abendmahlslehre', *Exegetische Versuche und Besinnungen*, I, 1960, 11–33.

495. Cf. Weiss, ad loc.

496. Cf. J. Schniewind, '*Aggellein . . . kataggellein*', *ThWbNT*, I, 68–71.

497. Cf. E. Käsemann, op. cit. (n. 494); *contra* J. Jeremias, *The Eucharistic Words of Jesus* (E.T. by N. Perrin, 3rd ed. 1966), also, critique of H. Kosmala, op. cit. (n. 492).

retains the forward-looking orientation of the earliest Christian community which is more strongly accentuated in other versions of the tradition.[498]

27

eats . . . drinks . . . in an unworthy manner: Here again we face the problem of the precise nature of the Corinthians' activity. As I suggested above on vv. 17–34, Paul disapproves of the *factions* and *divisions* in the midst or the worshipping group as well as of their failure to provide for an equitable participation in the communal meal by rich and poor. In this action, Paul has pointed out, they *despise the church . . . and humiliate those who have nothing* (v. 22). Most commentators take this to refer to some form of sacrilege. It is most often taken to refer to the phrase *one who eats and drinks without discerning the body* in v. 29. I prefer, with Lietzmann and Moffat, to make the more obvious connection with the charges which Paul has already made against the Corinthians in vv. 21f. It is important to note that Paul has two different things in mind in vv. 17–34:

1. the abuses which he sees in the manner of worship;
2. the corrective which he applies from the tradition.[499]

These two matters of ethics and cultus are most intimately related, since they both involve external expressions of what the Corinthians affirm in faith about themselves as Christians. However, Paul can presuppose only an understanding of (1), since he is proposing (2) as a corrective to it. Paul therefore says that the person who participates in the communal meal in an unworthy manner is . . .

guilty of profaning the body and blood of the Lord: The Greek word here translated *guilty of profaning* is *enochs*, a legal term. It can mean guilty in the sense of 'proven guilty'. It can also mean 'culpable', i.e. 'responsible for'[500] or 'subject to'.[501]

Paul's interpretation of what the Corinthian worship really means (10^{15-17}) and the form in which it should be conducted (11^{23-5}) is his way of trying to correct the abuses which he sees in their present understanding and their present practice of worship. But Paul is also insisting that his interpretation is the correct one. And because this is true, the Corinthians are culpable or responsible for their participation cultically in the body and blood of Christ – as Paul has explained this to them.

498. Cf. Mark 14^{25}; Matt. 26^{29}; Luke 22^{15-18}. Cp. Did. 9^4.
499. Cf. above on vv. 23–5.
500. Cf. Jam. 2^{10}.
501. Cf. Heb. 2^{15}; the best analysis of this is in Edwards, ad loc.

28

This is the basis upon which they must *examine* themselves. They should *so eat . . . and drink*, that is they should participate in the common meal which is understood according to Paul's understanding and in the form which he has presented to them.

29f.

without discerning the body: Even if they do not do this, it is all the same. The *judgement* of God is still there. The nature of their community is such that they will pervert the meaning of it if they persist in their present behaviour. What Paul is doing here must be seen as more profound than making rules.[502] He is explaining to the Corinthians the true nature of their community in Christ and of their worship. The true nature of their community is reflected in their form of worship. It is one in which brother has concern for brother, where brother *waits* for brother. It is one in which, through their common participation in the bread and wine, the brethren *proclaim* the meaning of *the Lord's death*, even while they know his risen Presence. But this proclamation is both salvation and judgement.[503] The Lord who gave himself upon the cross is present as risen saviour and the judge who comes at the end of the world.

His *judgement* is already operative in the form of *chastening*.[504] Paul can say that, on this account, *many of you are weak and ill, and some have died*. In faith man can know that what we undergo in this life can be for our ultimate salvation.[505]

31

if we judged ourselves truly: Many commentators would insist that there is no consistency in Paul's use of the Greek word *diakrinein* translated here as *judge*. The inconsistency, however, is in the minds of the commentators. Paul uses *diakrinein* throughout to mean 'discern', as R.S.V. correctly translates it in v. 29. It is clear that the nature of the Christian community is not altered by our discernment or nondiscernment. We can do ourselves some good, however, by *truly* discerning ourselves, or the *body*, i.e. the church (v. 29), because then we will be able to avoid this operation of God's judgement which manifests itself as a *chastening*[506] or educating[507] of the community.

502. *Contra* E. Käsemann, op. cit. (n. 494). 503. Cf. ibid.
504. Cf. A. Ehrhardt, op. cit. (n. 451). 505. Cf. 5[4f.].
506. Cf. 2 Cor. 6[9].
507. Cf. 1 Tim. 1[20]; Greek, *paideuein*.

33

when you come together . . . [508]*wait for one another:* This is usually taken as referring to *each one goes ahead with his own meal* (v. 21). Instead they should start together.

34

if any one is hungry, let him eat at home: We must distinguish between this statement, which describes a person coming to the communal meal, and the statement in v. 21, which describes what happens at the communal gathering, i.e. some go without. This is in line with Paul's attempt to focus upon the true meaning of the Corinthians' worship, which took the form of a common meal. He points out that, though it takes the form of a meal, it is not one at which a hungry person should expect to satisfy himself.

Paul wants the Corinthians to fulfil their intention to conduct their worship in the form of a supper in honour of the Lord. But in order to do this they must remember that it is not only the risen, triumphant Lord who is present in their assembly, but also the crucified Lord. It is the Lord's will therefore that at the centre of their worship should be the repetition of what he did at his last supper with his disciples. For in this supper there is established the new covenant of God with all men. But it is not established without the giving of Jesus's life, his body and blood. Furthermore this remembrance will have its proper setting only in an assembly where the brethren are more concerned with each other's needs than with their own. It is only in this setting that the meaning of the Lord's death can be truly proclaimed.

About the other things: It is unlikely that Paul has covered all the problems connected with the worship of the Corinthian Church. The *other things* are, one suspects, however, small details compared with what he has done. Even Paul probably did not recognize the extent to which he had set the form of worship in the Western church for at least the next 1,500 years.

508. Cf. above, on 8[11], 11[17f.].

Chapters 12–14

In Chapters 12–14 Paul takes up the problem of the Spirit. In previous sections of the epistle he has shown how an unrestrained exercise of their newly found freedom has led the Corinthian Christians to do things or to approve behaviour which he considers contrary to God's will.[509] Along with this freedom, the Corinthians also experienced an influx of power which Paul calls the *Spirit* (2¹²). He refers to those *inspired by . . . the Spirit* (12¹¹) as *spiritual men* (2¹⁵, 3¹). However, there was a tendency among the Corinthian Christians to identify the presence of the Spirit only with its ecstatic manifestation in glossolalia or *speaking in tongues* (14⁶).

As I have indicated in the Introduction,[510] the first gentiles were admitted into the church because they had already received the Spirit. As far as we can tell from the account in Acts 10 and 11, the external manifestation of Spirit-possession was *speaking in tongues*.[511] If the Corinthian Christians had some such experience as this associated with their reception into the church, or if, as the evidence of Acts indicates, this was the very basis upon which they were admitted, it is not surprising that they placed a high value upon this particular manifestation of the Spirit. It is quite possible that on this basis they were even prepared to exclude or downgrade those who could not show evidence of this particular gift.[512] Paul must therefore give the Corinthians a broader perspective from which to view the activity of the Spirit. He does this in three ways:

1. He draws upon the analogy of the human *body* in order to express the unique relation which Christians have to Christ and also to one another.

2. He then describes the Christian life in terms of *love*, with which he contrasts the behaviour of the Corinthian Christians.

3. He uses another gift of the Spirit, *prophecy*, as a foil against which he plays off *speaking in tongues* in order to set in relief its essentially private, i.e. non-community-oriented, nature.

---

509. Cf. above on 8⁹. 510. Cf. above, general Introduction, pp. xxviff.
511. Cf. 10⁴⁶, 11¹⁵. 512. Cf. below on 12³.

The problem which the Corinthians have raised has special reference to the worship of the church.[513] They have inquired of Paul concerning the proper place of *speaking in tongues* in their *church assemblies*, when they *come together*. In order to answer their question fully, however, Paul explains the nature of the church into which they have come by Baptism (12^{13}). This nature he describes at its deepest level as the love which *does not insist on its own way* (13^5).[514] It is also the Spirit which allows men to *speak ... to God* ($14^{2f.}$) but who seeks even more the *up-building and encouragement and consolation ... [of] the church* ($14^{3f.}$). The church in turn is a community of men in which God works primarily to reveal himself to those who do not yet know him ($14^{23ff.}$). Speaking in tongues should therefore be kept on the periphery of the church's life. It comes under the heading of what is traditionally referred to as private devotion. Only when there is also present one who can interpret to the congregation what the ecstatic is saying should speaking in tongues be a part of the public worship of the church ($14^{27f.}$).

The concern out of which Paul wrote these three chapters was a pastoral one. There was a particular problem which had arisen in connection with the worship of the church in Corinth. The approach which he uses to deal with this particular problem was strongly influenced by the particular set of circumstances in which the problem arose. Paul chose his approach with the particular situation of the Corinthian Church in view. This should be kept in mind when one attempts to make any broad application of Paul's statements here regarding the church.

[1]*Now concerning spiritual gifts, brethren, I do not want you to be uninformed.* [2]*You know that when you were heathen, you were led astray to dumb idols, however you may have been moved.* [3]*Therefore I want you to*

513. Cf. $14^{23, 26}$; cp. $11^{17f., 20}$.
514. Cf. G. Bornkamm, 'Der köstlichere Weg', *Das Ende des Gesetzes*, 1952, 93ff.

*understand that no one speaking by the Spirit of God ever says 'Jesus be
cursed!' and no one can say 'Jesus is Lord' except by the Holy Spirit.*

ᘒᘒ

1
Now concerning . . . Cf. above on 7¹.

spiritual gifts: Only the plural adjective *pneumatikoi* appears in the Greek
text. It could also be translated 'spiritual men'. If the Corinthians were
distinguishing between matters within the church, then *gifts* is the best
translation.[515] If, however, one were distinguishing between those who
were spiritual and those who were not, i.e. not really in the church,[516]
then 'men' gives the best sense. One suspects the Corinthians asked
about 'men' and Paul instructed them about 'gifts'. The best translation
would then be 'matters spiritual'.

2
The construction of this sentence in Greek is most confused.[517] Paul's
point is that the influx of power is a sensation common to Christianity
and paganism.

dumb idols: Cf. Hab. 2¹⁸; Psalm 113¹⁵; 3 Macc. 4¹⁶.

3
'Jesus be cursed': If anyone said something like this, there is little doubt
about his source of inspiration – it is not God's spirit. Commentators
have been quite exercised over the possibility that someone actually
said this. It is more likely that Paul sets this up as the hypothetical opposite[518] of the following confession of faith.[519] Whether one were an
ecstatic or not, such a statement would disqualify one as a Christian.

'Jesus is Lord': This confession of faith, which may represent a pre-
Pauline credal formula,[520] is a sufficient indication of the Spirit's

515. Most commentators favour this translation.
516. Cf. Hurd, Weiss.
517. Cp. translation of J.B.: 'You remember that, when you were pagans,
whenever you felt irresistably drawn, it was towards dumb idols?'
518. Cf. J. P. M. Sweet, 'A Sign for Unbelievers: Paul's Attitude to Gloss-
alalia', *NTS*, 13 (1967), 241. Also Hurd.
519. But see Schmitals, op. cit. (n. 10), 117ff. Other possibilities in Barrett,
Schlatter.
520. Cf. Rom. 10⁹. Also O. Cullmann, *Early Christian Confessions*, 1949.

presence. There is no necessity to exhibit the ability to speak in tongues. This, as Paul will show, is only one of many gifts of the Spirit.

12[4-11]   OPERATION OF THE SPIRIT

4 *Now there are varieties of gifts, but the same Spirit;* 5*and there are varieties of service, but the same Lord;* 6*and there are varieties of working, but it is the same God who inspires them all in every one.* 7*To each is given the manifestation of the Spirit for the common good.* 8*To one is given through the Spirit the utterance of wisdom, and to another the utterance of knowledge according to the same Spirit,* 9*to another faith by the same Spirit, to another gifts of healing by the one Spirit,* 10*to another the working of miracles, to another prophecy, to another the ability to distinguish between spirits, to another various kinds of tongues, to another the interpretation of tongues.* 11*All these are inspired by one and the same Spirit, who apportions to each one individually as he wills.*

The Corinthians have become too attached to one manifestation of the Spirit – speaking in tongues. Paul emphasizes in what follows that *there are varieties of gifts.* He emphasizes the word *variety* by using it three times. This is clearly a rhetorical device. Commentators are struck, however, by the occurrence of the three terms *Spirit, Lord,* and *God,* which resemble the designation of the three persons of the Trinitarian formula. There can be no doubt that *Spirit, Lord,* and *God* all refer to the divine source of the gifts. However, one notes an ascending order in the terms, *service* and *working,* which is probably also rhetorical.[521]

༃

7
To each is given the manifestation of the Spirit for the common good: The emphasis here is rightly placed upon *to each.* It is the diversity of gifts which is being emphasized as contrasted with the exclusivism of those who speak in tongues. One is reminded of those zealous souls who

521. Cf. I. Hermann, *Kyrios und Pneuma, Studien zur Christologie der paulinischen Hauptbriefe,* 1961, 71ff.

would deny the designation 'Christian' to anyone who has not had a 'conversion experience'.

the manifestation of the Spirit: Most commentators take this to mean: showing that the person really has the Spirit. It can also mean: the particular manifestation (gift) given by the Spirit. The ambiguity goes back to the same problem noted above in v. 1.

8ff.
This list of spiritual gifts, as well as the analogy of the human body which follows, is Paul's way of describing and justifying the diversity of operation within the church. This diversity is an essential part of God's plan.[522] There is a purpose in this diversity. It is that there may be *care for one another* (12^{25}). That is, the *gifts* are complementary and are so by design of God, who is their sole source. Paul emphasizes, however, that within this diversity one *gift* is no more evidence for the existence of the *Spirit* than any other.[523]

Paul lists gifts of the Spirit in three places.[524] A comparison of these three lists would indicate that we have in 12^{8-10} a list constructed for the occasion, as are the other two. No two lists correspond, either in terms of gifts mentioned or in the order of their appearance. With the most generous allowances for differences in terminology, only two of the gifts, *prophecy* and *teaching*, appear on all three lists. Paul prepares this list of spiritual gifts in an attempt to show their diversity on the one hand and their equal 'validity' on the other. Probably, since the Corinthians put a top priority on speaking in tongues, Paul puts this gift last and next to last (respectively) in the two lists on which it appears (in Chapter 12).

utterance of wisdom . . . of knowledge: Whatever the distinction may be between *wisdom* and *knowledge*, the important word here is *utterance*. Wisdom and knowledge will not be for *the common good* unless they are communicated.[525]

9
faith: This is an unusual use of this word in Paul's letters. In Paul's letters *faith* is usually that response of man to God's acts of salvation through Christ which is the basis of his Christian life. Most commenta-

---

522. Cf. $12^{11,18,24}$.
523. Cf. the emphasis on Spirit in *the Spirit* (v. 8), *the same Spirit* (vv. 8f.), *the one Spirit* (v. 9), *one and the same Spirit* (v. 11).
524. 1 Cor. 12^{8-10}, 12^{28}; Rom. 12^{6-8}.
525. Cf. Schlatter, *ad loc.*

tors suggest that this particular usage is paralleled in I Cor. 13² and Matthew 17²⁰, i.e. 'faith to move a mountain'. Paul could also have reference to those who help others in the church who are weak in the faith.[526]

10

the ability to distinguish between spirits: Some see this as the ability to distinguish one type of spirit from another in terms of their comparative value. This is what Paul does in his comparison of prophecy and speaking in tongues in Chapter 14. Most, however, agree that the primary function of this gift was to distinguish between the false Spirit and the true.[527]

11

Cf. above on vv. 8f.

DIVERSITY AND UNITY

¹²*For just as the body is one and has many members, and all the members of the body, though many, are one body, so it is with Christ.* ¹³*For by one Spirit we were all baptized into one body – Jews or Greeks, slaves or free – and all were made to drink of one Spirit.*

The nature of Paul's use of the image of the body and its place within his theology has been a subject of endless discussion and debate. Broadly speaking the discussion moves between two extremes:

1. The Body of Christ is a key, if not the key, idea in Paul's theology. What we see in I Corinthians in germinal form is not significantly different from the notion that the church equals the Body of Christ, which we find developed in Ephesians and Colossians. The Body of Christ is a collective term and is meant to embrace all those baptized into Christ. Baptism constitutes our entrance into this body.[528]

2. Body of Christ is not a key term in Paul's theology. It represents one of four images by which Paul seeks to describe the unity of the church. Further, every mention of Body of Christ is not a reference

526. Cf. Rom. 14¹.
527. Cf. I Thess. 5²¹; Did. 11⁸; cp. I John 14ᶠ·; I Tim. 4¹.
528. See Allo, ad loc.

to the church. Sometimes, as in 1 Cor. 12¹²ᶠ·, Paul means the body of Jesus – the one which hung on the cross. The image is best understood as addressed to the specific situation of the church in Corinth and was not necessarily meant for general application.[529]

At the risk of over-simplification, we might say that one extreme states that we belong to Christ because we are members of his body (the church), and that the other extreme asserts that we can speak of ourselves as members of his body because we belong to Christ (by faith).

ממ

12

The principal difficulty in this verse is its relation to v. 27: *you are the body of Christ*. If we assume that the idea of v. 27 underlies v. 12, then body in v. 12 probably means 'body of Christ'. However, if this is the case why does Paul end v. 12 with a statement about Christ and not a statement about the church? On the other hand, some have recently suggested that v. 12 does not depend upon v. 27 for its meaning. If this is so, what is the sense of the statements *the body is one* and *the members . . . are one body*?

One point should be clearly made. As we noted above, Paul's formulation of the working of the Spirit was deeply influenced by the particular situation to which he wrote. He is not therefore forging a doctrine of the church when he speaks here of the one Body and the Body of Christ. He is rather using these terms to elucidate the situation of the Corinthian Christians. The Body-image is therefore a means to an end. The end in view is the description of a proper view of the gifts of the Spirit.

There may have been a number of reasons why Paul used this particular image of the Body. It was a familiar one in antiquity. It was employed among Roman writers to describe the proper functioning of the state.[530] Some have suggested that the Gnostic idea of the archetypal man may have been current at this time. In this view, all men were really bits or sparks; originally part of this heavenly being.[531] It has also been pointed out that the Jews thought in terms of the corporate

529. Cf. M. Barth, 'A Chapter on the Church – the Body of Christ', *Int*, 12 (1958), 131–56.
530. Cf. Livy, II, 32; other references in Lietzmann, ad loc.
531. Cf. R. Bultmann, *Theology of the New Testament* (E.T. by K. Grobel, 1951), I, 178. E. Käsemann, *Leib und Leib Christi*, 1933, 159ff.

personality both of the patriarchs and of those figures who would come to save God's people at the end of the world.[532] They also speculated about the figure of Adam, who was glorious in his pre-fallen state and who would, at the end of the world, regain his glory.[533]

Whatever the source of the Body-image in Paul's writings, the more immediate motive for its use is clear: the Corinthian Christians needed to be shown how the Spirit actually worked and showed itself in the lives of the faithful. This needed to be done in the most concrete and specific way possible. The body-image was apt because of its concreteness, its illustration of the necessity of diversity, and because it leads man inevitably to be concerned with those others who are 'in the body' in the church sense or 'in a body' in the human sense.

13

Paul proceeds to substantiate what he has said about the diversity and unity of the Spirit's operation by reference to the beginning of the Christian's life.

by one Spirit we were all baptized into one body: The reference to Christian initiation is obvious enough in the term *baptized*. What most commentators do not see, however, is that the agent in this Baptism is the Spirit. Whatever the ceremony in which the Corinthians were formally inducted into the church they were baptized *by one Spirit*.[534] We have indicated above[535] that they received the Spirit and then they were baptized. They valued the gift of speaking in tongues because this had been the first manifestation of the Spirit working in them.

into one body:[536] This phrase can be seen as parallel to the statement in v. 27. It can also be understood as paralleling 6¹¹ above, in which Baptism, sanctification and justification take place *in the name of the Lord Jesus Christ and in the Spirit of our God*. If *body*, *spirit*, and *name* are taken as closely related terms, then the reference here is to the body of Jesus. This is Paul's way of saying that our Christian life is based upon what God did for us through Christ.

532. Cf. E. Best, *One Body in Christ*, 1955, 93f. Cp. E. Percy, *Der Leib Christi: in den paulinischen Homologoumena und Antilegomena*, 1942, 18–46; A. Schweitzer, *The Mysticism of Paul the Apostle* (E.T. by W. Montgomery), 2nd ed. 1953, cf. Best, op. cit., pp. 14ff.

533. Cf. W. D. Davies, *Paul and Rabbinic Judaism*, 2nd ed. 1955, 57.

534. Cf. M. Barth, 'A Chapter on the Church – the Body of Christ', *Int*, 12 (1958), 149ff.

535. Cf. general Introduction, pp. xxviff.

536. Cf. above on vv. 12f.

Paul does not distinguish as finely between the Spirit and Christ as later generations of theologians tended to. It is not always possible to say that when Paul uses the word Spirit he is not also implying the action of the risen Christ and vice versa.[537] This insight resolves some of the confusion in the twelfth chapter. When Paul speaks of the action of the Spirit, he is also referring to the action of the risen Christ. When Paul speaks of our baptism into Christ or into the body, he is also thinking of the way in which the Spirit becomes operative in the believer. One could explain the distinction on the basis of the particular way in which gentiles were admitted into the church in the first place.[538] Since the gentiles become Christians on the basis of their manifesting the Spirit, the Spirit became a particularly important part of their religious vocabulary. Paul on the other hand wants to be sure that their notion of the Spirit is firmly attached to the person of Jesus through whom God has acted for their salvation.[539]

all were made to drink of one Spirit: The Greek word translated here *made to drink* is *potizein*. It can also mean 'to water'. Many commentators have puzzled over a possible reference to Baptism or Eucharist. The imagery is in neither case satisfactory, since in Baptism one does not 'drink', and in the Eucharist the 'drinking' has reference to the blood of Christ and not the Spirit *per se*. In either case the meaning of *potizein* here is probably 'endued with' or 'saturated'. There is no problem if one sees the verb as referring to an event which preceded the formal introduction of the Corinthians into the church. They must not think, however, that this 'saturation' with the Spirit is something peculiar to them. The Spirit is the agent in all Christian initiation whether it be of *Jews or Greeks, slaves or free.*[540]

12¹⁴⁻²⁷   THE BODY OF CHRIST

[14]*For the body does not consist of one member but of many.* [15]*If the foot should say, 'Because I am not a hand, I do not belong to the body,' that*

537. I. Hermann, op. cit. (n. 521), 11–13.
538. Cf. above on v. 12; also general Introduction, pp. xxviff.
539. Paul makes the specific identification in 2 Cor. 3¹⁷: *the Lord is the Spirit*; cp. 1 Cor. 15⁴⁵.
540. Cf. Gal. 3²⁸.

would not make it any less a part of the body. ¹⁶*And if the ear should say, 'Because I am not an eye, I do not belong to the body,' that would not make it any less a part of the body.* ¹⁷*If the whole body were an eye, where would be the hearing? If the whole body were an ear, where would be the sense of smell?* ¹⁸*But as it is, God arranged the organs in the body, each one of them, as he chose.* ¹⁹*If all were a single organ, where would the body be?* ²⁰*As it is, there are many parts, yet one body.* ²¹*The eye cannot say to the hand, 'I have no need of you,' nor again the head to the feet, 'I have no need of you.'* ²²*On the contrary, the parts of the body which seem to be weaker are indispensable,* ²³*and those parts of the body which we think less honourable we invest with the greater honour, and our unpresentable parts are treated with greater modesty,* ²⁴*which our more presentable parts do not require. But God has so adjusted the body, giving the greater honour to the inferior part,* ²⁵*that there may be no discord in the body, but that the members may have the same care for one another.* ²⁶*If one member suffers, all suffer together; if one member is honoured, all rejoice together.*

²⁷*Now you are the body of Christ and individually members of it.*

Paul now elaborates upon his idea that the functioning of the Spirit in the faithful can be compared to the functioning of the human body. It is generally acknowledged by commentators that, in this extended analogy, Paul pursues two major themes:

1. Diversity is necessary in the body (14²⁰).

2. The members of the body are interdependent and interrelated (vv. 21–6).

It is plain, however, that this extended analogy of the body has elements of an allegory. That is, some of Paul's statements seem to reflect directly his concern over specific situations in the Corinthian Church. In vv. 14–20 we see that one segment of the Corinthian Church is excluding another. When Paul applies this principle of exclusion to the human body the absurdity is obvious. But the literary device of personifying members of the body is definitely allegorical in style. In vv. 21–4 this element disappears, and Paul slips back into using the body as an analogy. However, the allegorical style reappears in vv. 25f. where the members of the body are once again personified.

The question which seems to plague most commentators at this point is: How seriously are we to take this analogy with regard, not just to the Corinthian Church, but to the whole church? How one interprets this passage depends to a large extent upon one's view of the church.

The basic problem is: What part does one conceive the church to play in the process of salvation, since God is the principal agent in salvation, working through Jesus Christ? Jesus Christ, however, is not immediately accessible to the prospective believer. The church (in some form) therefore plays no small part in mediating to the prospective believer the message of the Gospel. Paul takes it for granted that, when one comes to believe in God through acceptance of the message of the Gospel, one is baptized and becomes a member of the church. At this point an important question must be raised: Is the church constituted by this accumulation of believers, or is the church a divinely constituted entity, i.e. the Body of Christ, before anyone ever believes?

Before we embrace either one of these alternatives, certain difficulties should be noted with respect to each. To take 'Body of Christ' in a purely collective sense, which tends to support the first of these alternatives, overlooks the givenness of the church in Paul and in the subsequent writings of the New Testament.[541] The Jewish background of both Jesus and Paul increases the probability that, for Paul and the early church, salvation was not just an individual matter.[542] On the other hand to see the church as a separate entity, which really exists prior to any believer, tends to separate the church, not just from individual believers, but also from Christ and God's action in Christ. This would be contrary to Paul's thought. The unity of believers is entirely dependent upon Christ.[543] The sacraments are meant to symbolize this unity of God's people which he brings about.[544]

It is necessary to see that, for Paul, the church was already a 'going concern' before his conversion. It has traditions and usages which antedate any of Paul's experiences as a Christian. It is clear that Paul

541. Cf. I. Hermann, op. cit. (n. 521), 80ff.

542. Cf. E. Käsemann, 'Gottesgerechtigkeit bei Paulus', *Exegetische Versuche und Besinnungen*, 1960–64, II, 104f.; E. Schweizer, 'Die Kirche als Leib Christi in den paulinischen Homologumena', *Neotestamentica*, 1951–63, 291; but see R. Bultmann, *History and Eschatology*, *The Presence of Eternity*, 1957, 40ff.

543. E. Best, op. cit. (n. 532), 106.

544. L. Cerfaux, *The Church in the Theology of St Paul*, 1959, 239.

used these traditions,[545] but was no more bound by them than he was by the Jewish scriptures.[546] In much the same way, Paul used the analogy of the body to express his thoughts upon the operation of the Spirit among the Christians in Corinth. His understanding of the church came before his use of the analogy, which he uses both allegorically and metaphorically as it suits his purpose. Paul is in no way bound to this analogy, but uses four different metaphors to describe the church.[547] The source of Paul's analogy of the body is most uncertain. Current scholarship is divided and undecided on this issue. E. Best[548] has the clearest exposition of the various positions and the problems involved in each of them.

୧୨

15f.

that would not make it: The R.S.V. translation glosses over a difficult problem here. It is created by the Greek phrase *para touto*. Literally this phrase would mean 'along this'. Here it seems to mean 'on account of this'. 'This' could refer either to what the member says or to that fact of the matter upon which the member comments. Most commentators would refer it to what the member says. It is, however, the facts of the matter which form the basis for this comment of 'not belonging' here and the comment of exclusion below[549] and are Paul's main concern. Paul is not interested in the subjective state of the rejected member, any more than he takes seriously the idea that a hand or an eye can talk.

22

the parts of the body which seem to be weaker: Paul probably refers to the more delicate organs of the body.[550]

23

invest: i.e. clothe.

less honourable ... unpresentable parts: Must refer to genitalia. This part of the analogy is the most forced. One can see what Paul is saying here about clothing those parts of the body which are specific to one's sex and have to do with reproduction. The indirect allusion to Genesis 3[7,10,21] is also clear. Paul's real point, however, is not in the fact that we wear clothes to cover these parts. His words must be seen as euphemisms

545. Cf. 11^{23ff.}, 15^{3ff.}.   546. Cf. 10¹⁻⁴.
547. Cf. L. Cerfaux, op. cit. (n. 544), 239ff.   548. Op. cit. (n. 532), 83ff.
549. Vv. 21ff.   550. Cf. Barrett, ad loc.

which express, somewhat haltingly, the concern which one has for one's sexual organs whose value lies more in function than in appearance. Paradoxically, then, one has the greatest care or concern for the least presentable parts of one's anatomy. Paul's analogy breaks at this point because the agent in transferring *honour* from the *more presentable parts* to the *inferior part* is the individual himself, not the parts. However, Paul's point here is to illustrate the strategy of God in putting the body together in this particular way.

25
discord: The Greek work here is *schisma*, 'division'. *Discord* is misleading and changes the emphasis of Paul's argument.

the same care for one another: The opposite of division is care for one another. It is not a situation in which there is mere consensus. The community of faith does not operate on the basis of compromise, but of loving concern.[551] Paul envisages a community in which everyone cares about the other person. This love, which is the highest manifestation of the Spirit at work, is the source of the church's unity.

27
the body of Christ: There is no article, *the*, in the Greek text. It reads: *You are body of Christ*. This could mean that Paul is addressing himself to the specific situation in Corinth, with no thought of a wider application of the body analogy. That is, you are like the human body, but in this case it is a body which belongs to Christ. He is the source of its life and the director of its operation.[552] This analogy is elaborated considerably in the Pseudo-Pauline Epistles to the Colossians and Ephesians. As Barrett notes, however,[553] the idea of Christ's direction of the church is maintained.

12^{28-30} THE ECONOMY OF THE SPIRIT

[28]*And God has appointed in the church first apostles, second prophets, third teachers, then workers of miracles, then healers, helpers, administrators, speakers in various kinds of tongues.* [29]*Are all apostles? Are all prophets? Are all teachers? Do all work miracles?* [30]*Do all possess gifts of healing? Do all speak with tongues? Do all interpret?*

551. Cf. Chapter 13.   552. Cf. R.-P., ad loc.   553. Ad loc.

Paul illustrates his view of the operation of the Spirit by listing once more some of the gifts of the Spirit.[554] Again, we do not have here any more than a sampling. However, Paul seems to give a certain priority to the first three gifts in this list. His main point would seem to be that each receives his own gift and that this may or may not be shared by someone else.[555] There is only one thing in which all share, and that is in the Spirit from whom all gifts come. One cannot comprehend the Spirit by viewing it through only one of its gifts, such as the gift of tongues. Paul must find a much broader category for this, which he does in Chapter 13.

කෲ

28

in the church: Most take this to indicate a widening of perspective on Paul's part. He refers now to the whole church.

God has appointed: The point is not in some kind of ordered or hierarchical arrangement, but in the ultimate divine purpose in creating diversity.[556]

first apostles: In Paul's view, the apostle (Greek, *apostolos*, literally 'one who is sent') is a person commissioned by the Lord Jesus to bring the message of the Gospel to those who have not yet heard it. Their message is like that of Jesus in that they announce the end of this world and the coming of the new world.[557] The consummation of this process involves the carrying-out of this commission by these apostles.[558] The apostle is sent by Christ. In Jewish thought there was no basis for thinking that an apostle could send or commission anyone else in turn.[559] This is an idea which arose later in the church when it became apparent that 'this age' would not end for a long time.[560]

---

554. Cf. above on vv. 8–10.
555. Cf. Rom 12^3.
556. Cf. E. Schweizer, *Church Order in the New Testament* (E.T. by F. Clarke), 1961, 100. Also Hurd, 198.
557. Gal. 4^4; cp. Mark 1^{14f}.
558. Cf. A. Fridrichsen, *The Apostle and His Message*, 1947, 16. Also Bultmann, op. cit. (n. 531), I, 307.
559. Cf. T. W. Manson, *Ministry and Priesthood: Christ's and Ours*, 1958.
560. Cf. C. K. Barrett, 'The Apostles in and after the New Testament', *Svensk Exegetisk Årsbok*, 21 (1956), 47f.

second prophets: A prophet in the early church was one through whom the risen and exalted Christ spoke and made his will known in particular instances. It is quite possible that many Christian communities were first led by prophets, perhaps in conjunction with teachers.[561] There is some evidence that these prophets provided the first laws for the early Christian communities.[562] The prophets are second to the apostles because they presuppose the existence of a Christian community within which to function. This community is founded by apostles.

third teachers: These are the preservers, transmitters and interpreters of the tradition.[563] In the beginning this tradition consisted primarily of the scriptures inherited from Judaism. As time went on, there would also be a larger and larger body of specifically Christian tradition[564] including those words spoken by Christian prophets.

Commentators worry a great deal about the extent to which these gifts of the Spirit were connected in any permanent way with individuals. The relation between office and Spirit-led action is a perennial problem.[565] As we stated above, Paul is not pointing in this passage or elsewhere to any order or hierarchy in these gifts of the Spirit. However, he also emphasizes by the rhetorical questions of v. 29 that there is a certain 'economy' involved in the manner in which the Spirit operates. It is at variance with the ordering proposed by some of the Corinthian Christians, who wished to make speaking in tongues the test for the Spirit.

It is the church's task to recognize and respond to the obvious gifts of persons within it.[566] It is the task of the individual within the church to recognize those among the gifts he has from the Spirit which are of the greatest service to the community. Paul will lay down the practical guide lines for this determination in Chapter 14.

then workers of miracles: There is a change in tone here glossed over in the R.S.V. Paul shifts from the personal, prophets, etc. to the impersonal, miracles, etc. This could mean that these gifts are less closely associated

561. Cf. H. Greeven, 'Propheten, Lehrer, Vorsteher bei Paulus', *ZNW*, 44 (1952–3), 38f.

562. Cf. E. Käsemann, 'Sätze heiligen Rechtes im Neuen Testament', *Exegetische Versuche und Besinnungen*, II, 69–82. Also below on 14¹³, ²⁸,³⁰,³⁵,³⁷: cp. Rom. 2¹².

563. Cf. H. Greeven, op. cit. (n. 561), 28.

564. Cf. I Cor. 11²³ᶠ·, 15³ᶠ·.

565. Cf. H. von Campenhausen, *Ecclesiastical Authority and Spiritual Power* E.T. by J. A. Baker), 1968.

566. Cf. E. Schweizer, op. cit.(n. 556), 103.

with specific individuals than the first three. Given Paul's view of the interdependence of the members within the church, it does not mean that they are less important.[567]

helpers, administrators: Some have seen in these two functions the precursors of the later deacons and bishops. In the beginning, it is fairly certain that administration was not exercised in any hierarchical fashion, involving supervision or representation.[568] Rather it is more probable that some prophets and teachers were also leaders within certain communities.[569]

speakers in various kinds of tongues: Cf. the introduction to Chapters 12–14 and below on Chapter 14.

29f.
A series of rhetorical questions expecting the answer 'No'.

$12^{31}-13^{13}$ THE SPIRIT IS LOVE

[31]*But earnestly desire the higher gifts.*
    And I will show you a still more excellent way.
    13 [1]*If I speak in the tongues of men and of angels, but have not love, I am a noisy gong or a clanging cymbal.* [2]*And if I have prophetic powers, and understand all mysteries and all knowledge, and if I have all faith, so as to remove mountains, but have not love, I am nothing.* [3]*If I give away all I have, and if I deliver my body to be burned, but have not love, I gain nothing.*
    [4]*Love is patient and kind; love is not jealous or boastful;* [5]*it is not arrogant or rude. Love does not insist on its own way; it is not irritable or resentful;* [6]*it does not rejoice at wrong, but rejoices in the right.* [7]*Love bears all things, believes all things, hopes all things, endures all things.*
    [8]*Love never ends; as for prophecy, it will pass away; as for tongues, they will cease; as for knowledge, it will pass away.* [9]*For our knowledge is imperfect and our prophecy is imperfect;* [10]*but when the perfect comes, the imperfect will pass away.* [11]*When I was a child, I spoke like a child, I thought like a child, I reasoned like a child; when I became a man, I*

---

567. Cf. above on vv. 14–26.   568. Cf. H. Greeven, op. cit. (n. 561), 35.
569. ibid., 38. Also Rom. 12[8]; I Thess. 5[12].

gave up childish ways. ¹²*For now we see in a mirror dimly, but then face to face. Now I know in part; then I shall understand fully, even as I have been fully understood.* ¹³*So faith, hope, love abide, these three; but the greatest of these is love.*

Paul has now established a kind of theory of the Spirit's operation. He has demonstrated the interdependence and equal importance of those who belong to the body. He has shown in effect that there is no one gift of the Spirit in terms of which one may understand or test for the Spirit's operation. The next step would be to give practical application to what has been a theoretical discussion. This Paul does in Chapter 14. However, before he makes any particular application of his theory, Paul seeks to explicate, in a more profound manner, the operation of the Spirit. Since no one of the gifts of the Spirit suffices as a category for understanding the Spirit, Paul turns to the concept of *agapē*, usually translated 'love'.

Before attempting to deal with this section as a whole, we must first settle the serious problem of its place in the present context and the character of the transitional verse 12^{31}. Clearly this verse has nothing to do with what immediately precedes it in 12^{28-30}. It refers back to the discussion of *gifts* in general. The reference to *higher gifts* is in serious contradiction to what Paul has said about the status of gifts within the congregation. The phrase *earnestly desire* contradicts the whole idea of divinely granted gifts (v. 28). These two contradictions, plus the obvious break in continuity between vv. 30 and 31, have led some to consider Chapter 13 as an interpolation, and 12^{31} as a redactional gloss.[570] It is true that, if the section 12^{31}–13^{13} is removed, 12^{30} seems to fit well with 14^1. However, without Chapter 13, we are completely unprepared for the word *love* in 14^1. This suggests a sense of the term which would be wholly lacking if this section were removed.[571]

I favour the recent suggestion of G. Iber[572] that 12^{31a} be taken as indicative rather than imperative. Paul does not admonish the Corinthians to *desire the higher gifts*. Rather he points to the fact that they do.

570. Cf. E. L. Titus, 'Did Paul Write I Cor. 13?' *JBR*, 27 (1959), 299–302.
571. Of course, one could posit that 14^1 is also a gloss picking up the reference in 12^{31b}.
572. 'Zum Verständnis von I Cor. 12.31', *ZNW*, 54 (1963), 48.

This he has just shown to be a mistake. They do not understand the economy of the Spirit's operation. They think the Spirit can be understood with reference to the gift of tongues. No, says Paul, the Spirit's operation can be understood only in the most radical way – what R.S.V. translates as *a still more excellent way*. Paul does not mean to present a comparative notion here at all. The phrase which he employs here, *kath' hyperbolēn*, occurs in a number of crucial passages in Paul's epistles.[573] It almost invariably refers to pushing something to its logical or human limit. The sense is then, You desire the higher gifts (Corinthian terminology) and I will show you the most extreme way there is – this is the way to 'go the limit'.

Chapter 13

Love is introduced without definition or qualification. It is not described as a gift of the Spirit.[574] It is, however, something which one may *have* or *not have*. It was common in older commentaries[575] to refer to this section as the 'hymn to love'. More recent exposition has pointed out that the tone of the section is more descriptive than hymnic.[576] The description of love is indirect. It is fair to say that the description proceeds largely by way of contrast and negation. It has been suggested that in vv. 4–7 Paul is deliberately contrasting love with the behaviour of the Corinthians.[577] In vv. 8–9 he contrasts love with the spiritual gifts. In vv. 10–12 he contrasts love with that which is imperfect. Finally, in v. 13 Paul contrasts love with faith and hope.

In vv. 1–3 it is not so clear what Paul is driving at. Plainly he is not describing love, but rather the religious man in his highest possibilities.[578] Then Paul asks us to make a supposition. Suppose, he says, there is the most obviously religious man and he does not have love; that man's religion is worthless. He then proceeds to tell us what love

573. 2 Cor. 1⁸; Gal. 1¹³; Rom. 8¹³; 2 Cor. 4¹⁷.

574. Cf. A. Barr, 'Love in the Church, A Study of First Corinthians 13', *SJT*, 3 (1950), 418.

575. Cf. Edwards, et al., ad loc.

576. Cf. J. T. Sanders, 'First Corinthians 13. Its Interpretation since the First World War', *Int.*, 20 (1966), 160.

577. Cf. I. J. Martin, 3rd, 'I Corinthians 13 Interpreted by its Context', *JBR*, 18 (1950), 101–5.

578. Cf. G. Bornkamm, op. cit. (n. 514), 99.

is not. It is not what the behaviour of the Corinthians represents, and it is not any one of the gifts of the Spirit. It is not anything which is partial in character such as human knowledge – even self-knowledge. Positively (and only by implication) love can be identified with the knowledge which God has of us, a knowledge in which we can share only in the end-time, when God brings about the consummation of the old world and the creation of the new.[579]

ೞೞ

1

tongues of men and of angels: It is unlikely that Paul is introducing here the idea of human speech in a discussion of spiritual gifts.[580] It is more probable that he is giving this ecstatic manifestation of the Spirit the widest possible sweep.[581]

gong ... cymbal: Some see here a possible reference to instruments used in pagan worship. The point of comparison is that neither of these are intelligible communications.[582]

2

prophetic powers ...: Cf. above on 12²⁸.

mysteries ... knowledge:[583] These would seem to refer to the secrets of God revealed to the prophet regarding God's specific mode of operation, particularly regarding what happens at the end of the world.[584]

faith: Cf. above on 12⁹.

3

deliver my body to be burned: The reference here could be to martyrdom.[585] Or some see a possible reference to the contemporary self-immolation of two religious fanatics, one a Christian and the other an Indian.[586] Barrett is certainly correct when he characterizes this as a 'powerful climax' for Paul's description of the religious Christian.[587]

---

579. This is apparently the sense of the word *then* – cf. below on v. 12.
580. But cf. Martin, op. cit. (n. 577).
581. Cf. R.-P.; cp. 2 Cor. 4⁹.   582. Cf. Weiss.
583. Cp. 1 Cor. 2⁷, 4¹, 15⁵¹; Rom. 11²⁵, 16²⁵.
584. Cf. 1 Cor. 15⁵¹; cp. 1 Thess. 4¹⁵ᶠ.
585. Cf. Dan. 3²⁸; 2 Macc. 7.
586. Full discussions in Moffatt, Barrett, ad loc.
587. Cf. G. Bornkamm, loc. cit. (n. 514).

4–7

The subject of Paul's hypothetical description of the religious Christian in vv. 1–3 is 'I'. In these verses 'I' performs certain acts demonstrating piety, but does not *have love*. In the verses which follow, *love* is the subject and performs the acts. The performance of Love is nothing short of perfect, as Paul states in v. 10.

kind: The Greek verb *chrēsteuein* is used only here in the N.T.

jealous: The same Greek word is translated in 12^{31} as *earnestly desire*.

5

resentful: The Greek is *ou logizetai to kakon*, literally 'takes no account of evil'.[588]

7

bears all things: The Greek word translated here as *bears* is *stegei*. Its root meaning is 'to cover'. From this it develops also the meaning 'to endure', as in 1 Cor. 9^{12} and 1 Thess. $3^{1,5}$. It is perhaps akin to the thought of Proverbs 10^{12}: Love (*philia*) covers strife. Given its present meaning, this phrase and the one below, *endures all things*, are redundant.[589]

8–12

Love, which never comes to an end, is contrasted with those things which do.

ends: The Greek word *piptei* means literally 'fall'. The thought here is similar to that of Luke 16^{17}, '... one dot of the law to become void', where the same verb (*piptein*) is used. Love never disappears or goes away, it abides (v. 13).

Knowledge,[590] *prophecy*, and *tongues:* These gifts will *pass away*, they will not *abide* because they are *imperfect*. At the end of the world that which is *perfect* will supersede that which is *imperfect*.[591]

11

By way of analogy, Paul uses the phenomenon of human development. When a person grows up, it means that he 'gives up' his childhood state, which Paul considers as an imperfect state being superseded by a more perfect one. Whether in fact this is what happens as one passes

---

588. Cf. Zech. 8^{17}; N.E.B.: 'keeps no score of wrongs'.
589. Cf. J.B.: 'to excuse'.
590. Cf. above on v. 2.   591. Cf. $15^{53f.}$.

into adulthood is unimportant. Paul undoubtedly thought so, as did every one else until relatively recent times.[592]

12

The analogy of v. 11 now serves Paul as a springboard[593] for further application of his notion that perfection ultimately supersedes imperfection. The *now* refers to our life in this present world. The *then* refers ahead to the end-time. Just as a child becomes a man partly by ceasing to be a child, so our imperfect knowledge will become perfect when it is superseded by God's knowledge of us. For now we see in a mirror dimly: the partial character of our present knowledge is expressed by the figure of a mirror.[594] The Greek phrase translated here *dimly* is *en ainigmati*, literally 'in a riddle'. The point would seem to be that our present knowledge of things divine comes only by reflection.[595] We do not perceive these things directly, i.e. *face to face*.[596] This is true, even though *knowledge* and *prophecy*, etc. are themselves of divine origin. In the present order of things these are viewed as gifts of the Spirit.[597] But compared with what is in store in the world to come, they must be seen as only partial.

then I shall understand fully: Paul does not say that one's present knowledge will *abide*. He states quite carefully *now I know . . . (arti ginōskō), then I shall understand fully (tote de epignōsomai), even as I have been fully understood (kathōs kai epegnōsthēn).*[598]

The fact that Paul launches into a statement about one of the spiritual gifts is puzzling in the context of his overriding subject, which is Love. His purpose of course is to bring *knowledge* into relation to Love. Present knowledge is partial and therefore inferior to love,[599] as are all the gifts of the Spirit. However, in the end-time man will participate

592. Cp. use of 'I' in vv. 1–3, above.

593. Typical rabbinic argument of the type called *qal we homer*, 'light and heavy'; cf. R.-P., ad loc.

594. Mirrors in antiquity were thought to possess magical qualities; cf. H. Achelis, 'Katoptromantie bei Paulus', *Theologische Festschrift für G. Nathanael Bonwetsch*, 1918, 56–63.

595. Cf. J. Behm, who argues against any mystical or magical overtones in Paul's use of this particular analogy – 'Das Bildwort vom Spiegel, I Korinther 13, 12', *Reinhold Seeberg Festschrift*, ed. W. Koepp, I, 1929, 315–42.

596. Cf. Num. 12⁸; Exod. 38¹¹; Deut. 34¹⁰.

597. Cf. 12²⁸.

598. The change from *ginōskein* to *epiginōskein* indicates, not a different kind of knowledge, but the completeness of future knowledge (so Barrett).

599. Cf. R. Bultmann, '*Ginōskein*, et al', *ThWbNT*, I, 709f.

in the knowledge which God has of man. But Paul has shown in $8^{1ff.}$ that this fullness of understanding[600] is nothing less than Love of God. Knowledge, therefore, in its fullest sense is, in the end-time, brought into the most intimate relation with Love. For Paul, '... knowledge of the one God is not theoretical speculation ... but is genuine only when there is corresponding *agapē* ...'[601] The difference between *now* and *then* is that *now* we only recognize dimly the fact that God's knowledge of us is Love because our knowledge of God is not yet Love. In the end-time our knowledge will become Love just as God's is *now*.

13

So: The word translated here as *so* is the Greek *nuni de*. This can also be translated 'now' as opposed to 'then', as it is in v. 12. Most modern commentators prefer to take it with the logical connotations of 'so'.

abide: Most commentators interpret *abide* here to express the opposite of *pass away* in vv. 8–10 – i.e. 'remain', even after the end of this present world. However, if the word has this meaning, then it must follow that *faith* and *hope*, along with *love*, remain after the end-time. Paul, however, states expressly in two places that this is not the case.[602]

One solution to this problem has been to take the *nuni de* as temporal, so that these three only *abide now*. Another solution has been to assume that Paul is here quoting part of a formula current in Corinth which includes the three items *faith*, *hope*, and *love*. In either case the statement that *love* is the *greatest* is taken to imply that *love* will abide forever.

Paul's aim, however, in this chapter is not to explain love *per se*. The question of its duration is raised only by way of comparison with some of the spiritual gifts. These love outlasts. We know from other writings of Paul that he has already associated love with faith and hope by the time he wrote 1 Corinthians.[603] There is an intimate association of faith, hope, and love, just as there is in the case of knowledge (understanding) and love.[604] As we indicated at the beginning of this chapter, Paul is concerned to find a category within which to understand the working of the Spirit. It is simple to show that love outlasts the gifts of tongues, knowledge, and prophecy. Religion without love is unthinkable. Love is the direct opposite of the behaviour of the all-too-imperfect Corinthian Christians. It is in fact the source of faith and hope as well as of patience and endurance.[605] And love is a never-failing source (v. 8).

600. Cp. Gal. 4^9.   601. R. Bultmann, loc. cit. (n. 599).
602. Cf. Rom 8^{24}; 2 Cor. 5^7; cp. Heb. 11^1.
603. Cf. 1 Thess. 1^3, 5^8; cp. Gal. $5^{5f.}$; Rom. $12^{6,9}$.
604. Cf. above on v. 12.   605. Cf. above on v. 7.

It is because it is the source of faith and hope that it must therefore be considered the *greatest*. That is the only adequate way to understand the operation of the Spirit. Faith is the way in which Christian men live, but only because of the God who loves them and causes Christ to live in them.[606] Paul is not concerned with how long faith and hope abide in any absolute sense. They *abide* in so far as they outlast all the spiritual gifts. But only love is adequate to explain the working of the Spirit.

Chapter 14

We have indicated above that the matter of speaking in tongues was a serious problem in Corinth.[607] It was a touchy subject because of its intimate connection with the inception of Christianity among these gentile Christians. Paul does not, therefore, approach the matter head on, but prepares his readers rather carefully. Chapters 12 and 13 constitute this preparation. Once Paul has portrayed the proper ordering of spiritual gifts within the believing community, and once he has characterized the Spirit as the divine love, he is ready to deal with the specific problem of speaking in tongues. Paul has already established the principle of diversity of gifts within the congregation. Now he fastens on to one of them, prophecy. This he uses as a foil against which to play off his analysis of speaking in tongues.

14$^{1-6}$

1Make love your aim, and earnestly desire the spiritual gifts, especially that you may prophesy. 2For one who speaks in a tongue speaks not to men but to God; for no one understands him, but he utters mysteries in the Spirit. 3On the other hand, he who prophesies speaks to men for their upbuilding and encouragement and consolation. 4He who speaks in a tongue edifies himself, but he who prophesies edifies the church. 5Now I want you all to speak in tongues, but even more to prophesy. He who prophesies is greater

606. Cf. Gal. 2^{20}.
607. Cf. general Introduction, pp. xxviiiff., and also the introduction to Chapters 12–14.

than he who speaks in tongues, unless some one interprets, so that the church may be edified.

⁶Now, brethren, if I come to you speaking in tongues, how shall I benefit you unless I bring you some revelation or knowledge or prophecy or teaching?

෩෩

1

Make love your aim: This concludes what Paul has been saying in Chapter 13, in his digression on love.

earnestly desire the spiritual gifts: This admonition picks up the phrase *earnestly desire (the higher gifts)* of 12³¹. At the end of Chapter 12, Paul was not prepared to be quite so specific about what the *higher gifts* were. Now he is ready to say that prophecy is to be preferred to speaking in tongues, and to explain why this is so.

2

no one understands him: This is Paul's basic criticism of the one who speaks in tongues. There is no doubt but that he has the Spirit.[608] No one, however, can make sense of what he says.[609]

mysteries: The basis of comparison between prophecy and speaking in tongues is strengthened by the fact that both activities deal in things which are divine secrets revealed to selected individuals.[610] The difference between the prophet and one who speaks in tongues is that in the case of the latter the secrets remain hidden, while the former reveals them to his fellow believers.

in the Spirit: The Greek is inexplicit here. It is difficult to know whether the divine or one's human spirit is implied. The latter is certainly the meaning in vv. 14–16.

3

upbuilding and encouragement and consolation: These are not coordinate terms. The last two define what Paul means by upbuilding.[611]

608. Cf. below on v. 21f.
609. What was heard was probably some form of unintelligible speech rather than just inarticulate sounds; cf. Rom. 8²⁶.
610. Cf. H. Greeven, op. cit. (n. 561), 9.
611. Cf. Schlatter, ad loc. Cp. above on *the common good* (12⁷).

5

unless some one interprets:[612] This refers to someone, perhaps the person himself (Moffat), who has the gift to understand what is being said in tongues and to interpret this to the rest of the congregation. In this case, Paul admits that what he has said concerning the relative merits of prophecy and speaking in tongues would not hold true.

6

revelation or knowledge or prophecy or teaching: An artful arrangement of terms in which the first pair constitutes the usual product of the second pair.[613]

14⁷⁻¹²

⁷*If even lifeless instruments, such as the flute or the harp, do not give distinct notes, how will anyone know what is played?* ⁸*And if the bugle gives an indistinct sound, who will get ready for battle?* ⁹*So with yourselves; if you in a tongue utter speech that is not intelligible, how will anyone know what is said? For you will be speaking into the air.* ¹⁰*There are doubtless many different languages in the world, and none is without meaning;* ¹¹*but if I do not know the meaning of the language, I shall be a foreigner to the speaker and the speaker a foreigner to me.* ¹²*So with yourselves; since you are eager for manifestations of the Spirit, strive to excel in building up the church.*

Paul uses three analogies to make his point: (1) musical instruments; (2) the military trumpet; (3) human language. The first two are two versions of the same analogy.

❦

7f.
distinct notes . . . indistinct sound: If the ear cannot make out the melody or the 'call', the desired results will not be achieved.

9
So with yourselves: Paul refers to the Corinthians' status as humans who do have a voice – the primary purpose of which, he strongly implies, is communication.

612. Cf. above on 12^{10,30}.   613. Cf. R.-P., ad loc.

11

a foreigner: The word in Greek is *barbaros.* A *barbaros* was one who did not speak Greek and therefore was without the benefit of Greek culture.

12

eager for manifestations of the Spirit: The Greek is literally 'eager for spirits'. This is certainly an accommodation of language to the popular idiom of the hellenistic world.[614] Like v. 32 below, it betrays a touch of irony.[615]

14[13-19]

> [13]*Therefore, he who speaks in a tongue should pray for the power to interpret.* [14]*For if I pray in a tongue, my spirit prays but my mind is unfruitful.* [15]*What am I to do? I will pray with the spirit and I will pray with the mind also; I will sing with the spirit and I will sing with the mind also.* [16]*Otherwise, if you bless with the spirit, how can any one in the position of an outsider say the 'Amen' to your thanksgiving when he does not know what you are saying?* [17]*For you may give thanks well enough, but the other man is not edified.* [18]*I thank God that I speak in tongues more than you all;* [19]*nevertheless, in church I would rather speak five words with my mind, in order to instruct others, than ten thousand words in a tongue.*

Paul addresses himself now to the specific situation of being *in church* (v. 19) i.e. in the assembly of Christians gathered for worship.

ॐ

13

The implication here is that the person who *speaks in a tongue* might also be, were it granted him, the one to interpret.[616] The problem is what is the relation of *pray* (v. 14), *sing* (v. 15), and *bless* (v. 16) to speaking in tongues? Paul perhaps implies in 12[10] above that 'speaking' in tongues takes different forms, i.e. *various kinds of tongues.*[617]

Paul has certainly made it quite explicit throughout his discussion of this gift of the Spirit, speaking in tongues, that the setting with which

614. Cf. Weiss, *ad loc.*   615. Cf. R.-P., *ad loc.*
616. Cf. above on v. 5, and below on v. 27.   617. Cp. 12[28].

he is concerned is the worship assembly.[618] Paul would seem to be speaking somewhat hypothetically: if I [were to] pray [after the fashion of those who speak] in a tongue, who would profit? Even my own rational self (mind) does not profit but remains *unfruitful* (v. 14). The same argument holds in the case of singing.

16
Blessing, in the Jewish tradition, is a prayer which has God as its object, i.e. one blesses God for life, health, children, etc. To this prayer the congregation is to assent by saying *amen*.[619]

any one in the position of an outsider: The Greek word translated here outsider is *idiōtēs*. It can mean one who is a private citizen as opposed to an official. In religious circles it can refer to the 'laity' as opposed to the priests or 'clergy'. It can also refer to the person who lacks expertise as opposed to the 'professional' or trained person. It is this latter sense which fits best here. But it must be noted that from the congregation's point of view everyone was an *outsider* as opposed to the ecstatic.[620] This is most ironic on Paul's part, as the following verses show. But the gift of tongues does not initiate one into the speech of anyone else who speaks in tongues.

18f.[621]
Paul picks up the term *thanks* from above (vv. 16, 17). The tone could be somewhat ironic, i.e. this is the subject of his thanksgiving. What was a purely hypothetical statement in 13^1 now becomes an assertion.

19
The instruction of new or aspiring members of the community was probably a regular part of the activity associated with the Christian worship assembly.[622]

ten thousand: Cp. Matthew $18^{24ff.}$; 1 Cor. 4^{15}.

[20]*Brethren, do not be children in your thinking; be babes in evil, but in thinking be mature.* [21]*In the law it is written, 'By men of strange tongues and by the lips of foreigners will I speak to this people, and even then they*

618. Cf. $14^{4,12}$.   619. Cf. S.-B., ad loc.   620. N.E.B.: 'plain man'.
621. Cf. 2 Cor. $12^{1ff.}$.   622. Cf. Gal. 6^6; Luke 1^4; Acts 18^{25}; cp. Rom. 2^8.

will not listen to me, says the Lord.' ²²*Thus, tongues are a sign not for believers but for unbelievers, while prophecy is not for unbelievers but for believers.* ²³*If, therefore, the whole church assembles and all speak in tongues, and outsiders or unbelievers enter, will they not say that you are mad?* ²⁴*But if all prophesy, and an unbeliever or outsider enters, he is convicted by all, he is called to account by all,* ²⁵*the secrets of his heart are disclosed; and so, falling on his face, he will worship God and declare that God is really among you.*

෨෨

20

Paul calls here for a considerable degree of maturity on the part of the Corinthian Christians.[623]

be babes in evil: Their simplicity and lack of maturity is more in place as regards *evil* or 'malice'.[624] Paul may here refer to the example he used above in 13¹¹.[625]

21f.

The main problem in this section has to do with the relation of this paraphrase in Isa. 28¹¹f. to Paul's conclusion in v. 22 that . . . *tongues are a sign, not for believers, but for unbelievers.* . . . Paul cites Isa. 28¹¹f. in a form different from that in the Greek Old Testament as we know it (the Septuagint) and may have been using a version known to the Jewish translator Aquila.[626] The point of the quotation is usually taken by most commentators to be in the catch word *strange tongues* (v. 21), which Paul interprets in rabbinic fashion to refer to the gift of speaking in tongues. But it is also clear that the fact that *they* (in the Old Testament, the Israelites) will *not listen to me* (God) also represents for Paul the inability of anyone who does not have the gift of interpretation to understand what the ecstatic says. As most commentators admit, it is hard to see how this quotation substantiates Paul's conclusion that tongues are a sign for the unbeliever.

Sign is taken by most as a sign of judgement, as in Isa. 20³ or Luke 2³⁴. That is, it is not a sign by which men come to know God, but a means God uses to harden their hearts.[627] There are two problems with this:

1. It is difficult to see how speaking in tongues can be a sign only because people did not understand what the speaker meant. Paul under-

623. Cf. *mature*, 2⁶ above.   624. Cf. R.-P., ad loc.
625. Cp. Matt. 18³.   626. Cf. Origen, *Philocalia*, 9, 2.
627. Cf. Weiss, ad loc.

stands the Old Testament statement to mean that the strange tongues were a sign and the Israelites (some of them) did not hearken unto the sign.

2. Tongues were interpreted, as we have pointed out above, by the Corinthians in the most positive way, that is as a sign of God's (the Spirit's) presence. More particularly, as we have also conjectured above, speaking in tongues may have been intimately connected with the gift of the Spirit on the basis of which gentiles became fellow Christians with those Jews who had already accepted Jesus.

The gift of speaking in tongues had been a *sign for the unbeliever* in the sense that it provided him with his *entrée* into the Jewish-Christian community. It was a sign then and had a meaning for them. When they were unbelievers, i.e. not yet Christians, it was the sign that they were participants in God's spirit and could be admitted into the Christian community. But now that they are *believers*, speaking in tongues no longer has this function. In fact, speaking in tongues at this juncture only serves to confuse the *unbeliever* or the *outsider* who does not appreciate the meaning of the ecstatic speech.[628] Now that they are believers *prophecy* is more to the point, not only because it builds up the community,[629] but because of the effect which it has upon those who do not belong to the Christian community.

24f.
he is convicted . . . called to account . . . the secrets of his heart are disclosed: The question here concerns the precise nature of this occurrence. Is it something which takes place within the individual's conscience, or does it have an outward manifestation? Is some kind of mind-reading involved, or is this just inward recognition by the individual leading to his conversion? Some parallels to this seem to imply an outward manifestation along with a kind of mindreading.[630] In any event the result is a confession of faith in the God of the Christians.

God is really among you: This is a stereotyped confession in the biblical tradition.[631] It indicates the acceptance of one deity as opposed to another.[632]

628. Cp. Acts 2^{13}. On *outsider*, cf. above on v. 16.
629. 14^{2-5}.
630. Cf. John 4^{19}; Acts $5^{3f.}$; cp. John 16^8; Heb. $4^{12f.}$.
631. Cf. 1 Kings 18^{39}; Isa. 45^{14}; Zech. 8^{23}; Dan. 2^{47}.
632. Cf. 1 Thess. 1^9.

²⁶*What then, brethren? When you come together, each one has a hymn, a lesson, a revelation, a tongue, or an interpretation. Let all things be done for edification.* ²⁷*If any speak in a tongue, let there be only two or at most three, and each in turn; and let one interpret.* ²⁸*But if there is no one to interpret, let each of them keep silence in church and speak to himself and to God.* ²⁹*Let two or three prophets speak, and let the others weigh what is said.* ³⁰*If a revelation is made to another sitting by, let the first be silent.* ³¹*For you can all prophesy one by one, so that all may learn and all be encouraged;* ³²*and the spirits of prophets are subject to prophets.* ³³*For God is not a God of confusion but of peace.*

ະຂນ

26

each one: This should not be overemphasized. Paul is simply following his own principle of the variety of the gifts of the Spirit.⁶³³ His point here is that the diversity which is bound to exist within a community such as that at Corinth must serve its true purpose, which is *building up the church* (v. 12) or *edification.* This purpose Paul restates at the conclusion of this section as *peace* rather than *confusion.*⁶³⁴

27f.

The rules governing those who speak in tongues are similar to those governing the prophets. Only one may speak at a time, and no more than three in all may speak in any one assembly.

28

The other limitations on those who speak in tongues.⁶³⁵

29ff.

While no time limit is applied, the restrictions which Paul places upon the prophets may have been one way to enforce such a limit.⁶³⁶ One prophet must defer to the next.

let the others weigh what is said: Here we have the exercise of the gift mentioned in 12¹⁰, *the ability to distinguish between spirits,* i.e. whether

---

633. Cf. 12⁴ᶠᶠ· above. 634. Cp. 7¹⁵.
635. Cf. above on v. 5. 636. *Martyrdom of Polycarp,* 7.

they are true or false. In all probability *the others* here refers not to the *others* of the congregation but to the other prophets. The prophets probably constituted an identifiable group within the congregation in spite of the implications of Paul's wish in 14⁵ and his statement in v. 31, *you can all prophesy.* This is better taken in the sense that all who do prophesy can do so *one by one,* etc.[637]

so that all may learn: This refers to the content of the prophets' message, which was believed to be from the risen Lord himself.[638] One should probably distinguish this from the teaching gift, which concerned itself mainly with tradition.[639]

33a

confusion . . . peace: Again, following his general principle of mutuality within the believing fellowship,[640] Paul insists that different prophecies should be complementary to one another. It is conceivable that this is implied in the *all may learn* etc. of v. 31, that is one person would appreciate the words of one prophet, while another would appreciate the words of another prophet. The decency and order of which Paul speaks in v. 40 below is another version of this same thought. But this is no end itself. The ultimate end in Paul's thought is always the upbuilding of the whole congregation.[641]

14^{33b-35}

As in all the churches of the saints, ³⁴*the women should keep silence in the churches. For they are not permitted to speak, but should be subordinate, as even the law says.* ³⁵*If there is anything they desire to know, let them ask their husbands at home. For it is shameful for a woman to speak in church.*

The idea that women should be silent in the congregational assembly is in direct contradiction to Paul's statements concerning female prophets in 11²⁻¹⁶ above. This in itself would be a good *prima facie* reason for suspecting an interpolation[642] which represents more the thought behind 1 Tim. 2¹¹ᶠ· or Eph. 5²². Further, the continuity of thought between v. 33a and v. 36 is interrupted by vv. 33b–35. There

---

637. H. Greeven, op. cit. (n. 561), 10f.   638. Cf. above on 7¹⁰.
639. H. Greeven, op. cit. (n. 561), 28.   640. Cf. above on 12²⁵ᶠ·.
641. Cf. above v. 26.   642. Cf. Weiss, ad loc.

are two possible explanations for the contradiction of this passage with 11^{2ff}.

1. Paul has in mind different kinds of gatherings, the one in Chapter 11 being less formal than that in Chapter 14.

2. He has in mind different levels of discourse, the level in Chapter 11 being higher (prophecy) than that of Chapter 14 (mere chatter or conversation). The un-Pauline character, however, of the appeal to the law (v. 34), the contradiction implied with Paul's position with regard to the woman in marriage,[643] and the fact that the argument as to what is *shameful* (v. 35) is quite out of line with the rest of the chapter, all point to non-Pauline authorship for this section.[644]

14^{36-40}

[36]*What! Did the word of God originate with you, or are you the only ones it has reached?*

[37]*If any one thinks that he is a prophet, or spiritual, he should acknowledge that what I am writing to you is a command of the Lord.* [38]*If any one does not recognize this, he is not recognized.* [39]*So, my brethren, earnestly desire to prophesy, and do not forbid speaking in tongues;* [40]*but all things should be done decently and in order.*

If vv. 33b–35 are omitted, at least from their present context,[645] the thought of v. 36 refers to Paul's statements concerning prophecy in vv. 26–33. Paul reminds the Corinthians that they are neither the authors of the Gospel nor its sole recipients.[646] They are in no position to be the sole arbiters of their own procedures. Paul claims the authority, probably as a prophet himself or on the basis of someone else's prophecy, to legislate procedure for the Corinthian Church.[647]

ॐ

643. Cf. above on 7^{3-4}.
644. G. Fitzer, *Das Weib schweige in der Gemeinde*, 1963, 4–13.
645. Some manuscripts place them after v. 40.
646. Cp. 4^{7ff}.
647. Cf. 2^{10-16}, 7^{40}; cp. 2 Cor. 13^{3}.

38

If any one does not recognize this, he is not recognized: Here, in what looks like a legal formula,[648] Paul states the consequences of not accepting his *dicta* regarding spiritual gifts – rejection by God and lack of recognition by the community.

He sums up this section in a dialectical[649] fashion which is typically Pauline and representative of this period of rapid development of the church's life: (1) spiritual gifts are to be encouraged, not discouraged; but (2) the order of the proceedings is to be maintained.[650]

648. Cf. E. Käsemann, op. cit. (n. 267), 71f.

649. Cf. E. Schweizer, 'The Service of Worship. An Exposition of 1 Corinthians 14', op. cit. (n. 542), 342.

650. Cf. above on v. 33a.

Chapter 15

In this chapter Paul takes up the matter of the resurrection.[651] The chapter divides into four major sections. (1) Verses 1–11: statement of the tradition as Paul has received it and as he has in turn passed it on to the Corinthian congregations. (2) Verses 12–34: Paul's attempt to deal with those who deny the resurrection of the dead even while they profess Christ risen. (3) Verses 35–49: speculation by Paul on the manner of the resurrection, particularly the nature of the resurrection body. (4) Verses 51–8: a kind of coda, in which the resurrection at the last day is described in terms which can only be characterized as highly poetic.

15:1-11   THE TRADITION OF JESUS'S RESURRECTION

¹Now I would remind you, brethren, in what terms I preached to you the gospel, which you received, in which you stand, ²by which you are saved, if you hold it fast – unless you believed in vain.

³For I delivered to you as of first importance what I also received, that Christ died for our sins in accordance with the scriptures, ⁴that he was buried, that he was raised on the third day in accordance with the scriptures, ⁵and that he appeared to Cephas, then to the twelve. ⁶Then he appeared to more than five hundred brethren at one time, most of whom are still alive, though some have fallen asleep. ⁷Then he appeared to James, then to all the apostles. ⁸Last of all, as to one untimely born, he appeared also to me. ⁹For I am the least of the apostles, unfit to be called an apostle, because I persecuted the church of God. ¹⁰But by the grace of God I am what I am, and his grace toward me was not in vain. On the contrary, I worked harder than any of them, though it was not I, but the grace of God which is with me. ¹¹Whether then it was I or they, so we preach and so you believed.

The construction does not follow the pattern of Chapters 12–14, and 16, both of which begin with *Now concerning* followed by a statement

651. Cf. general Introduction, pp. xxi-xxv.

of the specific subject to be treated. This has led some to think that this chapter was not originally in this present context. It could come immediately after 11³⁴, since this chapter also deals with traditional material.⁶⁵²

א א א

1f.
I would remind: The Greek, *gnōrizē*, should be rendered *I make known*.

This obvious meaning conflicts with what Paul is about to say in v. 3, that what he is talking about is in fact part of a tradition (pre-Pauline) which he has imparted to them earlier. *I make known to you* must therefore have the nature of a 'gentle reproof'.⁶⁵³

The form of what follows is confused in the Greek. Much depends upon the punctuation. Some put the full stop after *saved*, others after *stand*. The second alternative makes *saved* part of the conditional *if you hold it fast* clause. This is probably not the emphasis of Paul. Rather, he places the conditional *if you hold it fast* clause towards the end of the thought. Its connection is with *the terms (in which) I preached to you*. This becomes clear from the great emphasis which Paul is about to place upon a formula-expression of the tradition (vv. 3–7), all the elements of which he considers to be essential. The full stop should therefore come after *saved*.

3
I delivered . . . what I also received: This is a tradition which antedated Paul. He does not feel bound by it, as he will show by the addition which he makes to it in v. 8 below. On the other hand, he feels it important for the Corinthian Church to take full cognizance of the precise form (see above vv. 1, 2) in which it has been handed down. This may represent a formula which was used by the rabbis to introduce traditional material.⁶⁵⁴

as of first importance: The preaching of the Gospel or the teaching of catechumens most probably began with those elements of the tradition which were considered primary. Other elements, such as the traditions discussed by Paul in Chapter 11 (vv. 23f.), could wait until later in the process of initiation.⁶⁵⁵

652. Cf. 11²ᶠ·,²³ᶠ·.   653. Cf. R.-P., ad loc.
654. Cf. Fr. Büchsel, '*Didomi . . . paradidomi*', *ThWbNT*, II, 173f. Also Mishnah, *Aboth*, I, 1.
655. Cf. Heb. 6¹⁻³.

158

Christ died: Cf. the general Introduction, on the Resurrection.

for our sins: Paul usually says *for us*, as in 2 Cor. 5^{21} and Gal. 3^{13}. Since this is the only occurrence of this particular usage in his letters, we may assume he means here *for us sinners.* This reflects the experience of the forgiveness of sins which was central to the experience of the early church,[656] an experience which was dramatized in the sacramental rite of Baptism and actualized in the mutual forgiveness of the members of the community.[657] It is this experience of forgiveness which Paul will use later in this chapter[658] to strengthen his argument concerning the resurrection of the dead.

in accordance with the scriptures: That Christ died was, so to speak, a matter of record in the early Christian community. This was not saving knowledge and would not have been necessarily according to the scriptures. The use of the phrase *in accordance with the scriptures* occurs again in v. 4, and refers to the phrase *on the third day.* That Jesus died, was *buried,* and was *raised* were the basic elements of the Christian tradition. That forgiveness of sins was somehow related to the belief that Jesus rose on the third day is a matter of interpretation. The process of interpretation involved searching the Jewish scriptures for clues as to the meaning of the events of the Passion, Death and Resurrection of Jesus.[659] The searching of the scriptures which underlies the phrase *in*

656. Cf. Acts 2^{38}, 5^{31}, 10^{43}, 13^{28}, 26^{18}; Eph. 1^7; Col. 1^{14}; cp. Mark 2^5 parr.

657. Cf. Mark 11^{25} par.

658. Cf. below on v. 17.

659. Cf. Luke 24^{25}. An early example of what this searching of the scriptures may have been like can be seen by a comparison of Mark 8^{12}, and Matt. 16^2 and 12$^{39ff.}$. In Mark 8^{12} Jesus is asked for a sign. He refuses to give one. In Matthew 16 the same scene is represented, except that Jesus's refusal is not categorical. He qualifies it by saying no sign will be given *except* the sign of Jonah (v. 2). In Matt. 12$^{39ff.}$, the occasion is the same: Jesus's enemies seek a sign, but this time *sign of Jonah* is interpreted in such a way as to be a type of the resurrection *on the third day.* One has only to compare the parallel in Luke 11$^{29-32}$ to see how the process of interpretation would and did take quite a different tack. Between the stage of the tradition represented in Mark 8^{12} and that of Matt. 16^2, someone had come to associate the 'sign' of which Jesus spoke with the story of Jonah. Between the stage of tradition represented in Matt. 16^2 and that represented in Matt. 12$^{39ff.}$ considerable interpretation of the 'sign of Jonah' had gone on in order to relate the sign of Jonah as a type of the resurrection *on the third day.* On the other hand the interpretation of the 'sign of Jonah' in the Lucan tradition proceeded to make it a type of repentance.

accordance with the scriptures was traced back by the tradition directly to the risen Lord[660] and therefore precedes the human witnesses to the risen Lord's appearances.[661]

5

he appeared: The Greek word translated here *appeared* is *ōpthē*. In the New Testament this word seems to have a special meaning. Apart from its use in connection with the resurrection appearances of Jesus, it is used exclusively in the New Testament of the appearance of objects in heaven and thus out of the sight of man.[662] By thus citing this part of the tradition, Paul is not proving that the resurrection took place. He is concerned to show his fidelity to the apostolic tradition and his own apostolic authority.[663]

Two different strands of tradition have possibly been fused together here in the process of transmission,[664] or perhaps even by Paul himself.[665] One comprises the appearances to Peter, the twelve, and the five hundred brethren. The other includes the appearances to James and all the apostles. The appearances of the risen Lord, as they are recounted in the N.T., are not just accounts to show that Jesus rose from the dead. They are rather, for the most part, accounts which include a word of commission and/or command from the risen Lord. This is also true in Paul's letters.[666] Paul is convinced that his encounter with the risen Lord has given him a commission quite on a par with that of the other apostles.[667] He may speak of himself as like one *untimely born* (v. 8) or as the *least of the apostles,* but he does not think of himself as any less an apostle. He is careful to point out in this connection that what he has been able to accomplish is more than all of them (v. 10).

to Cephas: Cp. Luke 24³⁴.

to the twelve: some early scribes attempted to change this reading to 'eleven'. The reference is to the apostolic college of twelve in the Gospel accounts.[668]

660. Cf. Luke 24^{25ff.}; Acts 1³.   661. Cf. Godet, ad loc.
662. Namely Moses and Elijah, Mark 9⁴ parr.; the ark of the covenant, Rev. 11¹⁹.
663. Cf. 9¹.
664. Cf. P. Winter, '1 Corinthians XV 3b–7', *Nov Test*, 2 (1957), 142–50.
665. Cf. E. Bammel, 'Herkunft und Function der Traditionselemente in I Cor. 15^{1–11}', *TZ*, 11 (1955), 401–19.
666. Cf. Matt. 28^{8–10}, 16²⁰; Luke 24^{13–25,36–49}; John 20^{11–17}, 21^{1–14}; cp.Gal. 1^{15ff.}; Acts 9^{15ff.}.
667. Cf. 1 Cor. 9^{1ff.}; cp. 2 Cor. 3^{1ff.}.
668. Cf. Mark 3^{14,16}, 4¹⁰, etc. Cp. Matt. 19²⁸.

6

to five hundred brethren: There is no other record in the N.T. of such an appearance. Some[669] have tried to associate this particular appearance with the account of Pentecost in Acts 2. This would not be totally impossible in the light of what is said in the Introduction concerning the resurrection.

most of whom are still alive, though some have fallen asleep: Along with the life in Christ, the life with the risen Lord, the life with the brethren, there remains, also as part of the Christian experience, death. That death among the brethren was a problem for some of the early believers is shown both in 1 Thess. 4¹³⁻¹⁸ and here in v. 29, where the concern is for those who have died. This clause is inserted here after the manner of an aside, not to prove anything, but to reinforce Paul's point about death – that it is a real thing which like Jesus they cannot avoid.

7

to James: There is no other reference to this appearance in the New Testament.[670]

to all the apostles: If the James referred to above is the brother of Jesus rather than the apostle, there would be considerable reason for a group looking to his leadership to characterize the leading group in the church as *the apostles* and not as *the twelve.* One can see in Luke-Acts that there was some problem in this regard.[671]

8ff.

For I am ... unfit to be called an apostle: The Greek word translated here *fit* is *hikanos.* It can mean 'sufficient' or 'suitable' (with sometimes the ancillary connotation of morally 'worthy'.[672] Paul's point in this section is to emphasize the parity of his apostolic credentials with those of Peter, the twelve, James and the apostles. On the face of it, Paul's persecution of the church[673] would have made him unsuitable to be an apostle. However, he emphasizes that apostleship is God's doing – *by*

669. Cf. E. von Dobschütz, *Ostern und Pfingsten*, 1903, 33ff. W. Schmithals, *Das kirchliche Apostelamt*, 1961, 177, 404.

670. But cf. *Evangelium ad hebraeos* in Jerome, *De viris illustribus 2.*

671. In Acts there is a group of qualified individuals from which members of the 'twelve' may be chosen. They are qualified by their intimate association with Jesus during his lifetime. Cf. G. Klein, *Die zwölf Apostel, Ursprung und Gehalt einer Idee*, 1967. Also Acts 1^{21ff.}.

672. Cf. W. Bauer, op cit. (n. 67), s.v.

673. Cf. Acts 8^{3ff.}.

the grace of God I am what I am. It is in this sense of suitability or un-suitability that we must understand the rather gross imagery of verse 8b.

as to one untimely born: This rather euphemistically renders the Greek *ektrōmati*, 'to one aborted'. The reference is to the aborted foetus. The temporal element of the analogy must not be pressed. The point of the analogy is in the occurrence of the event at a time other than the expected time, or in a way which is unexpected. The unusual element in the apostleship of Paul lay in the fact that he had *persecuted the church of God.*

15 12-19 THE RESURRECTION OF JESUS MEANS NOTHING, IF ONE DOES NOT BELIEVE IN THE RESURRECTION OF THE DEAD

[12]*Now if Christ is preached as raised from the dead, how can some of you say that there is no resurrection of the dead?* [13]*But if there is no resurrection of the dead, then Christ has not been raised;* [14]*if Christ has not been raised, then our preaching is in vain and your faith is in vain.* [15]*We are even found to be misrepresenting God, because we testified of God that he raised Christ, whom he did not raise if it is true that the dead are not raised.* [16]*For if the dead are not raised, then Christ has not been raised.* [17]*If Christ has not been raised, your faith is futile and you are still in your sins.* [18]*Then those also who have fallen asleep in Christ have perished.* [19]*If in this life only we have hoped in Christ, we are of all men most to be pitied.*

The two statements, (1) there is no resurrection of the dead and (2) Christ has been raised from the dead, seem to us, as we read them, to be mutually incompatible.[674] Nevertheless, it has been brought to Paul's attention[675] that some of the members of the Corinthian Church deny the resurrection of the dead. How could these people hold two seemingly incompatible notions? There are several possibilities. (1) The Corinthians, being gentiles, could not conceive of the

674. Cf. the general Introduction, pp. xxi–xxv.
675. It is not clear, because of the abruptness with which this subject is introduced, whether this subject had been raised by the Corinthians (cf. 7[1]) or was part of the material brought to Paul's attention by Chloe's people (cf. 1[11]).

bodily resurrection of a mere mortal. However, if Jesus were a special case and not a mere mortal, this would be no problem. (2) Paul had spoken, in his original preaching to the Corinthians, only of the resurrection of Jesus and had not included the idea of the resurrection for ordinary men.[676] (3) The Corinthians and Paul had a communications problem: either he had misunderstood them or they had misunderstood him, or both. As a result, the impression they gave was that they believed that the resurrection had, somehow, already occurred.[677]

In any case, the Corinthians were saying that whatever happened to Jesus, called resurrection, would not happen to Christians who had died or would die in the future.[678] Most commentators assume that Paul approaches this problem with the following syllogism in mind:

> There is no resurrection for dead men.
> Jesus was a dead man.
> Therefore, Jesus was not raised from the dead.

Paul's argument does not, in fact, operate in this fashion. Paul starts, not from some general principle or idea such as the resurrection of the dead, but from the specifically Christian experience of the Corinthian congregation.

The first experience of these Corinthian Christians was hearing the preaching of Paul (v. 14a). Their reaction to this preaching was one of faith (v. 14b). As we know from elsewhere in the epistle,[679] the Gospel was not primarily an intellectual quantity, but was conceived of as God's power, a power which emanated, so to speak, from the crucified and risen Lord as he found his faithful spokesmen in men such as Paul.[680] Part of the manifestation of this power, as it produced a faithful response in the hearers, was the experience of divine forgiveness and the hope that those who died in Christ had not perished.[681] Since both these happenings are presumably manifestations of the power of the risen Lord, if he is not risen then their faithful response

676. Cf. R. Bultmann, *Exegetische Probleme des zweiten Korintherbriefes,* 1963, 3-12.

677. Cf. H. J. Cadbury, 'Overconversion in Paul's Churches', *The Joy of Study,* ed. S. E. Johnson, 1951, 43-50.

678. Hurd, 229.   679. Cf. 2[4f.], 4[20]; cp. Mark 9[1].

680. Cf. Gal. 2[20]; cp. Rom. 8[9].   681. Cf. v. 17f.; cp. Mark 2[5] parr.

(in terms of being forgiven and their hope for the faithful dead) is vain, empty. This experience of forgiveness and hope would have, if Christ had not been raised, no ultimate meaning (i.e. it would be only in *this* life), and Christians basing their lives upon an illusion would be of all men the most to be pitied (v. 19).

The arguments of most commentators are generally unsatisfactory in regard to this passage, because they still insist on over-intellectualizing what Paul means here by preaching and faith and then trying to find the objective basis for this preaching and this faith in an event referred to as the resurrection. Paul is not arguing here about the resurrection of Christ. He is arguing about the faulty expression of the Christian Gospel, which has evidently gained credence in Corinth: Christ is risen, but the dead don't rise. If one cannot say, as part of the proclamation of the Christian message, that the dead are not raised, then it is meaningless to talk about Christ being raised. The life in Christ, when it is intellectualized to the point of having nothing to do with man's very human fear of death and his horror of ultimate extinction (i.e. a hope only in this life), becomes the biggest joke of all, because it is one which we play on ourselves.[682] Any thought which man has of the future is, after all, a projection on the basis of present experience. This present experience can issue either in faith, which projects hope, or in despair, which does not. Paul speaks here, as the first Christian theologian, of the legitimacy of the resurrection of the dead as an expression of this Christian hope on the basis of the experience of the risen Lord – preaching, forgiveness, hope for the dead.

15^{20-34}

[20]But in fact Christ has been raised from the dead, the first fruits of those who have fallen asleep. [21]For as by a man came death, by a man has come also the resurrection of the dead. [22]For *as in Adam all die*, so also in Christ shall all be made alive. [23]But each in his own order: Christ the first fruits, then at his coming those who belong to Christ. [24]Then comes the end, when he delivers the kingdom to God the Father after destroying every rule and

682. Cp. Apocalypse of Baruch 21[13].

every authority and power. 25*For he must reign until he has put all his enemies under his feet.* 26*The last enemy to be destroyed is death.* 27*'For God has put all things in subjection under his feet.' But when it says, 'All things are put in subjection under him,' it is plain that he is excepted who put all things under him.* 28*When all things are subjected to him, then the Son himself will also be subjected to him who put all things under him, that God may be everything to every one.*

29*Otherwise, what do people mean by being baptized on behalf of the dead? If the dead are not raised at all, why are people baptized on their behalf?* 30*Why am I in peril every hour?* 31*I protest, brethren, by my pride in you which I have in Christ Jesus our Lord, I die every day!* 32*What do I gain if, humanly speaking, I fought with beasts at Ephesus? If the dead are not raised, 'Let us eat and drink, for tomorrow we die.'* 33*Do not be deceived: 'Bad company ruins good morals.'* 34*Come to your right mind, and sin no more. For some have no knowledge of God. I say this to your shame.*

ຂໍ້

20
Christ has been raised from the dead: Paul proclaims the message of salvation; not this time by way of admonition, but as the word with power,[683] much as he probably proclaimed it when he first came to Corinth.

the first fruits of those who have fallen asleep: Paul interprets the meaning of the proclamation to show the relation between Christ risen and the evil powers of this age (especially death). Christ risen is the beginning of a process – *the first fruits.*[684] It is the *order* of Jesus to be first and his followers to come after (v. 23).

21
For as by a man came death: Paul mentions here only by allusion the process whereby he conceives that death, the ultimate power inimical to man, came into the world of man. He is more explicit in Rom. 5, where he points out that it was through Adam's sin that death gained its entrance to and domination over man.[685]

683. Cf. 2$^{4f.}$.
684. Paul uses the analogy of the representative offering of a sheaf of grain in the Temple on the morning of Passover. He uses this in the same way as he does the word *arrabōn*, 'earnest' or down-payment, Cf. 2 Cor. 1^{22}, 5^{5}; cp. Rom. 8^{23}, 11^{16}, 16^{5}.
685. Cf. Gen. 3$^{17-19}$.

22ff.

in Adam all die . . . in Christ shall all be made alive: Resurrection would presumably imply the reversal of the process begun by Adam's sin and the destruction of death. This is evidently conceived on a cosmic scale, since Paul says *all* die and *all* shall be made alive.[686]

But we know from Rom. 5 that Paul did not conceive of Christ as simply reversing the process begun by Adam, even though he can speak of Adam as the type of Christ.[687] Paul also emphasizes that the gift (Christ) is not of the same order as the transgression.[688] What begins in Christ comes to its conclusion only at the *end* (v. 24). The process is in one sense the reversal of the effects of Adam's sin to the extent that it involves the destruction of all those powers hostile to God including death (v. 24). But the end of the story is not the overcoming of death, but the granting of a new life – the re-creation of man. The resurrection is not to be identified with the destruction of death[689] but as the 'consequence and sequel of that destruction'.[690] Christ, *in his own order*, is alive, having been in himself triumphant over death. Our turn will come when he has defeated all our enemies. Then there will be an event analogous to the Creation of Adam.[691] This can only come, in Paul's Jewish way of thinking, when this world order, with its powers inimical to God and its men characterized as 'flesh and blood', has been brought to an end (v. 24). Then Christ hands over the rule of the world of God, who, according to Jewish belief in Paul's day, would create a new world.[692] That which characterizes the world to come in Jewish thought is God's rule or, as it is spoken of in the synoptic Gospels, the Kingdom of God. This is the world for which Jesus instructs his followers to pray.[693] This is the world, then, for which the church of Paul's day waited, which already had been revealed (as a foretaste only, to be sure) in Jesus's resurrection, of which one was afforded glimpses in the Spirit-filled life of the church.[694] It is a world which to a certain extent is already being formed for those who have faith.[695] This interim time is the time of the church. It is not necessary to think of a kind of millennium or 'Kingdom of the Messiah', as did

686. Cf. I Cor. 6^2, 11^{32}. Our thought is that the world is mentioned in these two passages and would present all men as participating in the general resurrection.

687. Cf. Rom. 5^{14}.   688. ibid., 5$^{15ff.}$.   689. *Contra* Allo, et al., ad loc.

690. Cf. N. Dahl, op. cit. (n. 457), 78, 4.   691. Cf. below on vv. 45ff.

692. Cf. W. D. Davies, op. cit. (n. 533 above), 49, 290.

693. Cf. Matt. 6^{10}; Luke 11^2.   694. Cf. Chapters 12 and 13.

695. Cf. J. A. T. Robinson, op. cit. (n. 287), 73ff.; M. E. Dahl, *The Resurrection of the Body. A Study of 1 Corinthians 15*, 1962, 115. Cf. 2 Cor. 4^{16}, 5^{17}.

Johannes Weiss[696] and Albert Schweitzer.[697] This interim time between the resurrection of Christ and the end of the world will see the preparation for God's absolute rule. All this has been prophesied in the scriptures.[698] Paul attempts to avoid any possible ambiguity concerning the word *all* in the quotation in his discussion of 'all things' in v. 27. *All things*, he says, does not include the one *who put all things under him.* There is still a measure of confusion, however.

In the Psalms the one who subjects is clearly God. It is also fairly clear that Paul understands that the one who does the subjecting (v. 27) is Christ, who then, having subjected all things to God, in turn subjects himself. Perhaps, as Allo suggests,[699] we should remember that the Father does not suspend his sovereignty during the reign of Christ.

28

The Son himself will also be subjected to him who put all things under him, that God may be everything to every one: One might contrast this expression of the final act of the drama of salvation with the picture in Philippians 2⁵ᶠᶠ·: there, the redeemer is equal with God to begin with, empties himself, becomes human, dies, is exalted, and receives a name above every name, all to the glory of God. Here, the redeemer reigns only until all things are made subject to him. Then he himself becomes subject to God. It may be significant in this connection that the main point of Paul's discussion here in 1 Cor. 15, the resurrection, is never mentioned in the above section in Philippians.[700] The end result of the reign of Christ is the establishment of God's rule. This is the case both in Phil. 2 and in I Cor. 15. The difference would seem to be that in Phil. 2 what is emphasized is the confession (by every tongue): Jesus is Lord; while in 1 Cor. 15 it is the defeat of the hostile powers. This is good evidence that the problems which Paul faced in Corinth were quite different from those he encountered in Philippi. There is a restraint[701] evident here in 1 Cor. 15 which Paul finds unnecessary in writing to the Philippians. The particular misunderstanding of the Corinthian Church[702] could best be handled by playing down the position of Christ as a heavenly figure.

696. Cf. Weiss, ad loc.
697. Cf. A. Schweitzer, op. cit. (n. 532), 75ff.
698. Cf. v. 25 (Psalm 110¹); v. 27 (Psalm 8⁷).
699. Cf. Allo, 444.
700. Cf. general Introduction, p. xxii.
701. Cf. K. Wegenast, op. cit. (n. 477), 83.
702. Cf. general Introduction, pp. xxivf.

29

what do people mean by being baptized on behalf of the dead?: Despite the many protests to the contrary,[703] it is evident here that there was in the Corinthian Church a practice of Baptism which was believed to have a vicarious effect upon the unbaptized dead.[704] Paul neither approves nor disapproves of the practice. Clearly, it was condemned eventually and survived only among some of the heretical sects.[705] It is upon this verse that Bultmann bases his claim that Paul has misunderstood the Corinthians' statement: There is no resurrection of the dead.[706] It is clear from this verse that the Corinthians were as concerned for the dead as were the Thessalonians whom Paul admonishes not 'to sorrow for the dead as those who have no hope'.[707]

30f.

Why am I in peril every hour . . . I die every day: We know that Paul had many trials and narrow escapes from death in the course of his life as a Christian.[708] He could refer to life as a Christian as a 'dying daily', evidently drawing upon Psalm 44 (43 in LXX)²³. There was perhaps, as Godet suggests, the constant danger of apprehension by the civil (Roman) or the religious (Jewish) authority. As one who had worked hard for the establishment in Jerusalem, Paul knew only too well what he was up against. *My pride in you:* Most take the word *you* here to be the object of *pride*, i.e. Paul has pride in what has been accomplished in Corinth.[709] The construction is awkward. Could it be that it means *your* in the possessive sense, i.e. Paul's many trials and tribulations are in fact a source of pride for the Corinthians just as they are for him? In any case it is of no avail if the dead are not raised, even to Paul's trials *with beasts at Ephesus.*

703. Many attempts have been made to change the obvious meaning of these verses: Godet – it really means 'baptism of blood'; Moffat – it refers to filling up the number of the elect by proxy; R.-P. – persons previously inclined to Christianity were baptized out of affection for some Christian now dead who had prayed for their conversion.

704. Cf. Goudge, ad loc.; 2 Macc. 12⁴³⁻⁵; Tertullian, *Contra Marcionem*, v. 10, 3.

705. Cf. Héring, Lietzmann, Weiss, ad loc.

706. Bultmann, loc. cit. (n. 676).

707. I Thess. 4¹³.

708. Cf. 2 Cor. 11²³⁻⁷; cp. Rom. 8³⁵.

709. Cf. 2 Cor. 3¹ᶠ·, where the Corinthians are described as Paul's letter of recommendation. Cp. 2 Cor. 4¹¹ᶠ·.

32

Does Paul mean here that he was literally in the arena in Ephesus?[710] Does he mean this in a metaphorical sense, that is that he contended with men who were like beasts?[711] Or is Paul here speaking hypothetically?[712] Speaking practically, Paul would not have survived an encounter with the beasts in the arena, Shaw's *Androcles* notwithstanding. Speaking grammatically, the third possibility is not a good one, since Paul uses the indicative rather than the subjunctive. Whatever he did in Ephesus, Paul states that it was *humanly speaking*. The 'if' must go here only with the verb, and not with the *humanly speaking* which modifies the verb. The tendency of commentators is to relate *humanly speaking* to the statement 'there is no resurrection of the dead'. As we have seen, that is something of a non-human statement. The problem is not that the Corinthians lack a super-terrestrial viewpoint, but that they are too much oriented in that direction. One suspects that if one is to fight with beasts, die daily, endure danger, all these things will be done humanly speaking. But they are also, from Paul's point of view and the Christian point of view, done in faith. It has been suggested that Paul here conceives of two possibilities, enduring these things from a human perspective, or enduring these things from a super-terrestrial, I-believe-in-the-resurrection perspective.[713] Clearly, these are not the alternatives which Paul has in mind. The alternatives are, humanly speaking, to endure hardships or to concentrate upon *eating and drinking, because tomorrow we die*. Paul thus emphasizes the inevitability of death. Now, he implies, if this means that death is one of the ultimate givens in the scheme of things, which is perhaps what underlies the Corinthian statement that there is no resurrection of the dead, then one should follow the words of scripture – Eat, drink, and be merry – tomorrow we die.[714]

But Paul's point in 1 Cor. 15 is that death, though humanly speaking inevitable, is not part of the ultimate character of God's creation. It will, through a series of events of which the resurrection of Jesus is the first, be destroyed, and man will be transformed.[715]

33

Do not be deceived: 'Bad company ruins good morals':[716] Paul cites this proverb with evident approval. If one associates with a group of corrupt people, one will eventually be corrupted (or repelled). Paul would

710. Cf. Godet, ad loc.
711. Cf. Allo, ad loc.; Ignatius, *Romans*, v. 1; Goudge, R.-P., ad loc.
712. Cf. Héring, ad loc.   713. Cf. Allo, Héring, ad loc.
714. Isa. 22¹³ (LXX).   715. Cf. Dahl, Robinson, loc cit. (n. 695).
716. Menander, *Thais*.

emphasize here that this is no matter of mere theory in which he is indulging himself. Rather, how one expresses one's Christian faith is intimately related to one's whole way of life. How one expresses one's Christian convictions influences and is influenced by how one lives. Paul thinks that there is something ultimately corrupting about a person who can say: Christ is risen from the dead and There is no resurrection of the dead.

15³⁵⁻⁴⁹ SPECULATION ON THE RESURRECTION BODY

³⁵*But some one will ask, 'How are the dead raised? With what kind of body do they come?'* ³⁶*You foolish man! What you sow does not come to life unless it dies.* ³⁷*And what you sow is not the body which is to be, but a bare kernel, perhaps of wheat or of some other grain.* ³⁸*But God gives it a body as he has chosen, and to each kind of seed its own body.* ³⁹*For not all flesh is alike, but there is one kind for men, another for animals, another for birds, and another for fish.* ⁴⁰*There are celestial bodies and there are terrestrial bodies; but the glory of the celestial is one, and the glory of the terrestrial is another.* ⁴¹*There is one glory of the sun, and another glory of the moon, and another glory of the stars; for star differs from star in glory.*

⁴²*So is it with the resurrection of the dead. What is sown is perishable, what is raised is imperishable.* ⁴³*It is sown in dishonour, it is raised in glory. It is sown in weakness, it is raised in power.* ⁴⁴*It is sown a physical body, it is raised a spiritual body. If there is a physical body, there is also a spiritual body.* ⁴⁵*Thus it is written, 'The first man Adam became a living being'; the last Adam became a life-giving spirit.* ⁴⁶*But it is not the spiritual which is first but the physical, and then the spiritual.* ⁴⁷*The first man was from the earth, a man of dust; the second man is from heaven.* ⁴⁸*As was the man of dust, so are those who are of the dust; and as is the man of heaven, so are those who are of heaven.* ⁴⁹*Just as we have borne the image of the man of dust, we shall also bear the image of the man of heaven.*

ಬಬ

35
But some one will ask: This is probably a rhetorical device and does not represent an actual occurrence.[717]

717. Cf. Allo, ad loc. Paul seems to employ from time to time literary devices borrowed from the style called the diatribe. Cf. R. Bultmann, *Der Stil der paulinischen Predigt und die kynisch-stoische Diatribe*, 1910.

How are the dead raised: The argument has proceeded one stage beyond
where it was in v. 12, i.e. if one were to admit the possibility of resurrection for those who have died, in what manner will it happen?

With what kind of body: This is to narrow the question down to the *kind
of body* with which a dead person will participate in the resurrection.
The Jewish mind had some difficulties with this question, which caused
the rabbis to speculate at some length on the nature of the resurrection
body.[718] There were Jews who denied the resurrection.[719] And there
were Jews in New Testament times who were influenced by Greek
thoughts of immortality.[720]

If the Corinthians were thoroughly gentile-Greek in their thinking,
it is hard to see them asking this kind of a question. They might have
asked, How are dead *bodies* raised? or, Why does the immortal soul
need a perishable body? But not, With what kind of a body? This is
strictly part of Paul's argument.

What follows is what the Jews would call *haggadah*[721] or 'speculation'
on the basis of an accepted religious idea, in this case the resurrection.
The section divides itself into three sub-sections, according to the
analogy which Paul uses: (a) 35–9, terrestrial creatures; (b) 40–41, super-
terrestrial creatures; (c) Adam 45–9 (vv. 42–4 constitute a transition in
the argument).

35–9
Paul makes two points in this sub-section:

1. the principle of life *through* death appears to be built into the
scheme of creation;[722]

2. living creatures are all given the kind of flesh which is appropriate
to them.

Paul uses the analogy drawn from terrestrial living creatures as a
springboard for thinking about the existence of resurrected man. The
obvious thing about living creatures is their different appearances,[723] to
which Paul refers first as *body* and then as *flesh*. He supplements his
observations about the appearance of terrestrial living creatures with
the same observation about the astral bodies and their appearance or
'glory' (vv. 40–41).

718. Cf. W. D. Davies, op. cit. (n. 533), 299ff.
719. Cf. ibid., loc. cit. – the Sadducees and the Samaritans.
720. Cf. Josephus, *Jewish Wars*, ii, 10, 11 – the Essenes.
721. Cf. M. Adler, *The World of the Talmud*, 2nd ed. 1963, 72ff.
722. Cp. Mark 8^{35}; John 12^{24}.   723. Cf. Godet, ad loc.

42

So is it with the resurrection of the dead: The fact that Paul is here involved in speculative thinking is shown by the rather 'associative' way
in which he proceeds. He has established that terrestrial and astral
creatures differ from one another in appearance – in the case of terrestrial
creatures he uses the terms *body* and *flesh,* and in the case of the astral
creatures he uses *body* and *glory.* When Paul then refers by analogy to
the existence of resurrected man, he maintains the word *body* and sets
up a series of four contrasts between the *body* which is *sown* and the
body which is raised:

1. perishable	—	imperishable
2. dishonour	—	glory
3. weakness	—	power
4. a physical body	—	a spiritual body

Paul carries over two terms, *sown* and *glory,* from the preceding analogy.
It is obvious, however, that in his discussion of the *physical body* and the
spiritual body these terms do not carry quite the same meaning as they
had in the analogy: *sown* referred to something quite specific in the
case of seed; now, however, it refers in a highly figurative manner to
a person. To try and understand it as referring specifically to either
interment or birth carries great difficulties, since of the first three sets
of contrasts, (2) and (3) would not apply to interment and (1) would not
apply to birth.[724] *Sown* must be understood here as Paul's rather imaginative way of referring to man's place and status in the created order. The
verb is passive – *is sown.* This often represents a circumlocution for the
active voice in which God is the subject.[725] This would contrast then
with the emphatic use of *you* in v. 36b, where the contrast is clearly
between *you* who *sow* and *God* who gives it a *body* (v. 38).

A problem immediately arises, because this makes God responsible
for *both* sides of these contrasting sets, i.e. the *perishable* and the *imperishable,* etc. The only answer to this difficulty is to admit that,
paradoxical as it may seem, this passage would seem to support the
idea that God is ultimately responsible for both sides of the contrast but
that it is his will that man moves from the one to the other. There were
many attempts on the part of Jewish-writers before Paul to explain this
anomaly. Paul's treatment of the problem is distinguished from theirs
by his concentration upon man's resurrected life, his life in Christ, and
his silence concerning Adam's status before the Fall.[726]

724. Cf. ibid., ad loc.
725. Cf. Blass and Debrunner, op. cit. (n. 302), 130 (1), 342 (1).
726. Cf. R. Scroggs, *The Last Adam,* 1966, 91.

Paul draws upon his own experience to describe the human situation as one characterized by perishability, dishonour, and weakness.[727] When he comes to describe the resurrection body, however, the items corresponding to the three characteristics of man's earthly condition are not, in two cases at least, mere opposites. Man is sown *perishable* and is raised *imperishable*. However, he is sown in *dishonour*, and will be raised in *glory*.[728] He is sown in *weakness*, and will be raised in *power*.[729] One is reminded of the point made by Paul in Romans 5^{12-21} in which he is at pains to contrast the human situation in which Adam sinned with the act of salvation by God in Christ:

> ... *God's act of grace is out of all proportion*
> *to Adam's wrongdoing* ...
> *The gift of God is not to be compared*
> *in its effect with that one man's sin.* ... (N.E.B.)

Paul saw this action of God, not as a restoration of man, but as an act of creation. Man, by faith in Christ, does not return to some kind of Eden or *status quo ante* but is 'a new creature'.[730] He receives, not only *honour* and *power*, but the very *glory* of God himself.[731] Paul sums this up by contrasting man's pre-resurrection body – a living body, made of flesh and blood – with the spirit – or spiritual, post-resurrection body (v. 50).

Just where the notion of a spirit-body as opposed to a life-body comes from is difficult to say. Paul did know the person of the risen Lord,[732] who is the first, presumably, to have received a spirit-body in his resurrection. Paul also knows the Spirit whom God has sent to those who have faith in Christ.[733] Paul does not draw any hard and fast line between the Spirit and Christ. It has been seriously suggested on the basis of 2 Cor. 3^{17} – the Lord is the Spirit – that he actually identified the two.[734] It is certainly true that Paul did not make the fine distinction between the 'persons' of the Son and the Holy Spirit which a later age was forced to make out of a concern to combat heresies and to establish a theological norm of faith.

The least one can say is that, in Paul's mind, the risen Lord and the Spirit were intimately connected, as they seem to have been in the preaching of the primitive church.[735] The synoptic tradition represents

727. Cp. Rom. 8^{21}; Gal. 6^8.   728. Cf. Rom. $8^{7,10}$.
729. Cf. 2 Cor. 12^9.   730. Cf. 2 Cor. 5^{17}; Schlatter, ad loc.
731. Cf. R. Scroggs, op. cit. (n. 726), 95f.; cp. Phil. 3^{21}; Rom. 1^4.
732. Cf. 15^8, 9^1; Gal. 1^{15f}.   733. Cf. Rom. 8^{15}; Gal. 4^6.
734. Cf. I. Hermann, loc. cit. (n. 521).   735. Cf. Acts 2^{32f}.

an intimacy of Jesus and the Spirit when he is endowed with the Spirit at the beginning of his public ministry.[736] An earlier age, knowing Jesus as 'risen', that is exalted, Lord, thought of his presence among them as 'Spirit'.[737] Furthermore, unlike the later developed synoptic tradition, an earlier age would have thought of the *exalted* Lord as Spirit, i.e. he became Spirit in his exultation (resurrection).[738]

This is the main thrust of Paul's speculation or Haggadah on Genesis 2[7]. The text of the O.T. is:

> *God formed man from the dust of the earth*
> *And breathed into his face the breath of life*
> *And* man became a living being.

On the basis then of the last five words quoted from Genesis 2[7], and of his experience of the risen Lord, Paul speculates upon the nature of the resurrection body. His experience of the risen Lord (the *Spirit*) allows Paul to affirm that the statement in Genesis 2[7] means: God will create a spirit-body (which he has already done for Jesus), just as he created a life-body for man (the first Adam). But there is a big difference. Adam's body was *alive* having had life breathed into it by God. Christ's risen (exalted) body was life-giving because he was Spirit. This continues the point made in v. 22: *For as in Adam all die, so also in Christ shall all be made alive.* In Adam, i.e. 'the human race before Christ', man knows a kind of life, the boundary of which is death. In Christ (i.e. the second Adam) man knows a life which produces not death, but more life[739] (i.e. Christ the life-giving Spirit).[740]

46

When Paul says the Spirit-man was not the first but the life-man, it is likely that he is answering some statement such as: The Spirit-man comes before the life-man. This would constitute an understandable Gnostic[741] interpretation of Paul's preaching. It would say, in effect, the earthly is as nothing; what is important is the Spirit, i.e. the heavenly. Let that which is perishing perish. This kind of attitude could very easily lead to strict puritanism, such as we find in 1 Cor. 7[1], or self-indulgent libertinism, such as is evidenced in 5[1] and 6[13]. Anyone therefore who would reverse the order of the Spirit-man and the life-man runs

736. Cf. Mark 1[9-11] parr.; cp. John 1[32].
737. Cf. general Introduction, pp. xxviiif.
738. Cf. Rom. 1[4]; cp. Acts 2[36].
739. Cp. John 10[10].
740. Cp. John 5[26].
741. Cf. the general Introduction, pp. xixf.

counter to the Christian experience and runs counter to the witness of scripture:

(a) The first man (Adam) became a life-being.
The second man (Christ) became a spirit-giving being.
(b) The first man was made of dust of the earth.
The second man was from heaven.

47
from heaven: indicates the source of the Spirit. The point is for Paul that in the order or timetable of salvation the Spirit-man from heaven comes *after* the living-dust-man.

Man's problem is that he is as the first Adam, made of dust. He has (and he knows he has) borne . . .

49
the image of the man of dust: But man finds himself in the in-between position – a descendant of the first Adam who also has faith in the second Adam (Christ), for whom God has conquered the enemies of man and who is even now in the process of conquering those enemies for all men.

But men have not yet become what they know Christ to be, the Spirit-man. Paul carefully points out that *We shall bear the image of the man of heaven.* The future tense here is important. This is not yet man's mode of existence. Only Christ has been granted this, because this is his place[742] in the scheme of salvation. Man's situation is one which is characterized by an ambiguity of 'already and not yet', or having *as if* not having.[743]

image: A term borrowed from Genesis 1 and which may refer primarily to God's revelation of himself.[744] The event whereby man will become what Jesus is lies still in the future.

15^{50-58} THE CHRISTIAN LIFE NOW

[50]*I tell you this, brethren: flesh and blood cannot inherit the kingdom of God, nor does the perishable inherit the imperishable.*

742. Cf. on v. 23, above.
743. Cf. C. K. Barrett, *From First Adam to Last*, 1962, 105ff.
744. ibid., 97ff.

51Lo! I tell you a mystery. We shall not all sleep, but we shall all be changed, 52in a moment, in the twinkling of an eye, at the last trumpet. For the trumpet will sound, and the dead will be raised imperishable, and we shall be changed. 53For this perishable nature must put on the imperishable, and this mortal nature must put on immortality. 54 When the perishable puts on the imperishable, and the mortal puts on immortality, then shall come to pass the saying that is written:

'Death is swallowed up in victory'
55 'O death, where is thy victory?
O death, where is thy sting?'
56The sting of death is sin, and the power of sin is the law. 57But thanks be to God, who gives us the victory through our Lord Jesus Christ.

58Therefore, my beloved brethren, be steadfast, immovable, always abounding in the word of the Lord, knowing that in the Lord your labour is not in vain.

Having set the timetable of salvation straight, Paul must now deal with the other side of his dilemma, our present flesh and blood composition. Paul anticipates the logical question: If at present we bear the image of the earthly Adam and yet know by faith that we shall some day bear the image of the second Adam (Christ), what is the relation between our present existence and our future one, and how do we move from the one to the other?

One suspects that this would have been no problem for the Jew who was already well acquainted with pictures of the end time which he knew from the apocalyptic literature of Daniel onwards. The gentile, however, would have been acquainted with none of these ideas. Therefore it is for him a *mystery* (v. 51) which Paul has to tell him. It is obvious from what Paul has said that he does not reckon that man as he is, earth-man or dust-man, even though he lives by God's breath, even though he knows and has received God's Spirit, can be resurrected. *Flesh and blood*, i.e. man formed from the dust of the earth, is not what will be raised (v. 44).

But this presents a problem. If what is *raised* is different from what is *sown*, in what sense is there any continuity between what is *sown* and what is *raised*? The continuity is expressed by Paul in two ways. First, the content of the mystery (secret) is: *we shall be changed*. God ensures the continuity of our identity by a divine act in which our mode of existence will be radically altered, but our identity will remain. Paul says that this will happen in a *moment* or *twinkling of an eye* and to the accompaniment of some heavenly trumpet.[745] Second, this change is not thought of as happening solely in the future. Christ has already been granted his resurrection body – he has become Spirit.[746] Those who know this are not mere observers of this cosmic process; they are, in faith, caught up in it. Paul can express this in a number of ways; namely being *in Christ* or the *body of Christ* or bearing the *image of Christ*.[747] The man of faith experiences this process of redemption, however, as a tension within himself, a tension which takes the form of simultaneous dying and living.[748] But even while our dust-earth man experiences death, we know life and another self is somehow being formed.[749] But this tension will not persist forever. Eventually good triumphs over evil, life over death. God-in-Christ will triumph over the powers hostile to man, and then the tension will be no more.[750] Then this[751] *perishable* and *mortal* will *put on* the *imperishable* and *immortality*. This is language which would be more familiar to the gentile Corinthians than the apocalyptic imagery of I Thess. 4¹³⁻¹⁷.[752]

Having used the terminology of his hearers, Paul returns to a more familiar Jewish background for his speculations. The change which will take place in the resurrection will (vv. 54f.) constitute the fulfilment of scripture. The question is: what Scripture? Neither the

745. Cp. I Thess. 4¹³⁻¹⁷. The imagery in this passage is more pictorial than that of I Corinthians, and is designed as an imaginative backdrop for the event of the resurrection. But the thought is the same. It strongly suggests that our present mode of terrestrial existence will be radically changed.

746. Cf. 2 Cor. 3¹⁷; cp. I Cor. 15⁴⁵.

747. Cf. C. K. Barrett, op. cit. (n. 743), 95ff.

748. ibid., 107. Cf. I Cor. 6⁸ff.; cp. Rom. 6³ff.; 2 Cor. 3¹⁸, 5¹⁷.

749. Cf. 2 Cor. 4¹⁶.   750. Vv. 25ff.

751. *This* is repeated four times in the Greek of vv. 53f. to emphasize continuity. Cf. Allo, ad loc. *This* refers, of course, to the individual believer.

752. Cf. above, n. 745. Cp. 2 Cor. 5¹ff. where Paul uses the image of *being clothed* (vv. 2, 4). Also the image of the mortal being swallowed up by life should be noted (v. 4).
The rabbis were accustomed to speculate on the reality of the clothing worn in the resurrection. Cf. W. D. Davies, op. cit. (n. 533), 305f. Greek thinkers, on the other hand, had already spoken of immortality as a garment. Cf. Moffat, ad loc.; cp. Odes of Solomon 15⁸.

Hebrew nor the Greek Septuagint of Isa. 25^8 and Hos. 13^{14} (although they are the closest approximations to what Paul writes) comes close to being rendered by Paul. Closer approximations can be found in the Greek versions of Theodotion (for Isaiah) and Aquila (for Hosea).[753]

As I have attempted to point out above, the process of redemption looks forward, in Paul's thought, to the End and the great change which will take place in the resurrection. To think about this future event requires Paul to speculate after the manner of the rabbis, stretching familiar human categories for the life to come. However, I also pointed out that this thought of the process of redemption also had in Paul's mind a definite reference point in the present. It is a process in which the believer is involved now.

56ff.

So Paul leaves his speculative mode and turns to the realities of everyday existence. The words which seem to trigger this change are *sting* and *victory*. In answering the question posed by the scriptures[754] Paul says that *the sting of death is sin*, which he associates with *the law*.[755] But the victory is ours through Jesus Christ our Lord.[756] The victory is ours *now* over sin, over the law, and over death. How? In some Gnostic, mind-over-matter, transcendental sort of way? No, it will be as we *abound in the work of the Lord*. It would be easy to think of Paul's statements in v. 58 as a kind of ethical addendum to his profound theological discourse-speculation of vv. 35ff. But if we look back over this chapter we see that the first major section, vv. 1–29, ended on just such a practical note, even a note of reproof. So here, at the end of what must have been even in its day a rather *recherché* bit of speculation, Paul ends with statements as to how the Christian experience expresses itself right here and now. That is, there is a *work of the Lord*, Christians are to *abound* in it because they know *in the Lord* that it *is not in vain*. Whatever the Christian does *in the Lord* we would take to mean the will of God, which the believer does because he knows it is the will of God. This, says Paul, is not done *in vain*, i.e. it is not without its ultimate consequences. We do not hope, as Paul points out in v. 19, only *in this life*, i.e. only from the vantage point of this life. Our perspective is that afforded by

---

753. Cf. Lietzmann, ad loc. 754. Cf. above on vv. 54f.
755. Cf. Rom. $5^{12ff.}$; $7^{7ff.}$. 756. Cf. Rom. $8^{37f.}$.

the resurrection of Christ and the whole process of redemption which God has initiated through that mighty act.

We know therefore that the work which we do *in the Lord* is not without ultimate consequences, in which we are personally involved through the resurrection of the dead. It is this faith which we have in the present meaning of Christ for our lives, a faith which expresses itself in our doing the *work of the Lord*, which allows us to hope for the ultimate effectiveness of what we do.

It is in this present time, in the process of redemption of which Christ is the beginning, that the believer is to stand firm and unmoved. The enemies of the Lord are being defeated. No matter how it may seem, in faith we believe this to be so. Because we believe this is so we believe that our steadfast faithfulness and pursuit of God's will is somehow taken up into that redemptive process and has its ultimate meaning and result.

Chapter 16

The sixteenth chapter of Paul's first epistle to the Corinthians has rightly been called an epilogue. In this chapter Paul discusses two more subjects about which the Corinthians have inquired.[757] He also brings them up to date on the movements of some of his fellow workers and on his own travel plans.

16¹⁻⁴ THE COLLECTION FOR THE CHURCH IN JERUSALEM

¹Now concerning the contribution for the saints: as I directed the churches of Galatia, so you also are to do. ²On the first day of every week, each of you is to put something aside and store it up, as he may prosper, so that contributions need not be made when I come. ³And when I arrive, I will send those whom you accredit by letter to carry your gift to Jerusalem. ⁴If it seems advisable that I should go also, they will accompany me.

Paul takes up first the question of the *contribution* to the church in Jerusalem. It is not altogether clear whether this collection was undertaken out of economic necessity or whether there were other motives as well. It is possible that the Christians in Jerusalem were boycotted[758] by their fellow Jews. There is some evidence for such a situation.[759] It is also possible that Paul had certain other motives, such as promoting the unity of the church[760] or furthering what he conceived to be the history of salvation in demonstrating the fullness of the gentiles.[761] It is clear from the other references to this subject that it was most important to Paul.[762]

ॐ

757. Cf. above on 7¹.   758. Cf. R.-P. and Schlatter, ad loc.
759. Cf. 1 Thess 2¹⁴.
760. Cf. D. Georgi, *Die Geschichte der Kollekte des Paulus für Jerusalem*, 1965, 39; K. F. Nickle, *The Collection*, 1966, 72f.
761. J. Munck, op. cit. (n. 6), 40ff.
762. Cf. 2 Cor. 8–9; Rom. 15²⁶; cp. Acts 24¹⁷ (11²⁹); Gal. 2¹⁰.

1

contribution: The Greek word is *logeia* or *logia* and means 'collection'. There is no doubt that Paul understands this as a free-will offering and wants the Corinthians so to understand it.[763] In terms of outward form, however, the Jewish temple tax offers the closest parallel.[764] It is clearly the activity of collection which Paul does not want going on while he is in Corinth (v. 2).

the saints: This is a typical designation for members of the Christian community in Paul's letters.[765] There may have been a sense in which these Christians were considered *the saints* in a special sense because of the status of the church in Jerusalem as the mother church,[766] or the congregation of those who stayed behind to await the end of the age and the second coming of Christ.[767]

Galatia: The best presentation of the problems connected with the location of Galatia is to be found in *The Introduction to the New Testament* by P. Feine and J. Behm and newly edited by G. Kümmel.[768] We have no evidence as to what these directions to the Galatians may have been.

2

the first day of every week . . . put something aside: There is no evidence here that this putting-aside had anything to do with a worship service on Sunday. It sounds more like a practical means of making sure that some kind of contribution would be there when Paul arrived. His rationale seems weak. It is simply easier for people of modest means to give a number of small contributions over an extended period of time than to give a relatively large sum all at once.

3

I will send those whom you accredit by letter: This is a possible translation. However *accredit by letter* is best taken with *I will send.* N.E.B. renders the sentence 'I will give letters of introduction to persons approved by you.'[769]

763. Cf. below on v. 4.
764. Cf. Nickle, op. cit. (n. 760), 99.
765. Cf. 1²; Rom. 1⁷; Phil. 1¹; cp. Col. 1²; Eph. 1¹.
766. Cf. Allo, ad loc.; Rom. 15²⁷.
767. Cf. Georgi, op cit. (n. 760), 26ff.
768. Op. cit. (n. 1), 191ff.
769. On this type of letter of recommendation, cf. 2 Cor. 3¹⁻³.

4

If it seems advisable: The problem is, What constituted the basis of advisability? Some have said the size of the offering,[770] while others see this as a reference to the attitude of the Corinthians.[771] In either case Paul assumes the authority for the mission. If he stays in Corinth he will *send* them and *accredit* them.[772] If he goes they will *accompany* him, i.e. as the head of the delegation.

16⁵⁻⁹   PLANS FOR THE IMMEDIATE FUTURE

> *5I will visit you after passing through Macedonia, for I intend to pass through Macedonia, 6and perhaps I will stay with you or even spend the winter, so that you may speed me on my journey, wherever I go. 7For I do not want to see you now just in passing; I hope to spend some time with you, if the Lord permits. 8But I will stay in Ephesus until Pentecost, 9for a wide door for effective work has opened to me, and there are many adversaries.*

᠎᠎᠎

5

The situation is that of Acts 19²¹. Paul has already mentioned his projected visit in v. 2f. and 11³⁴. There is evidence in 2 Cor. 1¹⁵ that he may at some point have had to alter his plans somewhat.

pass through: May represent a technical term for a kind of inspection trip. We find the same Greek word, *dierchomai*, so used in Acts 13⁶; 14²⁴; 15^{3,41}, 18²³, 19²¹, 20².

6f.

Paul now contrasts his tour of the Macedonian congregations with the visit he intends to make in Corinth. His Corinthian visit will be longer in duration. He may stay the winter.[773] At any rate he expects to *spend some time*. His Corinthian visit will also be more intense.

stay with you: The Greek work *pros* translated here *with* carries more the connotation of 'in active intercourse with'.[774] Paul uses this pronoun three times in vv. 5-7 for emphasis.

770. Cf. Lietzmann, Weiss, ad loc.
771. Cf. Georgi, op. cit. (n. 760), 41.   772. Cf. above on v. 3.
773. On the problems of winter travel in the Aegean, cf. R.-P., ad loc.
774. Cf. R.-P., ad loc.

speed me on my journey: The Greek word *propempein* rendered here *speed* can mean simply 'to give a send-off', or it can also involve providing material goods for the journey.[775] The first meaning is to be preferred here. It is clear from 2 Cor. 1$^{16ff.}$ that Paul's reasons for leaving on his Jerusalem journey from Corinth had to do with the Corinthians personally.

wherever I go[776]: It is also clear that Paul's mind was not made up at this point as to where he would go once he left Corinth (cp. 2 Cor. 1$^{16f.}$; Acts 19^{21}).

8

in Ephesus: From whence he writes this letter.

until Pentecost: Paul gives himself a good bit of time. The Jewish feast of Pentecost comes seven weeks after Passover, i.e. in late spring or early summer. He clearly does not intend to arrive in Corinth until some time in the autumn.[777] *Until* might include the possibility that he could stay on longer.

9

a wide door for effective work: Paul uses the metaphor of a door being opened. It must refer to some opportunity for preaching. He applies both of the adjectives, *wide* and *effective*, to the noun door, which makes the Greek text somewhat confusing. N.E.B. is to be preferred here. It drops the metaphor entirely and applies the adjective 'great'[778] to the implied subject, 'opportunity'. One can see in the Greek, however, how Paul shifted his attention from the figure of speech, door, to his subject, opportunity for work.

16$^{10-12}$ TIMOTHY COMMENDED, APOLLOS DEFENDED

10*When Timothy comes, see that you put him at ease among you, for he is doing the work of the Lord, as I am.* 11*So let no one despise him. Speed him on his way in peace, that he may return to me; for I am expecting him with the brethren.*

775. Cf. W. Bauer, op. cit. (n. 67), s.v.
776. Cf. 4^{19}; Acts 18^{21}; Jam. 4^{15}; Heb. 6^3. Cf. also R.-P., ad loc. for extrabiblical references.
777. Cf. above on v. 6.   778. R.S.V. *wide*.

12*As for our brother Apollos, I strongly urged him to visit you with the other brethren, but it was not at all his will to go now. He will come when he has opportunity.*

ॐ

10

When Timothy comes: The Greek word *ean*, translated here *when*, usually indicates a condition. There may have been some uncertainty in Paul's mind as to whether Timothy would ever reach Corinth. We know from 4^17 that he has already left Ephesus.[779] The letter will get there before he does, probably because it is sent by sea, directly across the Aegean.

he is doing the work of the Lord, as I am: Paul could speak with the authority of the risen Lord (14^37). He could also claim this authority for those who were his fellow workers. The Corinthians are therefore no more free to *despise*[780] Timothy than they are to disregard the command of the Lord given through Paul.[781]

11

with the brethren: It is difficult to decide whether this phrase should be taken with *expecting* or with *him*. Grammatically the Greek text points to the latter. In this case, however, we are at a loss to know who the other brethren were besides the Erastus of Acts 19^22.

12

As for our brother Apollos: The Greek would indicate that this was another subject of the Corinthians' letter to Paul.[782] In all probability they asked that Apollos return to Corinth.[783]

it was not at all his will: The Greek text has no adjective modifying *will*. The alternative reading of R.S.V. is to be preferred – God's will for him.[784]

when he has opportunity: Paul has already explained why he cannot come at the present time (vv. 8ff.). We do not know the details of Apollos's activity, but perhaps he did not consider them any less important than Paul's. The opportunity will come for him as for Paul – *if the Lord permits* (v. 7).

779. Cp. Acts 19^22.
780. Cf. 2 Cor. 10^10; Gal. 4^14; 1 Thess. 5^20.
781. Cf. above on 14^36ff..
782. Cf. above on 7^1.
783. Cf. Acts 18^24ff..
784. Cp. Rom. 2^18.

16^{13–14}   AN ADMONITION

¹³*Be watchful, stand firm in your faith, be courageous, be strong.* ¹⁴*Let all that you do be done in love.*

These are admonitions of a very general sort. Some are quite possibly borrowed from the Jewish scriptures, where there are a number of parallels.[785]

ℵℵ

13
Be watchful: This seems to be a peculiarly Christian usage and is related to the early community's belief that the end of the world was near.[786]

stand firm in your faith: On this particular expression, cf. above on 15^{1ff.}.

be courageous, be strong: This is a formula probably borrowed from the Old Testament.[787] The word translated here courageous is more aptly rendered 'act like men'.[788]

14
in love: Most commentators are quick to point to the general discussions of love in Chapters 13 and 8. On this, cf. the introduction to Chapter 13 and the commentary on 13¹³.

16^{15–18}   RECOGNITION FOR STEPHANAS'S HOUSE
FORTUNATUS AND ACHAICUS

¹⁵*Now, brethren, you know that the household of Stephanas were the first converts in Achaia, and they have devoted themselves to the service of the saints;* ¹⁶*I urge you to be subject to such men and to every fellow worker and labourer.* ¹⁷*I rejoice at the coming of Stephanas and Fortunatus and Achaicus, because they have made up for your absence;*

ℵℵ

785. Cf. below.
786. Cf. 1 Thess. 5⁶; Col. 4²; 1 Pet. 5⁸; cp. Mark 13 and 14.
787. Cf. 2 Sam. 10¹²; Psalm 30²⁵ (LXX).   788. Cf. R.-P., ad loc.

15f.

Paul's statement that everything *be done in love* (v. 14) offers us the key to these next two verses. As I tried to show in the introduction to Chapter 13, *love* for Paul is closely associated with the Spirit. It is the category within which he finds it possible to discuss the operation of the Spirit. The Spirit in turn is closely associated with the idea of one's function within the community, to which Paul refers as 'gift' or 'service' or 'working'.[789]

The word used here in v. 15 is *service*. It is qualified by the phrase *of the saints*. The phrase in Greek is *diakonian tois hagiois*. Paul makes it quite clear that there are different kinds of *service*.[790] He therefore usually qualifies the word *service*, as in Rom. 11[13] 'ministry'; and 15[31] 'my service'.[791] The closest parallels to 16[15] are to be found in 2 Cor. 8[4] and 9[1ff.], where the Greek is *tēs diakonias tēs eis tous hagious*, literally 'service for the saints'. The similarity to 1 Cor. 16[15] is obvious. The context of 2 Cor. 8 and 9 is the collection for the Jerusalem congregation. This is also the subject of 1 Cor. 16[1-4]. It would seem reasonable to suppose that Paul is here referring to the activity of Stephanas's household in connection with this collection. This also helps us to understand v. 16, which can then be seen as admonishing the Corinthians to cooperate with the household of Stephanas in this matter.

16

be subject to such men and to every fellow worker and labourer: This does not necessitate any kind of 'emerging concept of office'. Paul refers here to the specific service of the collection and urges cooperation with those who have taken this upon themselves as their special service or *diakonia.*

17

Stephanas, Fortunatus, Achaicus: Clearly these men constitute some kind of representation or delegation from the Corinthian Church (v. 17b). The latter two are not associated with the activity of the household of Stephanas as described in vv. 15f. These three in turn are not to be confused with *Chloe's people* in 1[11]. It is quite possible, as many have suggested, that these three men were the bearers of a letter from the Corinthians to Paul and were in turn bearers of his reply, i.e. 1 Corinthians. This would explain how they could refresh Paul's spirit as well as that of the Corinthians.

[18]*For they refreshed my spirit as well as yours. Give recognition to such men.*

789. Cf. above on 12[4].   790. ibid.
791. Cp. 2 Cor. 3[7ff.], 4[1]; 5[18], 6[8].

Give recognition to such men: i.e. recognize the arduous and dangerous character of their trip to Paul and back.[792]

16^{19-24}   GREETINGS AND SUBSCRIPTION

19 *The churches of Asia send greetings. Aquila and Prisca, together with the church in their house, send you hearty greetings in the Lord.* 20 *All the brethren send greetings. Greet one another with a holy kiss.*
21 *I, Paul, write this greeting with my own hand.* 22 *If any one has no love for the Lord, let him be accursed. Our Lord, come!* 23 *The grace of the Lord Jesus be with you.* 24 *My love be with you all in Christ Jesus. Amen.*

ಐಐ

19
The churches of Asia: While in Ephesus Paul had apparently been active elsewhere[793] in the province of which Ephesus was the capital.

Aquila and Prisca: These two had been helpful in the establishment of the church in Corinth.[794]

the church in their house: The congregation[795] which used their house as a place to meet.
    As he does in almost all his letters,[796] Paul concludes with greetings from the Christians in the place or general area from which he writes and the command to give greetings to one another.[797] Invariably, as he does here, Paul includes the invocation of *the grace of the Lord Jesus.* Here, too, as we noted in connection with the salutation,[798] Paul probably follows the epistolary conventions of his own day, which he modifies in accordance with Christian belief and practice.

20
All the brethren:[799] This may include all the Christians in those churches to which Paul makes reference in v. 19, or it may include only those of the congregation which meets in the house of Aquila and Prisca.
with a holy kiss: With one exception,[800] when Paul uses 'greet' in the

792. Cp. I Thess. 5^{12}.   793. Cf. Acts 19^{10,26}.   794. Cf. Acts 18^{2ff.}.
795. Cf. above on 1^2.   796. Galatians is the exception.
797. Cf. below on v. 20b.   798. Cf. above on 1^{1-9}.
799. Cf. 2 Cor. 13^{12}; Phil. 4^{22}.   800. Cf. Phil. 4^{21}.

imperative[801] he adds *one another with a holy kiss*. This leads one to think of some kind of ritual usage within the Christian community.[802]

21

I, Paul ... with my own hand: It was common in this period for letters to be dictated to a scribe. The author of the letter would usually append a greeting with his own hand.

22

If any one has no love for the Lord, let him be accursed. Our Lord, come! There is some reason to believe that this verse, interrupting the context as it does, and containing three non-Pauline words, represents an ancient liturgical formula.[803] Some would connect this with the *holy kiss* of v. 20 with which the eucharist in the primitive church may have begun.[804] The first two words, not found elsewhere in Paul's letter, are *philei* (*has ... love*) and *ētō* (*let ... be*). The third word, translated here *Our Lord, come*, is the Aramaic *maranatha*. This is best taken as *marana* (Our Lord) *tha* (come), though it could be construed as *maran* (Lord) *atha* (has come). It is possible that the phrase *maranatha* is introduced here to reinforce the exhortation to discipline of v. 22a.[805]

23

This is the one formula which Paul invariably includes in the conclusion of his letters.

The grace: This usually refers in Paul's writing to what God has freely done for man in the person of Jesus – especially in his death and resurrection. This central core of the Christian life can be combined in the conclusion of Paul's letters as it is here with Paul's own love for his fellow Christians (v. 24) or with a doxology;[806] it can be amplified with such phrases as 'the love of God and the fellowship of the Holy Spirit';[807] the *grace* of our Lord Jesus Christ remains, however, the one fixed element as Paul sends greetings to his fellow Christians. However they or he may interpret it, this remains the basis of their common faith.

801. Cf. Rom. 16¹⁵; 2 Cor. 13¹²; 1 Thess. 5²⁶.   802. Cf. below on v. 22.
803. Cp. Didache 10⁶; Rev. 22²⁰; Cf. G. Bornkamm, 'Das Anathema in der urchristlichen Abendmahlsliturgie', *ThLZ*, 75 (1970), 227–30. J. A. T. Robinson, 'Traces of a Liturgical Sequence in 1 Cor. xvi. 20–24', *JTS*, 4 (1953), 38–41.
804. Cf. Justin Martyr, *Apologia*, I, 65.
805. Cf. C. F. D. Moule, 'A Reconstruction of the Context of Maranatha', *NTS*, 6 (1959–60), 307–10; cp. C. Spicq, 'Comment comprendre *philein* dans 1 Cor. xvi. 22?', *Nov Test*, I (1956), 200–204.
806. Cf. Rom. 16^{25ff.}.   807. Cf. 2 Cor. 13¹⁴.

Index of References

THE BIBLE
OLD TESTAMENT

189

INDEX OF CLASSICAL LITERATURE

Index of Authors